DATE DUE

DEMCO 38-296

The People vs. Big Tobacco

How the States Took On the Cigarette Giants

by
Carrick Mollenkamp, Adam Levy,
Joseph Menn, and Jeffrey Rothfeder

of Bloomberg News

highlighted. **A high degree of legal and historical accuracy has been assured—largely as a result of relentless and uncompromising reporting.** I hope that they dissect the evolution of the settlement through Congress just as they pursued its birth. This is a **great read for anyone interested in the power of trial lawyers or the past behavior of the tobacco industry.**"

MARTIN FELDMAN
Tobacco analyst
Smith Barney

"This book gives a **behind-the-scenes look at how history is sometimes made.** It's not neat, it's not orderly; most of the time it's a lot more chaotic than we ever thought. This book is **a true account of the roller-coaster ride that turned out to be the landmark tobacco agreement.**"

JOHN COALE
Smokers' attorney who helped negotiate the tobacco settlement

"From the earliest breakfast meetings in New York City to the latest nights of negotiating in Washington, D.C., **Bloomberg reporters were there,** documenting every mile of the marathon of meetings between the states and the tobacco giants. **This is the true account of the struggle to hold Big Tobacco accountable for their sins. The People vs. Big Tobacco establishes for history the ups and downs, the losses and the victories.** Bloomberg Press should be proud that they documented this part of history. One day we hope that our children will read this and see how far we've come from the days of the Marlboro Man and the Misty girl. **The attorneys general of this country are proud to have prompted that monumental change.**"

ATTORNEY GENERAL GRANT WOODS OF ARIZONA

THE PEOPLE
vs.
BIG TOBACCO

THE PEOPLE

VS.

BIG TOBACCO

How the States Took On the Cigarette Giants

Carrick Mollenkamp

Adam Levy

Joseph Menn

Jeffrey Rothfeder

of

BLOOMBERG NEWS

BLOOMBERG PRESS

PRINCETON

Books are available for bulk purchases at special discounts. Special editions or book excerpts can also be created to specifications. For information, please write: Special Markets Department, Bloomberg Press.

BLOOMBERG, THE BLOOMBERG, BLOOMBERG BUSINESS NEWS, BLOOMBERG NEWS, BLOOMBERG FINANCIAL MARKETS, BLOOMBERG PRESS, BLOOMBERG PROFESSIONAL LIBRARY, and BLOOMBERG PERSONAL BOOKSHELF are trademarks and service marks of Bloomberg L.P. All rights reserved.

First edition published 1998
1 3 5 7 9 10 8 6 4 2

The people vs. big tobacco / Carrick Mollenkamp . . . [et al.].
p.   cm.

Includes bibliographical references and index.
ISBN 1-57660-057-2
1. Trials (Products liability) - - United States.   2. Cigarette
industry - - Law and legislation - - United States.   3. Cigarette smokers -
- Law and legislation - - United States.   4. Compromise (Law) - -United
States.   5. Cigarette industry - -United States.   6. Tobacco -
-Physiological effects.   I. Mollenkamp, Carrick, 1969-   .
KF226.P46   1998
346.7303'8 - - dc21   97-42358
                                                                                                    CIP

Book Design by Laurie Lohne / Design It Communications

To my family
—CARRICK MOLLENKAMP

To my father-in-law Roy Stubbs and his daughter
—ADAM LEVY

To my parents, all four of them, and my brothers
—JOSEPH MENN

To Alexis and Ben, my inspiration, always
—JEFFREY ROTHFEDER

Contents

Acknowledgments

T his book could not have been written without the extraordinary support of Bloomberg News editor-in-chief Matthew Winkler and company founder Mike Bloomberg, who freed all the authors from their daily assignments and coverage to put together the tale of the tobacco settlement. Winkler and Bloomberg both provided guidance, encouragement, and all the resources needed to write this book.

Not enough can be said about the contribution of John McCorry, Bloomberg's Princeton bureau chief. He not only provided crucial editing for this book, but for Bloomberg's entire tobacco litigation coverage as well. John's tireless enthusiasm, focused editing, never-waning support, and lucid thinking was an inspiring and motivating force for all of the authors.

Several other Bloomberg reporters and editors also contributed widely. Noam Neusner, Bloomberg's tobacco beat reporter, provided extensive hours and knowledge of the tobacco industry both in the reporting of this book and in the coverage of the settlement. Leslie Hillman and Galen Meyer also made valuable contributions, as did Karen Padley, Sylvia Wier, and James Greiff.

In Bloomberg's Washington, D.C., office, thanks go to Mark Willen, Richard Keil, Tom Ferraro, David Ward, Kristin Jensen, Kristin Reed, Dina Temple-Raston, and Robin Meszoly.

The support from Bloomberg Press—especially Bill Inman and Jared Kieling—was exemplary. They immediately realized how important this book is and backed the writers at every stage with excellent support and guidance.

We are indebted to Richard Marek for his editorial help. Marek was a needed steadying force on the book, adding key editing insights to what was at times a chaotic project.

A special thanks to Steve Matthews and Kathleen Sullivan in Bloomberg's Atlanta office for doubling their workloads during the duration of this coverage.

Marcia Anderson, Jen Wilson, Mark Hosny, and Leslie Fox provided valuable support from Bloomberg's Princeton newsroom, as did Bloomberg's library research team of William Merk, Mike Weiss, Larry Smitley, Arlene Goldhammer, Mike Novatoski, and Roy Thoden.

A final thanks to our families and friends who had to endure countless late nights, numerous missed dinners, broken dates, and a never-ending stream of arcane tobacco industry tidbits.

The Players

TOBACCO INDUSTRY OPPONENTS

State Attorneys General
   Michael Moore, Mississippi
   Grant Woods, Arizona
   Christine Gregoire, Washington
   Robert Butterworth, Florida
   Richard Blumenthal, Connecticut
   Hubert H. Humphrey III, Minnesota

Private Attorneys Representing States
   Richard "Dickie" Scruggs, Pascagoula, Mississippi
   Michael Lewis, Clarksdale, Mississippi
   John "Don" Barrett, Lexington, Mississippi
   Steve Berman, Seattle, Washington
   Ronald Motley, Charleston, South Carolina
   Joseph Rice, Charleston, South Carolina

Private Attorneys—The "Castano" Group
   Wendell Gauthier, Metairie, Louisiana
   John Coale, Washington, D.C.
   Hugh Rodham, Miami, Florida
   Russ Herman, New Orleans, Louisiana
   Stanley Chesley, Cincinnati, Ohio

Public Health Advocates
   Matthew Myers, National Center for Tobacco-Free Kids
   David Kessler, former Food and Drug Administration chief
   C. Everett Koop, former U.S. surgeon general

Whistle-Blowers
>   Jeffrey Wigand, former head of research, Brown & Williamson
>   Merrell Williams, former paralegal, Kentucky law firm representing
>   Brown & Williamson

TOBACCO INDUSTRY

Executives
>   Geoffrey Bible, CEO, Philip Morris
>   Steven Goldstone, CEO, RJR Nabisco Holdings
>   Martin Broughton, CEO, B.A.T Industries
>   Bennett LeBow, CEO, Brooke Group, Ltd.
>   Murray Bring, vice chairman and general counsel, Philip Morris
>   Robert Sharpe, general counsel, RJR
>   Steven Parrish, senior vice president, Philip Morris

Attorneys
>   J. Phil Carlton, tobacco industry settlement coordinator
>   Herbert Wachtell, Wachtell, Lipton, Rosen & Katz, counsel for
>   Philip Morris
>   Meyer Koplow, Wachtell Lipton
>   Arthur Golden, Davis Polk & Wardwell, counsel for RJR
>   Robert Fiske Jr., Davis Polk, counsel for Philip Morris
>   Marc Kasowitz, Kasowitz, Benson, Torres & Friedman, counsel for
>   Bennett LeBow

OTHERS

>   Bruce R. Lindsey, White House deputy counsel
>   Norwood "Woody" Wilner, Jacksonville, Florida, antitobacco trial
>   lawyer
>   Grady Carter, ex-smoker who sued Brown & Williamson
>   Trent Lott, U.S. senator (R-Mississippi)
>   William Osteen Sr., federal judge, Greensboro, North Carolina
>   James Hunt Jr., governor of North Carolina (Democrat)
>   Michael Easley, North Carolina attorney general (Democrat)
>   Jackie Thompson, Clarksdale, Mississippi, lung-cancer victim who
>   inspired Mississippi's Medicaid suit against Big Tobacco

The Companies at a Glance

These are the companies involved in the tobacco settlement. Sales and profits are for the year ended December 31, 1996; market share and number of employees are as of July 1997.

PHILIP MORRIS COS.
- —Headquarters: New York City.
- —Chairman, chief executive: Geoffrey Bible.
- —Major tobacco brands: Marlboro, Merit, Basic, Virginia Slims, Cambridge.
- —U.S. cigarette market share: 47.5 percent in 1997, up from 46.3 percent in 1996.
- —Cigarette division: Philip Morris USA.
- —Financial highlights: Net income of $6.3 billion, or $7.68 a share, on sales of $68.9 billion.
- —Other businesses: Kraft Foods, Inc., the largest U.S. food company (Oscar Mayer, Jell-O, Post cereals, Maxwell House); Miller Brewing Co., the No. 2 U.S. brewer (Miller, Red Dog, and Löwenbräu); financial services and real estate.
- —Number of employees: 154,000.

RJR NABISCO HOLDINGS CORP.
- —Headquarters: New York City.
- —Chairman, chief executive: Steven Goldstone.
- —Major tobacco brands: Winston, Camel, Doral, Salem, Magna.
- —U.S. cigarette market share: 25.4 percent in 1997, down from 26.5 percent in 1996.
- —Cigarette division: R. J. Reynolds Tobacco Co.

—Financial highlights: Profit from operations of $898 million, or $2.62 a share, on sales of $8.89 billion.

—Other businesses: Owns 80.5 percent of No. 1 U.S. cookie and cracker maker, Nabisco Holdings Corp. (Oreo, Ritz, Snackwells).

—Number of employees: 79,700.

B.A.T INDUSTRIES PLC

—Headquarters: London.

—Chief executive: Martin Broughton.

—Major tobacco brands: GPC, Kool, Lucky Strike, Misty, Capri.

—U.S. cigarette market share: 16.1 percent in 1997, down from 17.3 percent in 1996.

—Cigarette division: Brown & Williamson Tobacco Corp.

—Financial highlights: Pretax profit of $4 billion.

—Other businesses: Insurance and financial services (Allied Dunbar and Eagle Star in the U.K. and Farmers Group in the United States).

—Number of employees: 164,000.

LOEWS CORP.

—Headquarters: New York City.

—Cochairmen: Laurence Tisch and Preston Robert Tisch.

—Major tobacco brands: Newport, Kent, True, Old Gold.

—U.S. cigarette market share: 7.9 percent in 1997, up from 7.8 percent in 1996.

—Cigarette division: Lorillard Tobacco Co.

—Financial highlights: Net income of $1 billion, or $11.91 a share, on revenue of $20.4 billion.

—Other businesses: Insurance (CNA Financial), Loews hotels, Diamond Offshore Drilling.

—Number of employees: 35,300.

BROOKE GROUP LTD.

—Headquarters: Miami.

—Chairman, chief executive: Bennett LeBow.

—Major tobacco brands: Eve, Lark, Chesterfield, L&M.

—U.S. cigarette market share: 1.6 percent in 1997, down from 1.8 percent in 1996.

—Cigarette division: Liggett Group.

—Financial highlights: Loss of $62.5 million, or $3.28 a share, on revenue of $452.7 million.

—Other businesses: Real estate and finance (New Valley Corp.).

—Number of employees: 1,740.

UST INC.

—Headquarters: Greenwich, Connecticut.

—Chairman, chief executive: Vincent Gierer Jr.

—Major tobacco brands: Copenhagen and Skoal snuff.

—U.S. smokeless tobacco market share: About 80 percent.

—Financial highlights: Net income of $464 million, or $2.42 a share, on revenue of $1.4 billion.

—Other businesses: Wines (Chateau Ste. Michelle and Village Mt. Eden) and pipe tobacco products (Dr. Grabow pipes).

—Number of employees: 4,467.

Sources: Company reports; Securities and Exchange Commission; Hoover's, Inc.; PaineWebber analyst Emanuel Goldman.

Prologue

Smoking is cool. I saw everyone else smoking and that's when I started smoking a pack a day. I won't stop. Others won't either. There's no advertisements for drugs and no Joe Camel for drugs, and a lot of people do drugs.

—SPENCER WOLFE

a 17-year-old New York City smoker

Thomas E. Sandefur Jr. died on a stormy, windswept morning in Louisville, Kentucky, July 1996—the kind of unpredictable day that only a native Southerner could appreciate.

His death was a signpost for the region and, indeed, the nation: It marked the end of a time when the U.S. tobacco industry was run by men (mostly from states in the Deep South) who defied public opinion, disputed medical evidence that smoking killed, and lied or dissembled when questioned about tobacco and addiction.

Sandefur was the former chief executive of Brown & Williamson, whose British parent, B.A.T Industries Plc, is the world's second-biggest cigarette maker. Two years before his death, on April 14, 1994, Sandefur—and six other top tobacco executives—outraged the people of the United States when he sat before a House committee and in a calm Georgian drawl, without hesitation, said, "I believe nicotine is not addictive."

Sandefur knew better; his own company's research proved differently. But he was a corporate executive from an industry that so far remained nimbly above the law. Sandefur was the last of the southern tobacco barons, master of an empire that tied together thousands of farms, warehouses, auctioneers, brokers, factories, wholesalers, distributors, and retailers—and the marketing geniuses who drove home to generation after generation the excitement of smoking.

He was born in December 1939 in the flat, central Georgia plains town of Cochran and began his lifelong career in tobacco peddling cigarettes and cigars in the north Georgia mountains. He married a minister's daughter and quickly rose through the ranks at R. J. Reynolds Tobacco Co., displaying a fierce work ethic and genius for marketing. In 1982, realizing that another man stood in his way to rise any higher at R. J. Reynolds, Sandefur went to work for Brown & Williamson. Eleven years after he joined the Louisville, Kentucky company, he was named chairman.

In his adopted hometown of Louisville, a city that takes an unflinching pride in its two biggest businesses—bourbon and tobacco—Sandefur was a quiet presence, shying away from the civic boosterism of so many business leaders in mid-sized southern cities. His picture was in the *Louisville Courier-Journal* just once in the 12 years before he appeared that day in 1994 on national television, right hand upraised as he swore to tell the truth and nothing but about tobacco.

But despite his low profile in Louisville, Sandefur was an international power broker. He was responsible for billions of dollars in shareholder money that he wielded with little restraint to make sure that politicians in Washington, D.C., protected the interests of cigarette makers, and still more money that his company used to prop open domestic and overseas markets.

Sandefur's undoing—and Big Tobacco's—began in President Clinton's first term with a troubled man named Merrell Williams, a paralegal who stole Brown & Williamson documents from a Louisville law firm that worked for the cigarette company.

These records, disseminated on the Internet in July 1995—a little more than a year after the tobacco executives testified in a crowded wood-paneled hearing room on Capitol Hill—showed that the industry knew far more about the harmful effects of smoking than it ever admitted.

Then, on November 29, 1995, another whistle-blower, Jeffrey Wigand, the former research chief at Sandefur's Brown & Williamson, opened the door further to the secrets hidden deep in the cigarette company's executive suite.

On that day, Wigand was deposed by Ron Motley, a Charleston, South Carolina, trial attorney working for Mike Moore, the Mississippi attorney general who had filed the first of what would be 40 state lawsuits against Big Tobacco.

Motley: "Let me ask you sir: How many conversations would you say you had between 1989 and 1993, when you were dismissed by Mr. Sandefur, about cigarette smoking and the addictive nature of nicotine?"

Wigand: "There have been numerous statements made by a number of officers, particularly Mr. Sandefur, that we're in the nicotine addiction delivery business."

Motley: "And did he express that view on numerous occasions?"

Wigand: "Frequently."

Motley: "Do you see where I have highlighted where Mr. Sandefur swore to tell the truth under oath under penalty of perjury what he told the Congress of the United States?"

Wigand: "Yes, I do."

Motley: "He said, 'I do not believe that nicotine is addictive.' Do you see that?"

Wigand: "Yes, I do."

Motley: "Is that the opposite, contrary to what he has expressed to you numerous times?"

Wigand: "That is correct."

Motley: "It is not true, is it?"

Wigand: "It is not true."

Tommy Sandefur had little time to dispute Wigand's testimony. Seven months later, at the age of 56, he was dead of a rare blood disease.

For a time after Sandefur's death, tobacco executives stuck with their line: Cigarettes aren't addictive, and no one has ever proved that smoking is dangerous. It was a code of silence that they refused to break.

Rarely did a tobacco executive put on a more brazen display than in April 1997, when James Morgan, head of Philip Morris USA, testified in a Florida tobacco trial. In that suit, flight attendants were seeking $5 billion in compensation for lung cancer and other diseases they claimed to have contracted after breathing passengers' smoke. Under oath, Morgan said that cigarettes are no more addictive than Gummy Bears, those sugary, chewy candies that dentists tell parents not to give their children.

"I don't like it when I don't eat my Gummy Bears," Morgan said, "but I'm certainly not addicted to them."

This was the public face the industry always wore. And yet, the tobacco business wasn't the same anymore: No longer were men like Sandefur, born and raised in the South, in control.

Around the time of Sandefur's death, the guard had changed at every major tobacco company. At the world's biggest tobacco company, Philip Morris, the new boss was Geoffrey Bible, a wily Australian-born executive who spent most of his career in Europe. The No. 2 cigarette maker, RJR Nabisco, meanwhile, handed power to Steven Goldstone, a veteran New York lawyer. Tommy Sandefur's Brown & Williamson had a new boss: a British executive.

The new tobacco chiefs were pragmatists, not zealots. With neither the passion nor the hubris of those who came before them, they weighed the costs of fighting the mountain of lawsuits against the gains. They chose compromise.

Publicly, though, tobacco executives continued to have difficulty embracing this choice. Testifying in the Florida flight attendant tobacco trial, Andrew Schindler, president of RJR's tobacco unit, said that he once took his father—who had circulation problems, smoked three packs a day, and refused to quit—to the doctor. "You can either stop smoking, or I can cut off your hands and feet some day," the doctor told his father. But despite this firsthand experience with the lethal habit, Schindler said in court tobacco is no more addictive than coffee or carrots.

"Carrot addiction?" the lawyer grilling Schindler asked incredulously.

"Yes," Schindler answered. "There was British research on carrots."

Four days after Schindler testified, a morning sea breeze blew across Figure Eight Island, an exclusive North Carolina enclave. In a 25 mph wind, carpenters installed ceiling tile at Schindler's three-story, half-million-dollar vacation house there.

One of the carpenters took a drag on a cigarette and continued working. Shortly before noon, they broke for lunch and drove to town for sandwiches.

Moments later, a worker at another house noticed smoke floating over the ocean and called for help. By the time the firemen crossed the drawbridge to the island, it was too late: Schindler's house was consumed—only blackened pilings remained—as the salty wind whipped the fire into an afternoon fury.

Investigators later guessed the fire was caused by a still smoldering cigarette butt left by one of the workers.

Divine retribution? Hardly. But perhaps the incident was indicative that things were burning out of control for Big Tobacco.

FROM MAIN STREET to Wall Street, from Tobacco Road to Pennsylvania Avenue, tobacco has a powerful grip on America. It's the country's sixth-biggest crop—fetching $2.5 billion for growers—and the No. 1 nonfood crop. Tobacco is remarkably profitable: Farmers earn $4,000 an acre from tobacco vs. only $400 an acre from strawberries.

More than three million nonfarmers—or 2.6 percent of the country's labor force—work in the tobacco business, making and distributing cigarettes or developing the advertising to entice new generations of smokers.

If it were a country, the U.S. tobacco business would have an economy as big as Turkey's or Austria's. All told, the industry generates $200 billion a year in revenue.

Big Tobacco pays tens of billions of dollars in taxes each year. And it's one of America's largest donors to politicians.

Cigarette makers are America's 20th-century Medicis, sponsoring symphonies, art exhibits, dance, and theater troupes. When the British director Peter Brook wanted to stage a nine-hour adaptation of the Sanskrit epic the *Mahabharata* in the United States and England, Philip Morris footed much of the bill.

Big Tobacco had also found a willing partner in professional sports. The Virginia Slims women's tennis circuit took its name from the Philip Morris brand, before dropping that association in the 1990s to distance itself from cigarettes. RJR, meanwhile, had the Winston-brand logo emblazoned on NASCAR race cars and the uniforms of drivers and pit crews. Television shots of baseball scoreboards often took in cigarette billboards in the background.

Communities, towns, even cities owe their very existence to tobacco. In the rural South of the late 19th century, warehouses, some as big as football fields, sprang up in areas near tobacco farms to sell the crop at auction. Related businesses moved in nearby to dry, stem, and clean tobacco. Banks were founded to finance the crop. Soon cigarette, pipe, chewing-tobacco, and snuff makers arrived. Trucking companies were started and railroads were built to carry the finished products across the country.

Winston-Salem, North Carolina, population 144,000, is one of the largest cities tobacco built. Thousands work at RJR, which has dominated the town for a century. On warm summer days the musk of drying tobacco hangs in the air. There's even a nearby community called Tobaccoville, named in the 1870s after the town's lone landmark: a chewing-tobacco factory.

In another tobacco city, Durham, North Carolina, Duke University, one of the finest in the South, was built from a $40 million endowment given by tobacco industry chieftain James Buchanan Duke. He headed up American Tobacco Co., which controlled 92 percent of the U.S. cigarette business in the early 1900s.

And in Macon, Georgia, where Brown & Williamson has the world's largest cigarette factory, it's "pretty hard to not find the company's presence," says Paul Nagle, president of the Macon Chamber of Commerce. Among many other things, the company sponsors the city's annual Cherry Blossom Festival in March. "I don't know what we would do without our Brown & Williamson," says Carolyn Crayton, executive director of the festival.

To drive in America in this century was to experience the sights and images of cigarettes, conveyed by the billboards lining the roadside.

Cities, too, had cigarette-promotion landmarks. For more than 25 years, millions of people gawked at a single Camel billboard in Times Square, in the heart of New York City. Two stories high, between 43rd and 44th Streets, a smoker blew yard-wide rings of vapor 24 hours a day.

Philip Morris, with the help of its advertisers, made "Marlboro Country" shorthand for the freedom of the Wild West. Always keen to tie smoking with youthfulness, RJR went to new extremes with Joe Camel, a caricature of a smoking camel dressed in hip gear and always found in ultracool and trendy situations. It didn't take long for Joe Camel to endear itself to U.S. children and become the second-most recognized cartoon character after Mickey Mouse.

Cigarettes alighted in pop culture as well. Everyone over a certain age knows that smokers will "walk a mile for a Camel," and that "Winston tastes good like a cigarette should." Women, fighting for equal rights, were empowered by the Virginia Slims slogan: "You've come a long way, baby."

The country's stars and heroes puffed away. Humphrey Bogart, Lauren Bacall, Sharon Stone, Rod Serling, and Bruce Willis all glamorized smoking in public and in the movies. Al Jolson, Amelia Earhart, Joe DiMaggio, and Mike Wallace promoted it. In his prime, Jackie Gleason would take a deep drag on a Marlboro and exclaim, "How sweet it is."

AMERICA'S PASSION FOR tobacco began to cool in the 1950s, when medical research first suggested a link between smoking and debilitating and often fatal diseases, particularly emphysema and lung cancer.

The initial attack on tobacco came from an unlikely source: the federal government, which once gave cigarettes to soldiers and doled out subsidies to tobacco farmers. The opening round came in 1964, when a U.S. surgeon general, Luther Terry, issued a report that said what many had known all along: Cigarettes make people sick. Though the industry denied any link between cigarettes and disease, every pack carried a warning label from then on.

That wasn't enough for the Federal Trade Commission, which noted that every American household with a TV set was exposed to 800 cigarette commercials a year. In 1971, cigarette advertising was banned from television and radio.

Then people like Betty Carnes weighed in.

Carnes helped run a hospital in Scottsdale, Arizona. In the early 1970s, she secured three floors exclusively for nonsmokers, a tiny victory that foreshadowed tobacco's retreat from public buildings.

She dispensed thousands of "Thank You for Not Smoking" signs. One ended up on the U.S. surgeon general's desk. Tens of thousands more were pasted on walls, bulletin boards, and doors across America. After two years of lobbying, Carnes persuaded Arizona's legislature to ban smoking in elevators, libraries, theaters, and buses. Other states followed.

By the mid-1980s, tobacco was public health enemy No. 1, and smokers were becoming social outcasts. Smoking on domestic flights was banned. Many restaurants restricted smokers from lighting up. Boeing Co. was among the first U.S. corporations to forbid smoking in their offices and factories; thousands more followed.

THROUGH IT ALL, the tobacco industry ceded nothing. There was no reason to. Though the percentage of U.S. adults who smoked was in decline—half of all adult Americans smoked after World War II, while only one in four did in 1997—profits rose steadily. When the industry was barred from advertising on TV, cigarette companies found other ways to market their products.

And Big Tobacco was invincible in court, defeating every lawsuit from individual smokers for decades.

To legal scholar Donald Garner, a professor at Southern Illinois University School of Law who has studied the tobacco industry's legal history, Big Tobacco's winning streak was uncanny—especially recently, considering changes in the country's legal system.

"The industry that markets the most dangerous product sold in America," he said, "is the only industry completely sheltered from the storm of 20th-century product liability."

But from 1994 to 1997, the industry was beset by a string of withering events: more lawsuits than in the preceding 30 years, leaks of confidential records, defections by whistle-blowers, an increasingly activist Food and Drug Administration, the rise of a new breed of consumer-minded and ambitious state attorneys general, and the reelection of Bill Clinton, antitobacco president.

By June 1997, the industry that could never lose suddenly had no choice but to surrender. It caved in to a whopping $368.5 billion settlement of lawsuits—which could go much higher before Congress and the president okay it—that effectively labels Big Tobacco as an outlaw business, largely banned from promoting or marketing its product.

And Big Tobacco's new breed of CEOs began to sound a lot different than any cigarette executive had before—even to the point of admitting publicly that cigarettes make people sick and may kill.

RJR's CEO Steve Goldstone was the first to confess this on the record, speaking during a deposition in the Florida flight attendants' trial. "I do believe that today, that cigarette smoking plays a role in causing lung cancer," Goldstone said.

Philip Morris CEO Geoff Bible's testimony was even more dramatic.

Q.: "Would Philip Morris agree that a single American citizen who smoked their products for 30 or more years has ever died of a disease caused in part by smoking cigarettes?"

Bible: "I think there's a fair chance that one would have, yes. Might have."

Q.: "How about a thousand?"

Bible: "Might have."

Q.: "A hundred thousand?"

Bible: "Might have."

How did Big Tobacco go from being invincible to being this vulnerable?

How could a handful of companies that dominated the politics of several states and cowed or emboldened the most powerful members of Congress let a small group of lawyers with little experience on national cases back them into a corner, all within the space of three months, behind closed doors, and to the tune of a third of a trillion dollars?

It started where it all began: Tommy Sandefur's Deep South.

THE PEOPLE
vs.
BIG TOBACCO

1
THE PEOPLE vs.
BIG TOBACCO

Can I have a cigarette?

—SUZY LOCHRIDGE

Suzy Lochridge's first words after an operation in 1995 to
remove a lung tumor. A year later, Lochridge died of cancer

The locks of brown hair.

Jackie Thompson's daughter Alice couldn't get the sight of them out of her mind. She saw the clumps, refuse from cancer patients' scalps after chemotherapy, lying on the floor while visiting her 49-year-old dying mother at Baptist Central Hospital in Memphis, Tennessee. Jackie, once a pretty brunette with friendly eyes and a mischievous smile, had been withered by the disease.

When Jackie's friend and attorney, Mike Lewis, came to visit her at the intensive care unit on a May afternoon in 1993, he too was appalled by what he saw.

Jackie's mouth was weak and trembling, her pupils looked small and distant; she weighed 90 pounds; her skin was a sickly yellow, and she had no hair. Cancer had robbed this vital woman not just of her radiance, but of her self.

Lewis couldn't shake one thought: How many fewer cigarettes—in her case, Salems—would it have taken for Thompson not to be where she was today, less than a year from her grave? He knew she was a heavy smoker, knew that her cancer was a direct result of her habit, knew that there was nothing he, her dear friend, could do to help her. And it made him angry.

Jackie and Mike talked, about the weather, about the attorney's work-a-day practice in the slow-moving central Mississippi town of Clarks-dale, about the mass of visitors in town braving the spring break to line up hundreds deep at Graceland. They didn't speak about the inevitabil-ity of her death from cancer, or of its certain cause—cigarettes.

For Lewis, 50, it was difficult to stay focused on their conversation. He watched his friend struggle to breathe through the ventilators and pumps attached to her nose and lungs and listened to the diagnostic devices beeping from seemingly every corner of the room.

It suddenly hit him that the costs of treating people dying from tobacco-related cancers were enormous.

Perhaps it was the lawyer in him—always counting the dollars and cents in human suffering. But this wasn't only about money, it was about the death of a good friend. And this scene—a dying patient, visitors who could barely look at their loved one without revulsion—was being played out in tens of thousands of hospital rooms across the country. Lewis felt his anger rise. He wanted to apportion blame. He wanted revenge.

The long hospital stays, the teams of doctors and nurses trying to squeeze out a few more days for patients, the expensive equipment pumping life and feeling for vital signs, the last days at hospices. All of that added up—in Jackie Thompson's case, to about $1 million in state money. Someone had to be held responsible, Lewis said to himself.

He knew the answer. This was the fault of the cigarette makers, Philip Morris, RJR Nabisco, Brown & Williamson, and the others. It was their product and their single-minded efforts to addict everybody to it— even though they knew it was dangerous—that landed Jackie Thompson and 425,000 others on their deathbeds every year.

Big Tobacco was making tens of billions of dollars annually from sell-ing Marlboros, Winstons, Merits, and the dozens of other brands. Who better to hold responsible for the pain and suffering cigarettes caused? But how could he—how could anyone—get back at them? Others had tried, all futilely.

Restless now to come up with a way to stand up to Big Tobacco, Lewis couldn't stay in the hospital room much longer. The still air made him claustrophobic; the antiseptic smell singed his nostrils. It was almost unbearable to look at his emaciated friend or to witness her daughter's suffering. He said goodbye to Jackie and walked slowly down the hospital's old tile hallway toward the elevator.

It wouldn't be easy to tap the tobacco companies' deep pockets, the lawyer reflected. Until 1996, the cigarette makers had never had to pay any money as the result of lawsuits—and they had lost only twice in the courts. All of the courtroom strategies and theatrics thrown at Big Tobacco by attorneys on behalf of dead and near-dead plaintiffs had repeatedly failed to convince judges and juries that the industry was guilty of killing people.

But during his short ride in the hospital elevator, Lewis hatched a plan different from any tried so far: Instead of arguing that Big Tobacco should be punished for murdering with its product, he would get his home state of Mississippi to sue tobacco companies to recoup public money spent treating people—the indigent, the aged—who got sick from smoking.

The tobacco companies had easily fended off decades of lawsuits by claiming that smoking is a personal choice; they shouldn't be held accountable for people's behavior and voluntary decisions, the companies argued. Besides, they said, there was no proof that cigarettes killed smokers.

Lewis decided to skirt this defense by focusing not on individuals and the choices they made but instead on the states—by pressing for reimbursement of the billions of dollars the states spend to pay for the medical care of sick smokers. Surely, Lewis reasoned, there are dozens of top-tier doctors who would testify that tobacco was a major contributor to many of the most expensive illnesses and thus was costing the states a lot of money.

It was such a simple, unique idea that it rattled Lewis. And as he stepped into the cool, late-afternoon air, hung with a faint scent of sweet magnolia, guilt gripped him, because he felt more alive after this visit with a near-dead friend than he had in years.

Lewis, balding, with a slight middle-aged paunch, didn't look or act the part of the high-octane attorney, the kind that typically thrives on signing up hundreds of people to sue big corporations. He preferred wearing polo shirts and khaki pants rather than suits at work. And most of his clients in Clarksdale, population 20,000, were local citizens with real estate, personal injury, and small-business problems.

Lewis was comfortable in small-town America. He grew up in Belzoni, Mississippi, the "Catfish Capital of the World." His house didn't have running water until he was seven.

Lewis joined the U.S. Air Force as a young man and ended up flying jets in Southeast Asia. He later graduated from the University of Mississippi Law School, where he became close friends with several students who would become well-known lawyers in the state, among them Mississippi Attorney General Michael Moore and his associate Richard Scruggs.

Despite his mostly grassroots practice, Lewis made a name for himself in at least one big case: In 1992, he settled a multimillion dollar fraud case, for an undisclosed amount, against a group of insurers, including Blue Cross Blue Shield of Arkansas, who had sold medical policies to an insolvent company.

But that was easy compared to what he was considering now. Taking on the tobacco companies would require hundreds of hours of research, and Lewis knew that would prove too costly for his practice. He would have to have allies, men and women equally committed to his cause.

Lewis gunned his Chevy Blazer, screeched out of the hospital driveway, and began the return trip to Clarksdale from Memphis. After driving only two blocks, Lewis had to pull off the road because his hands were shaking with excitement. He sat in the parking lot of a car dealership, thinking about his plan, trying to calm himself. After a few minutes, he turned on the ignition again and slowly began the 90-minute drive south on Highway 61, past fields where John Deere tractors stripped lines in the soil for cotton, wheat, and soybeans; past bulldozers ripping rocks and turning dirt to hollow out foundations for casinos, Mississippi's latest hope for an economic miracle.

There were lots of questions: How do you prove damages when the cigarette companies had never even admitted—and there was no satisfactory proof—that smoking was dangerous? On what basis would the defendants be made to pay? On the market share of their products? The number of sick smokers in the states? Who would finance the legal attack on Big Tobacco? What penalties should be sought? How much money should Mississippi demand?

These were tough issues. But Lewis had an ace in the hole: Mike Moore, his Ole Miss friend who in 1988 had been elected the state's attorney general and was still in office. Moore was an activist who loved causes that grabbed publicity; he could spearhead the case, Lewis figured.

Moore, 10 years Lewis's junior, was as iconoclastic as Lewis was conservative. On campus in the mid-1970s Moore wore his hair long and played keyboard in a rock 'n' roll band. Lewis was a married former air force pilot by that time and tended to hang out in the library, not blues clubs.

And while Lewis's practice involved mostly local cases that never made headlines, Moore was a Southern populist politician, catching the eye of Mississippians through high-publicity schemes—like nailing warnings on telephone poles that drug dealers would be busted, while photographers snapped pictures to run in the state's newspapers. He became Mississippi's top legal officer by promising to be the people's attorney general, tough on crime and fighting for safe streets.

Moore, the oldest of five children whose father was a real estate developer in the Gulf town of Pascagoula, was one of the new breed of Mississippi politicians who took office in the late 1980s—young, aggressive, reform-minded people like Ray Mabus, who became governor with the dramatic campaign vow, "Mississippi will never be last again," and Mike Espy, the first black elected to Congress from the state in this century. (Espy later was named President Clinton's agriculture secretary but was forced to resign after becoming entwined in a graft scandal.)

When Moore became Mississippi's youngest attorney general in more than 75 years, he and the other up-and-coming state politicians were featured in a *New York Times Magazine* article: "The Yuppies of Mississippi: How They Took over the Statehouse."

Moore was a trim 45-year-old with thick, brown hair and earnest, farm-boy looks. His energetic, head-bent stride lent an air of tirelessness, and he lived up to that image: Between 1988 and 1997, he made more than 2,000 appearances in schools to talk about the evils of drug abuse and smoking. Fulfilling his promise to be the attorney general for all Mississippians—not just special, old-line interests—Moore halted the state's long tradition of fighting all civil rights lawsuits, a move that cleared the way for blacks to win judgeships and other elected positions.

Political observers in and outside Mississippi compare Moore to Bill Clinton. Both were young southern Democrat lawyers with the ability to draw voters across party lines. Both also suffered sobering losses early in their political careers: Clinton was defeated in his first gubernatorial reelection bid in 1980; Moore was beaten in a 1989 congressional race.

Moore's friend Mike Lewis was betting that taking on Big Tobacco, with the surefire headlines and obvious David vs. Goliath analogy, would fit well with Moore's ambitions—whether they led to the state-house or the White House.

Two weeks later, from his office, Lewis telephoned Moore. "I need a reality check," he said, and in 60 seconds laid out his idea to sue the tobacco companies for reimbursement of the state's Medicaid costs to treat poor patients who were sick and dying from cigarettes. "Does this make sense?" Lewis asked. "Do we stand a chance? Will you work with me?"

Moore said he was intrigued. He invited Lewis to visit his office later in the week so they could talk about Lewis's plan in detail. Two days later, Lewis and his wife, Pauline (who was also an attorney), climbed into their four-seat Mooney 205 plane and flew to Jackson, Mississippi.

In a fifth-floor office, Moore and the Lewises spoke for an hour. Moore had some problems with the plan. The biggest one was that the state wouldn't be able to pay any money to the private attorneys working on the case unless they prevailed. "The people in the state of Mississippi don't like the idea of paying lawyers' fees," Moore said.

Lewis said that wouldn't be a problem. Any work he did on the suit would be on a so-called contingency basis: He'd take a percentage of the amount awarded to the plaintiffs after the case was, hopefully, won. Most tobacco suits are handled that way, so almost every attorney will likely agree to this, Lewis added.

Moore also had a suggestion: get Richard "Dickie" Scruggs involved. Scruggs, their Ole Miss law school pal, had made millions toppling Ingalls Naval Shipyard and other asbestos users in 1992 in a series of health liability cases, and it was health liability they were talking about here.

In the next days, Lewis and his wife drove their Cadillac to Greenville, Mississippi, where Scruggs, and yet another Ole Miss law school friend, Don Barrett, were trying a tobacco case on behalf of Anderson Smith, who was diagnosed as a paranoid schizophrenic and began smoking while hospitalized. Scruggs and Barrett were arguing that cigarette companies shouldn't be allowed to employ their usual defense that Smith made a personal decision to smoke, because their client's mental state was impaired. (That contention failed to sway the jury, and Anderson Smith lost the case.)

The Lewises watched the trial for half a day and then met with Scruggs and Barrett at a Hampton Inn.

In the crowded motel room, Lewis laid out his unorthodox and untried plan. He didn't have to work hard to convince the Mississippians.

Scruggs and Barrett had tried several times to get past the industry's defense of pinning individuals with the responsibility of choosing to smoke. The plan to take on Big Tobacco by suing the cigarette companies to pay for the medical costs of the state's 200,000 Medicaid smokers seemed perfect. The industry's argument that smoking was a personal decision couldn't be an issue here.

"Eureka!" said Barrett. "The state of Mississippi has never smoked a cigarette."

That meeting set in motion a year of quiet planning for a lawsuit that everybody in the room—and Mike Moore as well—knew would make or break their careers. Failure on such a public stage and against the high-powered East Coast legal counsel that the cigarette makers would throw against them would be embarrassing. They knew they'd be ridiculed as a bunch of inept southern attorneys with the foolhardy notion that they could actually beat some of the nation's biggest corporations.

Success, on the other hand, would instantly catapult them into the ranks of the nation's boldest and brightest attorneys. And for Mike Lewis, it would avenge Jackie Thompson's death.

It took the Mississippi lawyers almost a year to assemble their case. In May 1994, after thousands of hours of preparation, Moore, Lewis, and the others were ready to go public with their lawsuit.

At a session the attorneys came to call the "Alamo meeting," Moore gave them one last chance to turn back. He stole an idea from the 1950s movie about a group of Texans who made a stand against the Mexican army, in which Col. William Travis (played by Laurence Harvey) draws a line in the sand. Those who crossed it were in the fight; there would be no quitting. Those who didn't could walk away before it was too late.

In Moore's office, Moore, Scruggs, Barrett, and Lewis stepped over the line and shook hands.

On May 23, 1994, Moore walked into the Chancery Court of Jackson County, Mississippi, and filed his landmark lawsuit against 13 tobacco companies as well as wholesalers, trade associations, and industry public relations consultants.

No one was there to represent Big Tobacco. Philip Morris assistant general counsel Steven Parrish told the *New York Times* that a state would have the same burden of proof as an individual, and that could prove difficult. Besides, he added, "no jury has ever concluded that illnesses are directly caused by smoking."

Later that day, at a press conference, Moore said: "This lawsuit is premised on a simple notion: You caused the health crisis, you pay for it. The free ride is over. It's time these billionaire tobacco companies start paying what they rightfully owe to Mississippi taxpayers."

Moore couldn't say he completely believed his own words—this was a case that was far from a sure thing. But bravado made good political theater, and anyway now there was no turning back. They had crossed the line.

MOORE REPLAYED THAT rash moment many times in his mind as the legal battle against Big Tobacco heated up. And on June 20, 1997— three years after filing the Mississippi suit—as he stood in his suite at the ANA Hotel in Washington, D.C., picking out the perfect blue tie to wear before a nationwide TV audience to announce that a settlement with the tobacco industry had been reached, Moore was thinking about how much things had changed.

In 1994, he and his colleagues were alone among the states in taking on the cigarette companies. Since then, 38 other states had mimicked Mississippi's suit and a federal class-action suit, representing individual smokers who accused the tobacco companies of knowingly turning them into cigarette addicts, had splintered into massive local class actions in 17 states.

The surge in legal activity at the state level frightened the cigarette companies into taking their adversaries more seriously, even if Big Tobacco had never before lost a case. The federal government had also stepped up the pressure, launching criminal grand jury probes of the companies and their executives and winning regulatory control of nicotine in a contested courtroom showdown. Those moves helped bring the two sides to the bargaining table.

But the biggest difference for Moore on June 20 was that the doubt was finally erased. Big Tobacco and its foes had forged a settlement. The industry, in large measure, had capitulated.

Hard-won confidence suffused Moore as he walked into the jammed ANA ballroom.

What Moore was about to say was stunning. In a landmark legal settlement, tobacco companies had agreed to pay $368.5 billion over the first 25 years to smokers and states to cover medical costs for cigarette-related illnesses—all of this growing out of the Mississippi suit and Moore's persistence.

This was the all-important first step that no one else had been able to take. There was no going back now, for anybody. Congress would have to approve the settlement, in one form or another. President Clinton would have to back it. And in fact, by mid-September, after a lengthy review amid infighting among his advisers, the president called a press conference and lauded the accord, asking that certain provisions related to teen smoking and the Food and Drug Administration be strengthened. That could add as much as $100 billion to the price tag of the agreement. Big Tobacco didn't flinch; the settlement, cigarette makers said after Clinton's announcement, was still something they could work with.

Mike Moore had clearly tamed what was once a ferocious industry— a marketing machine as powerful as the automakers—and some of the highest-paid corporate attorneys in the world. The concessions that Moore squeezed out of the tobacco companies were remarkable. For one thing, billboard advertisements, vending machines, sports promotions, and ads with people and cartoon characters such as the world-renowned Marlboro Man and Joe Camel, would be banned in the United States. And the cigarette makers promised to help reduce teen smoking by cracking down on retailers that catered to minors and footing the bill for a massive antismoking campaign targeted at kids. The goal would be to deter the 3,000 teens who light up for the first time each day. If the campaign failed, the cigarette companies would have to pay billions of dollars as punishment.

In return, Philip Morris Companies, Inc., RJR Nabisco Holdings Corp., B.A.T Industries Plc's Brown & Williamson unit, and other U.S. tobacco companies would be freed from the shadow of four decades of legal wrangling with smokers and health organizations. The companies no longer would have to worry about class-action lawsuits or state

Medicaid cases and would never have to pay more than $5 billion a year in awards and settlements to individuals.

In other words, for the first time, tobacco companies would know that they couldn't be wiped out by a hostile judge or unsympathetic jury. And they could still make steep profits: In 1997, it cost approximately 20 cents to manufacture a pack of cigarettes that companies then sold for about $2. And after the settlement was approved, they could raise the price.

On the face of it, Big Tobacco would pay dearly for its peace of mind. The agreement's price tag equals the combined annual gross national product of Greece, Ireland, Chile, New Zealand, and Kenya. Each year, the U.S. tobacco companies would ante up to states, federal agencies, public health groups, and smokers—who get to enroll in free programs designed to help them quit the habit—an average of $14.7 billion. If the companies were paying in midsize family sedans, the line of cars would stretch from Los Angeles to Cleveland. In dollars, the settlement was more than 10 times larger than the biggest corporate takeover in history.

Despite these monumental numbers, though, the impact on the companies was likely to be limited. Cigarette makers would pass on the lion's share of the massive settlement bill to consumers in the form of price increases of at least 62 cents a pack. That was expected to result early on in one out of every eight smokers kicking the habit in the United States—but sales would likely remain steady beyond that.

"After the shock of the 15 percent drop over the next couple of years, we'll be back to normal," predicted B.A.T Industries' chief executive Martin Broughton.

There's evidence to support his position. British smokers pay $4.90 a pack, and their numbers are growing.

Even so, on the June afternoon that the settlement was announced, Mike Moore was big news. After all, the tobacco settlement didn't just change the way cigarettes are advertised and regulated, it transformed the role of cigarettes in American society. A "smoke" would no longer be considered an enduring "grown-up" symbol—a macho icon—or even a way to overcome social ineptness, but a highly regulated, dangerous, drug delivery device.

Little wonder that everywhere in the United States—even in Washington, where lots of deals are cut each day—the settlement and Mike Moore had center stage.

At about 3.30 P.M. East Coast time, ABC television broke away from its regularly scheduled *Oprah Winfrey* show to broadcast the news conference. The other networks followed suit soon after, sending millions of viewers to this breaking story.

At the White House, on Capitol Hill, in stock exchanges and corporate boardrooms worldwide, people clicked their remote controls to CNN's minute-to-minute coverage. Editors at the *New York Times* set space on its front page for a double-banner headline, something usually reserved for wars, disasters, and elections.

Mike Moore made the most of the moment. As the cameras whirred and photographers snapped dozens of still pictures, he led a group of seven attorneys general to a bank of microphones on the podium.

The first to speak was Moore. Members of the media, few of whom had seen him before, were taken by his striking resemblance to John F. Kennedy Jr. In his Mississippi drawl, softened a bit for the national audience, Moore started slowly but gradually picked up the pace: "Today is V-Day for the American people in the war on tobacco. This agreement will do more for the public health of our nation than all of our lawsuits combined—even if we had won all of our individual suits. If enacted by Congress, it will save more lives than any public health initiative in memory."

Moore said the agreement had the support of public health groups, which for decades had battled to reduce smoking by warning that it caused lung cancer, emphysema, and other lethal diseases. Tobacco companies, he said, would stop lying about the addictive nature of the nicotine in cigarettes. The U.S. Food and Drug Administration would gain full regulatory authority over nicotine—a huge concession that tobacco companies made in the last weeks of the eight-month negotiations.

As Moore warmed to the topic and the TV audience, he sounded more comfortable by the second. There would be more than 15 minutes of fame attached to this moment, he was certain. Now, he was a household name and finally a player in something more than a small southern pond; this was a huge rushing river, 10 blocks from the White House.

Meantime, hundreds of miles away, in a Sardis, Mississippi courtroom, at just past 4:00 P.M., Mike Lewis was listening to the closing arguments of an opposing defense attorney in a whistle-blower case. Lewis's clients, Sue Sumner and Carolyn Willard, had uncovered wrongdoing at Paracelsus Health Care.

A paralegal slipped into the courtroom and handed Lewis a note. Scrawled on the paper: "CNN just reported a national settlement with tobacco companies for $368.5 billion."

Lewis, still focused on the closing argument, calmly passed the note to his wife, who was helping him try this case. He smiled at her, thinking to himself that he knew he chose well when he turned his idea over to Mike Moore. A short time later, the jury awarded Lewis's clients $3 million.

Some of the nation's most powerful corporate executives, public health advocates, and lawmakers were listening to Moore from their offices and homes. Several had played critical roles in the settlement talks, which began quietly in hotel rooms in Memphis and Washington and on conference calls—and then expanded to big meetings in Chicago, Dallas, and New York as the momentum for an agreement had built.

Among them was former FDA Chief David Kessler, who since 1994 had made tobacco companies his main adversary. He was already working with former U.S. Surgeon General C. Everett Koop to organize a review of the agreement. Removed from the action, they both watched on TV, wondering if their one-time allies had been too easy on Big Tobacco. Within weeks, they would be blasting the accord for leaving in too many loopholes that could prevent the FDA from effectively regulating nicotine.

At the White House, Bruce Lindsey, President Clinton's trusted aide and liaison to the talks, had helped shape the final agreement and persuade the president to say the accord had promise. But Lindsey wasn't around to accept a signed agreement. He had flown off to Denver, Colorado to join the president at a meeting of the Group of Seven (G-7) industrialized nations. Domestic policy adviser Bruce Reed collected the 68-page document.

Some participants in the talks were dejected. Hillary Clinton's brother, Hugh Rodham, who was one of the lawyers representing the plaintiffs in the talks, had been asked by his colleagues not to attend the press conference because consumer advocate Ralph Nader had blasted Rodham's involvement in the negotiations as a blatant conflict of interest for the White House. Rodham was in a hotel conference room across the street, watching the announcement on television.

Bennett LeBow, CEO of Brooke Group, which controls Liggett, the nation's fifth-biggest tobacco company, watched the announcement on an airport TV without sound. LeBow had broken ranks with the industry in 1996 by settling his company's lawsuits with the states before the much larger agreement was negotiated. In that settlement, LeBow agreed to become the first tobacco executive to testify that cigarette smoking is addictive and harmful.

Jeffrey Wigand, former head of research at Brown & Williamson, who became the highest-ranking official to disclose that the tobacco companies manipulated cigarettes to make them more potent and that the cigarette makers knew their product was addictive and dangerous, stood to one side of the packed ANA Hotel ballroom, fighting back tears.

Just before all sides had signed the agreement, Arthur Golden, an attorney with Davis Polk & Wardwell, and RJR Nabisco's point man in the negotiations, called RJR CEO Steven Goldstone. "The deal's done," Golden said. Goldstone replied, "I hope we are doing the right thing."

At the same time, in a hotel room, Murray Bring, Philip Morris's vice chairman and top lawyer, called his boss, CEO Geoffrey Bible. He described the final events leading to the settlement.

Bible, the tough-talking Australian who had kept his competitors in line during the long negotiations, listened to Bring detail the last provisions of the accord, asking few questions. Then, in his 22nd-floor Park Avenue office in Manhattan, after Bible hung up the phone, he leaned back in his chair and lit up a Marlboro Menthol Light.

2

THE THIEF

Today with education, kids are much smarter than they were 10 or 15 years ago. But there are always going to be a small group that smokes. I don't think the settlement will have much of an impact.

—JOANNE LEE

a 34-year-old Wilmington, Delaware, resident who began smoking as a teenager

On the morning of January 6, 1988, Merrell Williams's alarm rang at 6:00 A.M. He showered, dressed, then stood in front of the mirror. This is more like it, Williams thought, admiring his white shirt, tie, neatly pressed pants, and houndstooth blazer. He felt ready for his first day on the job as a paralegal at the Louisville, Kentucky, law firm of Wyatt, Tarrant & Combs. A lot had changed in a month: Just 30 days before he was digging grease pits at a Buick car dealership for $4.50 an hour and raking leaves after work for extra cash.

The position at Wyatt Tarrant wasn't particularly prestigious— Williams would be reviewing eight million pages of documents in a warehouse on the outskirts of town, for $9 an hour—but at least he could go to work in something better than jeans, and he wouldn't come home smelling of motor oil. More importantly, Williams hoped that being at the law firm would give him credibility with the courts in his attempt to win custody of his two daughters from his ex-wife.

With his stubbled chin, receding hairline, pot belly, and droopy eyes, 56-year-old Williams had more in common with country and western songs than John Grisham thrillers.

He was booted out of the army for attacking his sergeant with his helmet. He'd been divorced three times, the first time from a woman he met on a Tuesday and married that Saturday. He couldn't hold a job for long, even though he was well educated as a drama major at Baylor University in Texas and had a Ph.D. in theater from the University of Denver.

He taught drama for a while at Jackson State University in Mississippi, took a trip to England and, inspired by what he saw there, opened an English-style pub in Oxford, Mississippi. He sank $40,000 into the business, borrowing 20 percent from his father and raising the rest by shipping cars from England and selling them at a profit in the United States. The pub failed.

But that was where he met his second wife, Mollie Thurman, who worked at the bar. When the pub was sold, Merrell and Mollie Williams moved to Louisville, to be near her family. They had two kids before divorcing. Unable to find a steady job, Merrell went back to school, taking law courses.

A friend told Williams about the opening at the Wyatt Tarrant law firm. It paid almost as much as teaching, and while there were no benefits he could work a flexible, 40-hour week. The job involved research, which Williams enjoyed.

Williams wore a wool pinstripe suit he had bought in 1976 to the interview at the law firm. He was asked if he had ever smoked cigarettes. "I smoke now," he replied. "But I could quit."

Ironically, that was the perfect answer from Wyatt Tarrant's worst-ever hire. Within months, he would be secreting out of the warehouse confidential documents that showed Wyatt Tarrant's tobacco company clients knew the health dangers of cigarette smoking.

But on that cold, bleak January morning, Williams was anxious to get to work. He turned the ignition of his 1982 Nissan, which he purchased at the car dealership he had worked for, and headed for his new job. The car had 90,000 miles on it and reeked from the cigarette smoke of the previous owner. It cost $2,000, a step up from his prior car, a 1971 Toyota he had bought for $260.

In his 10-mile drive to work on the interstate, Williams passed through downtown Louisville, an Ohio River city that was more Rust Belt than Sun Belt. The home of Churchill Downs and the Kentucky Derby, Louisville had been a major trading and industrial center in the 19th century. But it fell on bad times in the 1970s and early 1980s as businesses fled further south where the labor was cheaper.

By the late 1980s, however, things improved as service industries moved in, attracted by the city's aggressive redevelopment of its downtown area and tax and real estate incentives. United Parcel Service opened a giant distribution center. An impressive skyline sprang up, dominated by the hospital chain Humana's corporate headquarters, complete with 2,000-year-old Roman statues. Historic warehouses were made over into loft housing for employees of the new companies moving in. Merrell Williams pulled off the interstate. He was early. He sat at a nearby McDonald's sipping coffee.

In Wyatt Tarrant, Williams was about to join Kentucky's biggest law firm, a white-shoe partnership with 215 lawyers and roots tracing back to the 1800s. Its partners liked to say that it's a law firm for the people: "The firm's offices are within a day's drive of more than half the population of the United States," they boasted.

One of Wyatt Tarrant's most important accounts, however, was as corporate as they come—Brown & Williamson Tobacco Corp., maker of Kool, Carlton, and Misty cigarettes. With $4.2 billion in annual revenue, Brown & Williamson was one of the state's largest companies, employing more than 600 in Louisville alone. In Kentucky, some 60,000 farmers cultivated the golden leaf for a living, and it was the state's No. 1 cash crop.

When he arrived at the law firm, Williams was put on a team of 10 people who were dividing years of internal Brown & Williamson's documents into categories. This would make it easier for Wyatt Tarrant attorneys to read through the presorted memos and see which would help or hurt them in court. Williams's group put documents dealing with disease in the "D" category; those covering addiction were coded "DA." Anything to do with cancer was put under "DD." And, documents discussing ads targeted to smokers younger than 18 were coded "ABEG."

Williams was warned that the Brown & Williamson memos were secret and must not be shared with anyone outside Wyatt Tarrant. The work was tedious, little more than thoughtless filing after a key word in a document was identified. To break the monotony, some on the research team shot rubber bands and putted golf balls in the office. Williams, though, was never bored. Unlike his colleagues, he read these documents word for word. And the more he read, the more he wanted to know.

It didn't take Williams long to see why the files were confidential: Among them were hundreds of thousands of pages documenting the lengths to which tobacco company executives had gone to hide the risks of smoking.

One of the memos, dated July 1963, was from Brown & Williamson general counsel Addison Yeaman to a research conference in Britain discussing fresh reports of a new cigarette filter: "Scientists now say that tobacco has not only tranquilizing effects, but unique tranquilizing effects. It works more broadly and mildly than what the pharmaceutical companies have come up with. Moreover, nicotine is addictive. We are in the business, then, of selling nicotine, an addictive drug."

Others told of nicotine's sweeping effects on the central nervous system. One, a 1963 report, compared nicotine to how tranquilizers work on the brain. Some executives were worried, the document said, that tranquilizers "may supersede tobacco habits in the near future." And others boasted that nicotine had advantages over drugs like morphine in that its powers to addict were slower and steadier.

One 1985 document was written by a Brown & Williamson executive designating dozens of documents to be shipped out of the country because they could cause legal problems for the company.

Williams was sickened by what he read. He had smoked for nearly four decades, hooked on a pack of Kools a day since the age of 19. His father gave him a carton of smokes every Christmas. And now Williams was seeing firsthand, on paper, Brown & Williamson's cavalier attitude toward the harm cigarettes cause.

For Williams, the subject of these documents proved as addictive as nicotine. He began driving to the University of Louisville library on Saturday mornings to read patent filings and transcripts of congressional hearings held in the 1960s, when lawmakers debated whether or not to put warning labels on cigarettes.

In the spring of 1988, Williams started writing notes from the memos he was sorting, outlining what they said on small pieces of paper or envelopes that he could shove into his pockets. Then he got bolder, taping originals to his body and copying them at the Kinko's store after work. Later he got even more daring, sneaking in to the office on Saturdays to photocopy documents and walk out with a stack of copies.

In all, Williams stole upwards of 4,000 pages of documents.

He said he had no plans to do anything with the documents; he wanted them because he felt he was becoming a witness to a decades-long conspiracy.

All of this ended on February 11, 1992. With the work on the Brown & Williamson account winding down, Wyatt Tarrant gave Williams and two others on his team a month's notice. On March 13, Williams filed for unemployment benefits.

Ten months later, his unemployment checks ran out. Williams came close to taking a job at a Kroger supermarket, but instead decided to sell cars for a Mercury dealer. Then came the next big change in his life.

In March 1993, Williams went to a hospital complaining of chest pains. He was rushed into surgery for a quintuple cardiac bypass.

Williams said his heart attack was "a door opener" in which "God gave me a message"—apparently to use the tobacco documents to punish cigarette makers. He wanted to launch a personal injury lawsuit against Brown & Williamson and Wyatt Tarrant, claiming that the stress of the job had harmed him.

"Call it opportunity if you want, call it opportunism," Williams said. His Louisville lawyer, J. Fox DeMoisey, talked him out of filing the suit, saying his case was based on stolen documents that almost certainly wouldn't be admissible as evidence.

Williams and his attorney decided in favor of a more modest—and potentially lucrative—option: offer to return the documents to Wyatt Tarrant in exchange for $2.5 million.

Not surprisingly, Wyatt Tarrant called the demand extortion and refused to pay a cent. On September 29, 1993, the law firm filed suit against Williams in Jefferson County Circuit Court in Louisville, charging him with breaching his confidentiality agreement.

During this time, Williams kept the boxes of Brown & Williamson documents in his basement in Louisville, unsure of what to do with them. He thought of sending them to the *New York Times,* but realized his initials were on many of the stolen documents, making them easy to trace back to him. Williams was afraid that if the newspaper decided not to use the documents and declined to support him, he could be found and prosecuted. So he simply sent them to Nina Selz, a Baylor University friend in Orlando, Florida, for safekeeping.

Williams began sending cryptic messages, in which he hid his identity, to Richard Daynard, chairman of Northeastern University School of Law's Tobacco Products Liability Project, a group that helped antitobacco activists and attorneys plan cases against the industry. Williams had come across Daynard's name in his private research and wanted to meet him to see if Daynard knew what to do with the documents.

At first, Williams wrote to Daynard in the name of a woman. Then he recruited friends to call up Daynard on his behalf. After several months, Daynard finally consented to see Williams.

Though Williams had a mother-lode of internal documents, Daynard, an attorney, was careful. He never asked to view the stolen files. It could be an elaborate setup by the industry to undercut his work by making him appear unethical, Daynard feared.

Daynard was frank with Merrell Williams: "In the eyes of the law, you're a thief," he said. "You could go to jail."

Williams asked about approaching Congress. Maybe, he thought, the lawmakers would shield him from prosecution.

"There is no guarantee you are going to get congressional immunity," Daynard told him.

Despite his concerns, Daynard knew that the documents, if accurately described, offered an unprecedented opportunity to attack Big Tobacco. So he told Williams to telephone Morton Mintz, a retired *Washington Post* investigative reporter who had covered the tobacco industry. It was possible that Mintz would be willing to write about the documents, Daynard said. He assured Williams that Mintz wouldn't reveal to anyone what Williams had done, even if he wasn't interested in the memos.

Williams contacted Mintz, who was intrigued by the documents and considered using them as the basis for a book about Big Tobacco's duplicity. He backed off, though, after colleagues convinced him that the legal risk of writing a book based on stolen files was too high.

Running out of options, in March 1994, Williams anonymously sent a fax to the Lexington, Mississippi, law office of Don Barrett, the attorney, Williams knew, who was working with Mississippi Attorney General Mike Moore and Dick Scruggs to file the state's landmark

Medicaid suit against the tobacco companies. The fax, which Williams sent from a friend's dress shop, included newspaper articles from Louisville, detailing Williams's theft of the documents and the related lawsuit by Wyatt Tarrant.

A note attached to the fax said, "I've got something to talk to you about." It was signed, "A cautious friend."

Williams had come across Barrett's name in some of the Brown & Williamson documents. Barrett had twice sued Big Tobacco on behalf of a 50-year-old carpenter, Nathan Horton, who died of lung cancer. Barrett argued that the death of his client was caused by pesticides on the cigarettes he smoked for 30 years. To win, he needed nine of twelve jurors to agree. He fell one short. He tried again, this time blaming Horton's death on cigarettes themselves and not on pesticides. The jury sided with Barrett, but awarded zero in damages. After spending so much on this case and getting nothing back, Barrett was almost bankrupted.

Barrett noted the fax number at the top of the page he received from Williams and called an operator in area code 502. Sweet-talking the operator, Barrett managed to get a phone number in the same dress shop as the fax machine.

A woman answered the phone.

"May I speak to Merrell, please," Barrett said, taking a wild stab that it was Merrell Williams who had actually sent the fax.

The woman checked, then said he wasn't there. She gave Barrett a home number for Williams.

When Merrell Williams answered, he was so nervous at being caught sending an anonymous fax that Barrett had to fight to keep him on the phone.

"Don't—. Wait, don't hang up."

Barrett calmed Williams down, and they talked for an hour. Barrett spent most of the call trying to put Williams at ease. Each time he did, he pried out of Williams some more information about what was in the documents. After a second call, the two agreed to meet in Jackson, Mississippi, at the Old Tyme Delicatessen.

Barrett called Dick Scruggs. "I think you might want to fly to Jackson for this meeting," he told Scruggs. "I believe this guy has these documents."

At the Old Tyme, Barrett and Scruggs sat on a Naugahyde bench across from Williams, seated in a chair. Initially, Williams was skittish about Scruggs's presence. Although Barrett introduced him as his friend, an attorney, Williams believed that Scruggs might be an FBI agent. (The mistake was understandable to some degree: The 50-year-old Scruggs, dressed in a tie and with close-cropped hair, can look intimidating and officious.)

Scruggs grew up in Pascagoula, Mississippi, a shipbuilding town on the Gulf Coast, and later joined the navy. He was a fighter pilot in the early 1970s and saw some action in the Middle East when Egypt attacked Israel in 1973. In his heart, Scruggs never left the navy. From his beachfront office in a mansion in Pascagoula, he still gets transfixed by destroyers heading out to sea.

"That's one of ours," he says to anyone in the room. Then, he ticks off the specifications of the ship.

Out of the service in 1974, Scruggs entered Ole Miss law school, the same year as Mike Moore. After graduating, Scruggs jumped from one big commercial litigation firm in Jackson to another before returning to Pascagoula in 1980, where he launched a solo practice and began representing shipyard workers who claimed to have gotten sick after exposure to asbestos.

Scruggs won one trial and was consolidating thousands of other cases when, in 1988, Mike Moore gave his firm Mississippi's asbestos lawsuits aimed at recovering the cost of ripping the cancer-causing material out of state buildings.

In July 1992, almost 20 asbestos companies settled with the state, agreeing to pay $11 million. Scruggs received a $2.5 million fee. Critics carped that Scruggs—who had contributed $20,000 to Moore's campaign—was walking away with too much of the state's money. Scruggs, who took the case on a contingency basis, said the critics should have voiced their concerns four years earlier, when he began spending his own time and money to handle the lawsuit.

One thing is certain: The court victories padded Scruggs's lifestyle. In the early 1990s, he bought a Learjet and a $500,000 mansion on exclusive Beach Boulevard, looking out across the Mississippi Sound, which flows into the Gulf of Mexico.

As it would happen, Scruggs's family ties would play a role in his career. In 1971, Scruggs married Diane Thompson, whose sister seven years earlier had married Trent Lott, the future majority leader of the U.S. Senate. The two men's wives remained close, and the families often spent Christmas and other holidays together. Being the brother-in-law of such a key Mississippi politician only added to Scruggs's prominence as an attorney in the state—especially among those that wanted to keep in Trent Lott's favor.

Over sandwiches at the Old Tyme, Scruggs and Barrett tried to question Merrell Williams about the Brown & Williamson documents. But Williams, downing one dark beer after another, was evasive and wouldn't even admit he had the documents. Scruggs and Barrett were convinced he did, but knew better than to press this clearly troubled man. Nor were the attorneys sure they had any way to use the memos in court, since they were stolen, even if they got their hands on them.

Scruggs grew impatient.

"Why are you here?" Scruggs asked.

"I'm looking for a job," Williams said, characteristically inconsistent and cryptic.

More to get rid of Williams than anything else, Scruggs said he knew a junior college dean on the Gulf Coast. "I'll see what I can do," Scruggs said, exasperated.

Williams said he didn't have enough money to move to Mississippi, if he got a job there. Scruggs gave him $125, and the lunch ended.

After Williams left, Scruggs and Barrett were baffled by the strange man who had made absolutely no sense to them. They had met to talk about the documents, then Williams had done everything he could to avoid talking about them.

"What did he say?" Scruggs asked Barrett and laughed.

Barrett said he had a headache: "I feel like I've got a nail in my left eye."

While the two men didn't know what to make of Williams, they knew that he was probably holding explosive documents—memos that could make their case against Big Tobacco if they could get them introduced in court. So they remained receptive to hearing from him.

A month later, Williams called Dick Scruggs. He needed more money. Scruggs gave him $3,000 in cash and got him a job working for a Pascagoula law firm for $3,000 a month, as much as Williams had earned at Wyatt Tarrant.

In April 1994—just one month before Mike Moore and Dick Scruggs would file Mississippi's Medicaid lawsuit against Big Tobacco—Williams and Scruggs met for a buffet lunch at the LaFont Inn in Pascagoula. As Scruggs took a bite of fried okra, Williams finally dropped the news that Scruggs had been waiting for. Williams said he had the internal Brown & Williamson documents, all right; they were at a friend's house in Orlando for safekeeping.

"I'd like to get this stuff out of the hands of my friend," Williams said.

"I happen to own a former bank building with a vault in it," Scruggs said. "You want to store them there?"

"Great idea," Williams said.

"Well," Scruggs said, "let's get the Lear."

Williams's friend, Nina Selz, met the Learjet carrying Scruggs and Williams at an executive airport in Orlando. Inside the trunk of her Mitsubishi were the documents. She hugged Williams, who looked shaken, and watched as Scruggs loaded the boxes into his plane.

On the flight back to Pascagoula from Orlando, Williams sipped Southern Comfort.

After landing in Mississippi, the two men drove the documents to the old bank building. Scruggs wasn't sure he'd get to see the documents, much less get Williams's permission to use them.

Not long after, Scruggs telephoned Mike Moore and asked for his help in convincing Williams to sign over the documents to the Mississippi lawyers. Scruggs figured that Moore's political stature would sway Williams. Moore flew down to Pascagoula on a Sunday afternoon with Don Barrett. Moore and Williams met for 25 minutes in a dark room at the bank.

Moore assured Williams that Mississippi was a haven for those who had the courage to tell the truth, and he'd vow to protect him to the best of his ability. Williams believed Moore, trusted his earnestness, and signed the documents over to the attorney general.

Immediately, Moore, Williams, Scruggs, and Barrett began poring through the Brown & Williamson memos. To the attorneys, they were eye opening—shocking documents that told the hidden story of Big Tobacco from deep inside. It was a view of the cigarette companies— their most intimate secrets—that nobody had ever uncovered before.

Over and over Scruggs would say, "This is unbelievable."

For the first time, the attorneys were holding industry documents that showed executives knew nicotine was addictive, even as the tobacco companies argued that cigarettes didn't hook smokers. And there were memos detailing how Brown & Williamson officials routed research papers on the dangers of nicotine to company attorneys to prevent the results from being discovered by plaintiffs. This was clearly an abuse of attorney-client privilege and would weaken Big Tobacco's case—if he could somehow get the documents introduced as courtroom evidence, Scruggs thought.

After hours of combing through the documents, Scruggs was convinced that the memos proved the cigarette makers had lied, under oath, in case after case. Big Tobacco attorneys would no longer be able to argue that smokers made a personal choice when they lit up and that the cigarette makers knew of no reason to stop them. Moore and Scruggs's team could attack the industry for not disclosing facts that could have saved smokers' lives.

Merrell Williams got his reward later that week. Although he was broke, Williams purchased a drab, brown house on Diller Road in Ocean Springs, Mississippi, for $109,600 in cash. Scruggs picked up the tab.

Williams also bought a 30-foot Morgan sailboat and a Ford Mustang for himself, as well as a Dodge Neon for his daughter. Scruggs cosigned the loans.

"It sounds like a lot of money, but it wasn't to me," Scruggs said later. "I thought the guy had done a real brave thing. He was in a lot of trouble and needed some safe harbor."

Now that they had the documents, the Mississippi lawyers, too, were faced with a dilemma: The papers were stolen property and they'd never be able to admit them in court. Worse yet, the memos were written by and to Brown & Williamson's lawyers, meaning they were shielded by attorney-client privilege, which protects all communications between lawyers and their clients.

Scruggs and the other attorneys came up with an ingenious plan: copy the documents and disseminate them anonymously—put them in the public domain where anyone could read them. Once they were public, the lawyers figured, the documents could be used in Mississippi's lawsuit.

Within days, the stolen documents were showing up everywhere, including the desk of California Congressman Henry Waxman, who was tobacco's biggest opponent on the Hill. Waxman had just led the series of congressional hearings at which the chiefs of the seven biggest tobacco companies—including Brown & Williamson's Tommy Sandefur—swore nicotine wasn't addictive.

At the same time, an undisclosed federal government official called the Washington Bureau of the *New York Times* to speak with Philip Hilts, the newspaper's tobacco reporter. The official told Hilts he had documents, unbelievable documents, and invited him over to his house to view them.

On May 7—just 16 days before Mike Moore and Dick Scruggs filed the Mississippi lawsuit—the *Times* published a front-page story with the headline, "Tobacco Company Was Silent on Hazards," the first of several high-profile stories based on the Brown & Williamson memos.

That same week, Stanton Glantz, a University of California professor and a leading critic of the tobacco industry, received a set of the internal memoranda in the mail. The sender was a "Mr. Butts." On July 1, 1995, at 12:01 A.M., Glantz posted the documents on the Internet. Now they were available to the world.

THE TIMING OF the documents' release couldn't have been better for Norwood "Woody" Wilner.

Wilner, a lawyer at a tiny firm in Jacksonville, Florida, was about to launch the first of 200 suits he planned against cigarette companies using the classic product liability argument.

Cigarettes cause cancer; therefore, Big Tobacco should pay retribution to its victims, Wilner would argue. Of course, that same contention had failed to sway judges and juries 19 times.

But he had a wrinkle in his strategy that he thought might work. Wilner sought no punitive damages, as had the others who had sued and lost before him. In other words, he wasn't asking for money to punish Big Tobacco. He only wanted a modest cash award for his clients, reimbursement for their costs to fight cigarette-related diseases.

"I never planned to orchestrate an attack to destroy the industry," Wilner said. "I just wanted to take a simple case and ask for compensation."

Wilner, who was one of a half-dozen attorneys hired by Mike Moore and Dick Scruggs to consult on Mississippi's lawsuit, was actually taking a page out of their case—seek compensation, not punishment.

A rumpled, 49-year-old who owned only three suits and rode his bicycle six blocks to work at the Duval County courthouse, Wilner was one of the few attorneys who could say he had actually bruised Big Tobacco in court.

For 15 years, he had represented asbestos companies sued by cancer victims claiming they contracted the disease from working with the material. If the plaintiff was a smoker, Wilner would trot out pulmonary experts and pathologists to argue that cigarettes, not asbestos, were the main reason they had cancer. And in every case, the jury bought the argument and Wilner's clients, the asbestos makers, were found not liable. Now Wilner was determined to convince a court that the cigarette makers were not just passively culpable for causing cancer, as was determined in the asbestos cases, but actively responsible—and should pay for their actions.

Considering Big Tobacco's track record in court, Wilner's chances of success were minimal, he knew. That is, until he discovered the Brown & Williamson documents on the World Wide Web. With these memos, Wilner finally had proof that the tobacco companies were aware that cigarettes were dangerous—addictive and cancer causing—and that they had to tell smokers. That put Big Tobacco in the same category as, say, a ladder maker who knows that the fifth rung will break when 100 pounds of weight is put on it and doesn't warn anyone. By keeping what they knew hush-hush, the tobacco companies were liable for any deadly outcome from cigarettes, Wilner thought.

Now, Wilner needed a client—a sick Brown & Williamson smoker. He ran ads in newspapers across Florida looking for potential clients and then followed up by flying his two-engine Piper airplane across the state to interview candidates. One ad ran in the Jacksonville newspaper in February 1995: "Do you have a cigarette or other product-related illness or injury?" it read. That's how Wilner found Grady Carter.

Carter was anything but the traditional smoker who had taken on Big Tobacco. A fast-living former air-traffic controller who retired in 1990, Carter was known for his daredevil maneuvers while flying small airplanes over southeast Georgia's alligator-infested Okefenokee Swamp. On early Sunday mornings, when most of his neighbors were getting ready for church, he tore through the back streets of Jacksonville on his motorcycle, leaving skid marks on tight corners and kicking up dust on dirt roads.

Carter smoked cigarettes for 43 years—mainly Lucky Strikes, a Brown & Williamson brand. His wife begged him to quit and asked him to join a free smoking-cessation program offered by the Federal Aviation Administration. He refused. His son left newspaper clippings about the dangers of tobacco—one containing a picture of a black, cancerous lung—on the kitchen table so Carter couldn't avoid facing the truth about his habit before he left for the office.

Carter, 67, had always told himself he had a one-in-three shot of getting cancer. Not bad odds, he thought; I'll come out a winner. He was wrong. In 1991 Carter was diagnosed with lung cancer. Half a lung had to be removed. Carter quit smoking—he calls it one of the most difficult things he ever did—and still regrets having to stop: "I like to smoke. I liked the taste, and I didn't like how I felt when I wasn't smoking."

Three years after the surgery, Carter was watching the evening news and was shocked by what he saw: Seven executives from the major tobacco companies raised their right hands and swore to Congress that nicotine wasn't addictive.

It was April 14, 1994. The tobacco executives were in the middle of a six-hour hearing on Capitol Hill, jousting with Democrats and being stroked by Republicans on the House Energy and Commerce Subcommittee on Health and the Environment.

"The data we have been able to see has [sic] been statistical data that has not convinced me that smoking causes death," said Andrew Tisch, head of Lorillard Tobacco Company.

Congressman Ron Wyden, Democrat of Oregon, grabbed the microphone. He asked each of the executives about nicotine and addiction: "Let me ask you first, and I'd like to just go down the row, whether each of you believes that nicotine is not addictive."

William Campbell, head of Philip Morris USA, responded first: "I believe nicotine is not addictive, yes."

"Congressman, cigarettes and nicotine clearly do not meet the classic definitions of addiction," said James Johnston of RJR.

Joseph Taddeo, U.S. Tobacco: "I don't believe that nicotine or our products are addicting."

Edward Horrigan Jr., president of Liggett: "I believe nicotine is not addictive."

Thomas Sandefur, head of Brown & Williamson: "I believe nicotine is not addictive."

Donald Johnston, American Tobacco: "And I, too, believe that nicotine is not addictive."

The testimony was ludicrous to Grady Carter, who like other smokers, had tried to quit, only to give in to almost unbearable withdrawal pains. He seethed.

"I wasn't a crusader until that very minute," Carter said. "Then I became one. I had tried so hard to quit, and there they all were, saying it wasn't addictive. I knew for certain that I wanted to sue these guys."

Carter wasn't a particularly sympathetic plaintiff: He had a decent pension from the FAA, his cancer had been in remission for five years, and because he loved to smoke, he didn't solely blame the tobacco companies for his illness. "I chose to smoke, so I have to take some of the blame," Carter said. "But these guys lied and lied and lied and withheld evidence that might have helped me quit. I felt I wanted to get these liars."

He got his chance when Wilner chose him to be his client in a case against Brown & Williamson. At the trial, Wilner was the first attorney to introduce Merrell Williams's stolen documents as evidence against Big Tobacco. He produced 21 documents—showing in memo after memo that the tobacco company's top executives were clearly aware that cigarettes were addictive and harmful. Worse yet, they chose to bury this research, fearing a slowdown in sales if the information got out.

Brown & Williamson's attorneys fought to keep the documents sealed, arguing that they were illegally obtained. "Those records are confidential and have been stolen from us," said Brown & Williamson spokesman Tom Fitzgerald. "Anyone who is using those documents is continuing the crime."

Judge Brian Davis disagreed, ruling the documents admissible because they showed evidence of fraudulent or criminal conduct. He let the six-person jury use the memos in reaching its decision.

The trial took three weeks. On August 9, 1996, after deliberating for nine-and-a-half hours, the jury in the Duval County courtroom returned its verdict in the case of *Carter v. Brown & Williamson Tobacco Corp.*: "Liability for the lung cancer of Grady Carter is found against the tobacco defendant." Total damages: $750,000—money to reimburse Carter for his medical and related costs. For the first time since an ill-fated verdict a decade earlier, a smoker had defeated a tobacco company in court.

One juror—37-year-old architect Ronnie Fulgham—had been leaning in favor of Brown & Williamson, but the internal documents persuaded him to switch sides. "The documents explicitly spelled out the word addictive," Fulgham said. "Yet time after time, the tobacco companies denied knowing this. They told lies all those years."

Henry Waxman called the verdict "the beginning of the end of the industry."

It was a stunning defeat for tobacco.

Investor reaction was swift and harsh. On the day of the verdict, Philip Morris's shares plunged 12 percent, knocking $12 billion off the stock market value of the world's largest tobacco company. U.S. shares of Brown & Williamson's British-based parent, B.A.T, fell $.31 to $15.625.

"This trial was prejudicially tarnished by allowing the jury to receive inadmissible evidence and to hear testimony based on speculation," Brown & Williamson said in a press statement.

RJR issued a press release in support of its rival: "This verdict is ripe for appeal, and we have every confidence it will be overturned, given the number of significant legal ruling errors that riddled this trial. This ruling runs contrary to all but one previous tobacco verdict, and that was later reversed on appeal. We believe that this case will be no different."

Philip Morris called the verdict a fluke.

THE TOBACCO COMPANIES are hiding their panic, thought Mississippi Attorney General Mike Moore, when he heard the industry's nonchalant reaction to the *Carter* decision. He was certain the verdict wasn't an aberration. The Brown & Williamson internal documents detailed decades of covering up the truth by the tobacco companies, compelling evidence that would play well before any jury; it could be used to question the credibility of the cigarette makers in anything they said.

And by the time of the *Carter* verdict in 1996, it seemed almost certain that Big Tobacco would be spending a lot of time and money in court over the next few years defending itself in dozens of venues. Since Mike Moore's Mississippi lawsuit, filed two years earlier, more than a half-dozen other states had initiated similar cases.

For Moore, getting other attorneys general to follow him had become an obsession. Most of these suits were the result of Moore's hardball and soft-sell lobbying.

He and Dick Scruggs—"Mo" and "Scro" as they called themselves—zipped around the country in Scruggs's Learjet, relentlessly arguing that these cases could be won, especially if every state was onboard. Big Tobacco couldn't defeat the will of the public if the states, representing the people, were unanimously lined up against the cigarette companies, Moore asserted. And since no court case was a sure thing, the more Medicaid actions that were filed, the greater the odds that tobacco would lose at least once.

Minnesota was the second to file. Florida soon followed, aided by a unique law, slipped past most legislators in a midnight session, which said that if the state sued Big Tobacco, the cigarette makers would be barred in court from blaming smokers for their habit.

Some attorneys general, like West Virginia's Darrell McGraw, were easy to convince. Others took more prodding. Moore discussed suing the tobacco industry five times at length with Arizona Attorney General Grant Woods, a Republican populist politician with a local radio talk show who wasn't sure he could win in court and, at first, didn't want to take the chance.

Moore lobbied Woods at two sessions, first at an attorney general conference in Long Beach, California, and next, in June 1996 during a meeting of all the attorneys general in St. Louis, Missouri. By then, Woods had seen enough of the Brown & Williamson documents to feel that perhaps a lawsuit was winnable after all.

In St. Louis, Woods had lunch with Moore and Florida Attorney General Bob Butterworth.

The Democratic attorneys general homed in on Woods, telling him that they needed a strong Republican to file suit to make the attack on tobacco less partisan.

Woods nodded in agreement.

"I'll go ahead," Woods said.

A few days later, on June 19, Woods announced he would be suing the cigarette makers.

After filing his claim, Woods proved to have a sense of humor about his new tobacco foes. In February 1997, when dozens of Congressmen and aides flew to Phoenix, Arizona, to attend a golf junket sponsored by the cigarette makers at the posh Phoenician resort, Woods held his own outing 25 miles away. He joined 25 children on the green felt of the Castle N' Coasters miniature golf course at an event sponsored by the Coalition for Tobacco-Free Arizona.

Woods filed his suit the same day as another Republican attorney general, Carla Stovall of Kansas.

Moore became so obsessed with his war against Big Tobacco that it became almost a religious crusade. During one flight to meet a tobacco whistle-blower, Scruggs and Moore were in the cabin of the plane when they felt the jet sinking far too rapidly on its landing approach.

Scruggs, ranting at the pilots, shouted for the captain to yank the nose up.

The plane landed safely, but the passengers were shaken. Moore, however, was quiet, almost serene. He knew the plane wasn't going to crash, he said. He and Scruggs had a mission to finish: "It's God's work."

Moore had tinkered with his smoothly persuasive style in order to become more animated, almost Elmer Gantry–like, on the subject of tobacco. He'd roll up his sleeves and raise his voice to launch into a story, trying to convince anyone listening of the wisdom of his position.

And when Moore faced resistance, he could become unyielding—a tough negotiator, as the tobacco companies and even his fellow attorneys general found out during the settlement negotiations.

Indeed, Moore's favorite political anecdote shows how he thinks an opponent needs to be handled when the art of compromise and attempts to convince fail.

The story goes that a politician was attending a state fair, exhorting the crowd to vote for him and what he stood for, when he got pulled aside by a constituent. Spitting out a watermelon seed, the constituent said: "You'll never get my vote."

The politician launched into a tub-thumper of a campaign speech, telling the man why a vote for him was a vote for all that is good, true, and right about this great country of ours.

The man considered this for a minute, spat out another seed, and said: "You won't get my family's vote, either."

"Well, fuck you then," said the politician, and walked away.

MOORE WAS RIGHT that cigarette makers were getting worried about their legal liability in mid- to late-1996.

The industry faced several problems: Moore's single-mindedness in signing up state after state to sue; the disastrous verdict in Florida; the prospect of more trials and hundreds of millions of dollars spent defending itself and perhaps paying jury awards; the release of the Brown & Williamson memos; mounting criticism from people like David Kessler, head of the Food and Drug Administration, who wanted the agency to regulate cigarettes like a drug; and falling stock prices. In addition, the Justice Department had initiated five different grand jury investigations into the companies and their executives. Privately, the tobacco companies were cracking under the pressure no matter what they were saying in public.

Since 1995, tobacco company executives on occasion would discuss among themselves the merits of settling the lawsuits against the industry. Steven Goldstone, a longtime corporate attorney for RJR who was picked that year to run the food and tobacco giant, was far from opposed to the idea.

"It's silly to be in a state of siege, spending half your day fighting people," he told his law firm colleagues after joining RJR. "Nobody wants to ban cigarettes. We ought to be able to have rules and play by them."

And in July 1996, just as Grady Carter was about to defeat Brown & Williamson in the Florida courtroom, Philip Morris's CEO Geoff Bible and a few of his top lieutenants flew to Bermuda to discuss settling the mounting litigation against the company. By the end of the week, Bible was convinced that the idea made sense. "But I don't know how you get all the stars aligned," he told the group.

For Bible, this was a dramatic shift. After all, he posed with a lit cigarette in the company's 1994 and 1995 annual reports to buck the prevalent attitude that smoking—once a badge of hipness in the hands of Humphrey Bogart and James Dean—is an embarrassing habit. He also punctuated speeches with vows to keep scrapping with regulators and tobacco foes, rather than settle with them.

Though Bible was intrigued with the notion of settling the lawsuits against the tobacco industry after the meeting in Bermuda, he wasn't planning to do anything about it right away. Then, events overtook him.

In August 1996, days after being defeated in court by Grady Carter, Martin Broughton, the 50-year-old CEO of London-based B.A.T, telephoned Bible.

"There has to be some way to get this all behind us," Broughton said.

"I'm listening," Bible said.

"Have you given any thought to settling the tobacco cases?" Broughton asked.

"We have," Bible replied.

"You know, we have got to do something," said Broughton.

"I know," Bible replied.

"And if we do, we have to take care of all our problems once and for all."

Bible agreed: "First we have to make sure we're united."

Bible told Broughton he'd call RJR CEO Steve Goldstone and Laurence Tisch, CEO of Loews Corp., which owns Lorillard, the United States' fourth-biggest cigarette maker.

In September, the four CEOs began holding top secret meetings at The Plaza, St. Regis, and Four Seasons hotels in New York City. Almost nobody at their companies knew that these meetings were taking place; the executives wanted to make sure that investors and the press were kept completely in the dark about these sessions.

The CEOs didn't immediately decide that a settlement was the ideal alternative.

"Do we have other options?" Broughton asked, concerned that if the companies settled in the United States, they'd be open to massive amounts of litigation around the world, where B.A.T did most of its business.

The alternatives didn't look good, though: protracted legal battles, increased regulatory pressure from the government, criminal probes. The list went on and on.

By the winter, as a group, they decided a brokered peace was better than war.

3

BREAKING RANKS

We tried to diversify, and we'll keep trying, but there's nothing else we can grow that could keep (my brother) David and me here on the farm. We got workers' families in Mexico we're supporting off this farm and two families from town.

—RICHARD CONNOR

a 29-year-old second-generation tobacco farmer in Halifax, Virginia, worried
that the demand for his crop will fall if the settlement curbs smoking

The tobacco CEOs had another reason to settle their legal disputes with states and smokers at the end of 1996—their once-vaunted industry unity was shattering. Bennett LeBow, chief executive officer of Liggett Group, was cutting his own deals with the industry's opponents.

In March 1996, five months before Grady Carter and Woody Wilner beat Brown & Williamson in a Florida courtroom, LeBow stunned the other cigarette makers by settling out of court with class-action lawyers and with five states, including Mississippi. LeBow agreed to pay less than $26 million in all—$5 million over the next 10 years and as much as 7.5 percent of Liggett's pretax profit for up to 25 years. In exchange, Liggett would be freed from lawsuits filed to recover state Medicaid money spent treating sick smokers.

The other CEOs were unnerved. LeBow had kept the negotiations secret, to the point where his counterparts first heard of his deal on television.

For LeBow, it was a do-or-die strategy. Unlike the rest of Big Tobacco, his company was rapidly running out of money.

In the last decade, Liggett had tried to steal market share from its larger rivals by selling generic and discount cigarettes.

But Philip Morris responded in mid-1993, slashing prices of top-selling Marlboro and other brands by 40 percent. Unable to withstand this price war, by 1996 Liggett's market share had plunged to less than 2 percent, or one million smokers. The company made only $11 million a year in pretax profit, a fraction of its competitors' earnings. And Liggett was spending $10 million a year on legal bills.

LeBow figured if even one of the five states suing the tobacco industry prevailed in court, Liggett would go bankrupt paying its portion of the judgments. By settling separately for what amounted to at most 55 cents a year for each of the company's smokers, LeBow ensured Liggett's survival.

But for Big Tobacco, LeBow's capitulation shucked forever the myth that the industry is a monolith which would never change its position or admit any wrongdoing. With Liggett conceding defeat, all of the cigarette makers appeared more vulnerable.

The tobacco companies realistically shouldn't have been surprised by LeBow's actions, which weren't out of character. For one thing, the 59-year-old, bearded, 5-foot-7-inch LeBow—"5-foot-7½ in shoes," he liked to say—didn't have tobacco in his blood.

He was best known as a second-tier corporate raider, who tended to buy distressed companies on the cheap, rebuild them, and then try to sell them for a profit. LeBow didn't care what business he acquired as long as he made money on the deal. Since the early 1960s, he had purchased companies that made jewelry, computers, microfilm, planes, and trading cards.

A typical LeBow transaction was his takeover of Western Union.

In 1987, LeBow bought what was left of Western Union Telegraph Co. for $25 million. Some on Wall Street said that was $25 million too much, since the company had a negative net worth of $200 million: Its debt was far greater than its assets.

But LeBow somehow smelled opportunity—though it seems like more luck than acumen that made this questionable investment successful.

Even though the company's money-transfer business was wavering, Western Union had a good chunk of the telex business, a way to send text messages by telephone. So LeBow asked Drexel Burnham Lambert's junk-bond king Michael Milken to push the strength of telex to sell $500 million of low-grade, high-interest Western Union bonds. Investors bought the pitch and that enabled Western Union to refinance its debt and keep its creditors at bay—for a time, anyway.

By the early 1990s, however, fax machines made telex obsolete. So LeBow shut down Western Union's telex business and scraped up some needed cash by selling the company's electronic-mail unit to AT&T. He used the proceeds from this deal to buy back some Western Union debt from suffering bondholders, at 50 cents on the dollar. These moves were too late to prevent Western Union's bankruptcy in 1993. The company's stockholders were all but wiped out.

Suddenly, though, Western Union started to improve—mostly because its money-transfer business became popular among U.S. immigrants sending cash to their families overseas. And in November 1994, First Financial Management, an Atlanta, Georgia, data services company, paid $1.2 billion for the company—48 times what LeBow had bought it for. After retiring Western Union's debt and funding its pension system, LeBow walked away with $300 million in cash.

"I go after high-risk deals," LeBow said. "The returns are higher."

He became CEO of Liggett in 1986 when GrandMet USA, the American subsidiary of British conglomerate Grand Metropolitan Plc, put Liggett's U.S. cigarette operations on the block, having sold the overseas rights to its brands to Philip Morris earlier. Liggett was in such terrible financial condition that LeBow was able to buy the company for a measly $137 million. A year later, LeBow sold a 13 percent stake in the company to the public, raising $43 million and valuing the company at $330 million.

Liggett could ultimately prove to be a big winner for LeBow personally. By 1988, using revenue from cigarettes, LeBow was able to pay off a substantial portion of the debt he accumulated when he bought Liggett. Even now, he'd be able to sell Liggett for several hundred million dollars.

But none of that made him part of what he called "the little fraternity" of tobacco executives. "Everybody did what Philip Morris did," said LeBow. Liggett was "the peanut of the crowd."

And when Liggett broke ranks with the other tobacco companies in early 1996 and settled lawsuits with five states, smashing the notion of industry unity, LeBow had a ready answer for why he did this. "I'm an economic animal," he said. "I'm the chairman of a public company. We do what's good for the company. A traitor to the tobacco industry— I don't know what that means."

His irreverence toward the tobacco industry was evident in the days leading up to his secret settlement with the five states. Just prior to the announcement of the deal, LeBow's law firm had subleased new offices in New York City from RJR Nabisco.

LeBow couldn't let the coincidence go untouched. He decided to throw a party on the night Liggett's settlement was announced—at his law firm's new midtown Manhattan quarters. The irony of RJR's ignorance of this stunning adverse development, while a noisy party was being held on its property to celebrate it, suited LeBow's puckish sense of humor.

His delight lasted only a few months, however. By the fall of 1996, LeBow was getting nervous that the other tobacco CEOs could overtake him and forge a national settlement with the states suing it that would include Liggett—one that LeBow's cigarette company likely couldn't afford.

LeBow had his attorney Marc Kasowitz call Mississippi Attorney General Mike Moore to sound him out about whether Liggett could work out an agreement with the other states that were suing Big Tobacco before a broad agreement was reached with all of the cigarette makers. Because Moore had already reached an accord with LeBow, he told Kasowitz to call Arizona Attorney General Grant Woods. In that conversation, Woods agreed to work toward another separate settlement for Liggett.

On October 17, Bennett LeBow flew to Phoenix, Arizona, to meet with a small group of attorneys general at Woods's office. In the seven months since LeBow had settled with five states, nine more had sued the tobacco industry.

LeBow wasn't certain that the attorneys general would agree to another settlement, because there was some criticism that he engi-

neered the first deal with the states just to make his company an enticing takeover target.

Earlier in the year, LeBow had purchased 5.2 million shares of RJR
Nabisco, and fellow 1980s corporate raider Carl Icahn had acquired 13
million RJR shares. That gave LeBow and Icahn almost 7 percent of RJR's
stock and a leg up towards taking control of the company's board. LeBow's
plan was to take over RJR and then have RJR buy Liggett from him.

Although by October LeBow had already sold about half of his RJR
stock, he wanted the attorneys general to agree to a provision in their
new accord with him that they had okayed in the first deal: a stipulation
that extends the terms of his settlement to any company that acquires
Liggett, namely RJR.

The attorneys general rejected LeBow's power play. RJR was too big
a cigarette maker to let it be grandfathered into the kind of small settlement that Liggett would get.

LeBow's insistence on this was costly. RJR's shareholders rejected
LeBow's and Icahn's attempt to take control of the company's board.
That left LeBow with no chance to take over RJR—and have RJR buy
Liggett—and no settlement with the states.

Shut out by the attorneys general, LeBow came up with another
audacious plan to ease Liggett's woes.

He sent Marc Bell, the general counsel for Liggett's parent Brooke
Group, to ask Philip Morris attorneys if the tobacco giant would proffer
some financial help to head off another Liggett settlement with the states.

LeBow wasn't just being cheeky. Though a rival, in the past Philip
Morris had anted up as much as $10 million to cover Liggett's legal
costs. That was the industry's way of propping up its weaker colleagues
in return for keeping everyone in line.

On December 11, 1996, Bell met for an hour with two Philip Morris
attorneys at a site where they had something of a home-court
advantage—the Harvard Club, located at West 44th Street in New York
City, a few blocks west of Philip Morris's Manhattan headquarters.

The lawyers walked past the mahogany-paneled walls, festooned
with elephant heads and other trophies from Theodore Roosevelt's collection, as well as paintings of Harvard presidents dating back to the
19th century. They faced each other over coffee at a table in a dark corner of the club.

During a one-hour meeting, Bell said that Liggett needed more money to pay for defending itself from the suits against Big Tobacco. Not only that, Liggett wanted to be indemnified from future court losses that might bankrupt it. If Philip Morris refused to help, Bell said, Liggett would have to break ranks again.

LeBow KNEW THAT Philip Morris CEO Geoff Bible was furious with him. To Bible, LeBow was a turncoat, and he had to be mad to think Big Tobacco would help him now. It was the sort of tough-minded stance that tobacco executives had come to expect from Bible when he'd made up his mind about what was good or bad for the industry.

Shortly after becoming CEO of Philip Morris, Bible took on the ABC television network for a February 28, 1994, segment on its news magazine show, *Day One*.

The program reported that in the course of making cigarettes, tobacco companies took out some of the nicotine and then added back a greater amount, increasing the percentage of nicotine in cigarettes. ABC said that this amounted to nicotine "spiking," that is, fortifying cigarettes with additional nicotine and purportedly making smoking more addictive.

Geoff Bible couldn't ignore this charge. Soon after the show, Philip Morris lodged a $10 billion libel suit centering on use of the word "spiking." Bible won. The network—now owned by the Walt Disney Co.— eventually agreed to pay a $15 million settlement to cover Philip Morris's legal fees and issued a public apology for mistakenly reporting that tobacco companies add significant amounts of nicotine from outside sources.

Bible gloated in victory. Philip Morris's top executives and its legal team celebrated at the Rainbow Room, high above midtown Manhattan, dining on salmon and smoking cigars. Bible made an emotional speech praising the company's top outside lawyer on the case, Herbert Wachtell.

Later that year, Bible took on New York City Mayor Rudolph Giuliani when the city considered legislation to restrict smoking in public places. Bible told the mayor that the No. 1 cigarette maker would consider moving its offices from the city if the bill passed. A weaker bill passed, and the company's Park Avenue headquarters remained one of the few Manhattan office buildings where smokers can light up.

Bible's tenacity in many ways personifies Philip Morris, the industry kingpin that traces its history to 1847, when a Briton named Philip Morris opened a London tobacco store that sold pipes, cigars, and cigarettes. Seven years later, Philip Morris started making his own cigarettes with his name on the label.

When Philip Morris died in 1873, Leopold Morris bought the business from his brother's widow, sold stock to the British public, and led the company through 20 years of prosperity. In 1893, however, the firm went bankrupt after rival companies offered customers free cigarette samples and lower prices. A year later, U.K. industrialist William Thomson took control and started Philip Morris on a global marketing course, which a century later would become a hallmark of Geoff Bible's success.

Part of Thomson's strategy was to export Philip Morris cigarettes to the United States. One of its top-selling brands was a cigarette named after Marlborough Street in London, where the home company's factory was located.

Philip Morris remained just another player in a crowded U.S. market until the Depression, when other cigarette makers raised their prices—partly to pay for new cellophane wrappers on cigarette packs. Philip Morris countered by introducing inexpensive brands, and its sales took off. By 1940, the company rose to a solid No. 4 position with 10 percent of the market, buoyed by its namesake brand and Marlboro cigarettes.

The company used an early recognition of the power of advertising on radio and television to boost sales in the 1950s. It became inextricably linked to an ad campaign that featured bellboys bellowing, like town criers, one of the most-remembered lines in U.S. marketing—"Call for Philip Morris!"

An important expansion came in 1954, when Philip Morris bought Benson & Hedges, another cigarette manufacturer, for $22.4 million. The deal added the Parliament brand to Philip Morris's line, and Benson & Hedges President Joseph Cullman stayed on as an executive vice president. He became president three years later after company head Parker McComas died.

Cullman moved Philip Morris into other international businesses, such as American Safety Razor Co., one of the first makers of stainless steel razor blades.

In perhaps his most far-reaching product decision, Cullman hired the Leo Burnett Advertising Agency to breathe life into Marlboro cigarettes, then a lackluster woman's brand. Thus was born a marketing icon—the "Marlboro Man"—a lone cowboy dressed in a sheepskin coat, riding his horse through the rugged back country. Men worldwide fell for the campaign (no matter that some of the ads were actually filmed on New York City's very eastern Staten Island), and by 1975 Marlboro was the top-selling cigarette in the United States.

In 1969, Philip Morris acquired Miller Brewing Company for $227 million, adding Miller Beer, Milwaukee's Best, and Magnum Malt Liquor to its product mix. Sixteen years later, it turned its attention to food, paying $5.6 billion for General Foods. And in 1987, the company bought Kraft Foods for $13.1 billion.

Today, Philip Morris products can be found in most of the nation's kitchen pantries and refrigerators. They include Claussen pickles, Jell-O desserts, Kool-Aid drink mix, Kraft macaroni and cheese, Minute Rice, Oscar Mayer hot dogs, and Raisin Bran cereal.

But the company makes almost half of the cigarettes that Americans smoke each year, and about two-thirds of Philip Morris's earnings come from tobacco. That fact isn't lost on chairman Geoff Bible, an Australian by birth and an accountant by training.

Bible, 59, is small of stature, with wire-rim glasses and slick-backed gray hair—a Hollywood version of a number cruncher. He joined Philip Morris's overseas unit in 1968 as manager of finance and director of planning and left two years later to manage the Geneva office of a brokerage house. He returned to the tobacco company in 1976 as vice president of Philip Morris International's finance and strategic development.

Bible caught the attention of Philip Morris higher-ups with his successful marketing schemes. In 1981, Bible managed the company's tobacco business in Australia at a time when Rothmans, the company controlled by the South African Rupert dynasty, was gaining market share by keeping its cigarette prices low. To counter Rothmans, Bible put 30 cigarettes in a pack of Peter Jacksons, a Philip Morris brand, instead of the usual 20, and didn't raise the price. In effect, he reduced the price per smoke by 33⅓ percent.

Peter Jackson's market share nearly doubled instantly, and Philip Morris's overall sales in Australia skyrocketed. So did Bible's career.

In 1983, Bible was promoted to executive vice president; four years later, he was made head of Philip Morris's international tobacco operations, where he continued to prove his cunning by picking promising emerging markets in Southeast Asia and negotiating with foreign ministers to secure favorable long-term tax and royalty incentives for the tobacco company.

Bible spent $400 million on a large, new plant in Turkey, and Philip Morris sales in that country soon topped the company's performance in France and England combined. With the collapse of Communism in Eastern Europe in 1989, Bible poured cigarettes into the region and into the Soviet Union, marketing and advertising the brands with campaigns costing hundreds of millions of dollars.

Bible was named CEO of Philip Morris in 1994, after Michael Miles resigned under pressure from Philip Morris directors who thought that Miles was promoting the food business more than the cigarette unit and cutting into profit. Miles, a marketer and a nonsmoker, spent most of his career at Kraft and wanted to split Philip Morris into two companies— food and tobacco—to enable shareholders to invest in Kraft without worrying about the prospective costs of tobacco litigation.

As CEO, Bible dumped the split-off idea. Instead, he zeroed in on building profits at the company as a whole, getting rid of what he called "hippos"—slow-growing, less-profitable businesses like baked goods— and concentrating on "greyhounds"—high-margin products such as tobacco, cheese, coffee, and candy.

It worked. Since 1993, Philip Morris's sales have been up 14 percent to $69.2 billion; earnings have more than doubled to $6.3 billion.

By the last half of 1996, Bible's shrewd marketing decisions had helped Philip Morris overtake B.A.T Industries to become the world's largest cigarette seller. And Geoff Bible had become the mouthpiece and leader—the soul in many ways—of Big Tobacco.

CONSIDERING BIBLE'S TENACITY—and his well-known anger towards LeBow—it was foolhardy for Liggett attorney Marc Bell to think that his meeting with the two Philip Morris attorneys would shake loose any money for Liggett. But Bell did deliver a threat that he thought might carry some weight with Bible. At the Harvard Club session, he told the attorneys, James Cherry and Kenneth Handal, that unless Bible agreed to foot more of Liggett's legal bills, there was a strong chance that the company would have to seek protection from its creditors in bankruptcy court. There, a judge could release the company's stash of top secret industry documents.

"It's possible a bankruptcy trustee could have access to these documents," Bell said.

For much of the meeting, Philip Morris's attorneys had listened to Bell's plea for cash in stony silence.

As they got up to leave, Cherry said only: "We hear you. It is a persuasive argument. We'll get back to you."

Two weeks later, Bell was sitting at his office in the Miami, Florida, headquarters of Brooke Group, the parent of Liggett. A one-page letter came across his fax machine. The letter, signed by attorneys Cherry and Handal, wasn't the answer Bell or LeBow had hoped for.

The terse letter said simply that Philip Morris wasn't going to pay any more of Liggett's legal fees.

As LeBow should have expected, Geoff Bible had spoken.

4

THE BROKERS

It's like trying to hold the condom manufacturers responsible for kids having sex.

—GARY BLACK
Sanford C. Bernstein & Co. tobacco industry analyst

I n the summer of 1996, at the time that the CEOs were beginning their secret talks in New York about a tobacco settlement, Republican Senator Trent Lott of Mississippi had the same thing on his mind.

Two years earlier, the GOP swept the mid-term elections, snagging both houses of Congress by convincing the electorate that the Democrats were the party of special interests. Republican candidates told voters that the Democrats, headed by President Bill Clinton, had lost sight of grassroots concerns like balancing the budget, putting criminals in jail, simplifying the federal government, and slashing perquisites of power on Capitol Hill.

The GOP likened the 1994 election to a people's revolution, and won 54 percent of 435 House of Representative seats and 68 percent of the 35 vacant Senate seats. Lott became majority leader and Georgia

Representative Newt Gingrich was chosen Speaker of the House.

But the GOP ascendancy was short lived. By 1996, Clinton had turned the tables with some creative political jockeying. The President co-opted Republican positions and all but abandoned the liberal wing of his party. He jettisoned New Deal–like programs, including an ill-fated national health insurance plan, and supported welfare reform. Clinton even lobbied for Republican initiatives, such as the V-chip, which blocks objectionable TV programming in homes.

With the 1996 presidential and congressional elections approaching, Clinton was more popular than ever. Even early in the year, Lott knew that GOP chances for winning the White House were slim; an incumbent president—indeed, one who was an energetic, quick-witted campaigner with a high approval rating—would be tough to beat. The likely Republican nominee for president, former U.S. Senator Bob Dole from Kansas, was 20 years older than Clinton. While Dole's World War II record and long service to the country would win the electorate's admiration, Clinton was presiding over a five-year economic expansion. Clinton would be reelected, Lott was certain.

So, Lott focused on keeping the Republicans in control of Congress. A key liability, one that Democratic campaigners were certain to attack, was that Republicans were seen as soft on Big Tobacco because they were beholden to the industry.

After all, the tobacco industry contributed more than $5.75 million to Republican coffers for the 1996 election, more than five times as much as they gave to Democrats. Every chance they could, the president and cabinet members painted Big Tobacco as the evil face of corporate America, addicting the nation's young people to cancer-causing cigarettes. The few Republicans who discussed the issue at all were pro-tobacco, such as U.S. Senators Jesse Helms and Lauch Faircloth from North Carolina, both of whom argued for more subsidies for their states' tobacco farmers.

It didn't help that at the GOP 1996 convention in San Diego, cigarette companies were extremely visible, spending millions to entertain visiting politicians. Philip Morris took congressmen and senators for moonlight excursions on San Diego Bay on a catamaran called the *Mantis*. UST, the nation's largest smokeless-tobacco company, ferried delegates on its ninety-foot, two-deck yacht.

Philip Morris also sponsored a boisterous party at the San Diego Museum of Art, where a mariachi band strolled through the gardens as politicians ate turkey burritos. Outside the soiree, two dozen protesters hoisted placards that read: "This event is paid for with tobacco money" and "Tobacco kills; don't go in."

Somehow, Lott had to play down the GOP's relationship with Big Tobacco before the party paid for it at the polls. One way was to work with his Mississippi friends Mike Moore and Dick Scruggs to craft an expensive—but not too expensive—settlement of the states' tobacco suits, which included some wording about toning down cigarette advertising and teen smoking. He would then submit this accord as a Republican-sponsored bill in Congress. Even if it didn't pass before the end of the year, the GOP could go into the elections saying that while Clinton might be talking about the evils of tobacco, Republicans were doing something about it.

As Lott saw it, this was a plan that would be easy to put in motion. He knew from Scruggs, his brother-in-law, that Mike Moore and Scruggs were not particularly hopeful about winning their Mississippi Medicaid suit against Big Tobacco. The cigarette makers are just too formidable in court. A legislative settlement that gave Mississippi some of the money the state was asking for, and at the same time brought the tobacco companies to heel, would accomplish the lawsuit's aims and save the attorneys the embarrassment of losing.

The friendship of Lott, Scruggs, and Moore was strengthened by their shared roots in Pascagoula, Mississippi, a Gulf Coast town of 26,000 linked to Interstate 10 by a long bridge across the Escatawpa River. Pascagoula was named for an Indian tribe that committed mass suicide, joining hands, wading into a river, and drowning rather than be defeated by a rival tribe.

The biggest employer in Pascagoula was the Ingalls Shipbuilding Division of Litton Industries, builder of some of the huge warships that fought in the Persian Gulf War. The plant and its suppliers employed Lott's stepfather, Dick Scruggs's mother, and hundreds of others in Pascagoula.

Lott, Moore, and Scruggs went to the University of Mississippi in Oxford—a town noted for producing such varied southern literary lights as William Faulkner and John Grisham. The three sons of Pascagoula all received their undergraduate and law degrees from Ole Miss.

In early 1996, Lott talked to Scruggs about drafting a tobacco settlement bill. Lott told his brother-in-law that he couldn't be involved directly in the effort, because if it backfired or was seen as too soft on the industry, Republicans would be open to more criticism about their close ties to cigarette companies. But Lott said he did want to help.

Lott suggested that Scruggs get in touch with two Republican activists who could serve as liaisons to the tobacco industry in settlement discussions. One was Tommy Anderson, an old acquaintance of Scruggs's and yet another Ole Miss graduate. Anderson, a bespectacled redhead with a pronounced twang, was Lott's chief of staff for 17 years.

The other was John Sears, a White House lawyer in the Nixon Administration and a one-time Reagan campaign manager. Sears kept a hand in Republican politics but worked mostly outside the country, setting up joint ventures for U.S. firms and negotiating deals with Third World countries and former Communist bloc officials.

When Scruggs contacted Anderson and Sears, he was beginning to see that a national settlement could indeed be reached. Liggett's accord with five states showed that an agreement between tobacco companies and their foes was at least possible. And a comment that RJR's chief executive Goldstone made in the March 22, 1996, edition of the *Financial Times* regarding a possible settlement was also promising.

"I don't know of a way [a settlement could be found], but I do know that it isn't the kind of thing that the tobacco industry would try to obstruct," Goldstone said. "We know that litigation is not good for our companies."

In a conference call with Anderson and Sears, Scruggs told them: "I have two rules. First, total confidentiality. Second, you'll get paid only if a settlement becomes law."

Anderson and Sears agreed to Scruggs's stipulations. And in April, to get the talks in motion, Lott called RJR CEO Steve Goldstone and asked him to meet with Sears and Anderson as a personal favor. Goldstone consented.

Before meeting with the tobacco executives, Anderson and Sears conferred with Lott about their role. They didn't have authority to promise anything, Lott told them. Their mission was just to test the waters.

The meeting was held in early May at RJR headquarters on Sixth Avenue in midtown Manhattan. Sears, Goldstone, and RJR general counsel Rob Sharpe attended.

Sears, his white, stringy hair a bit unkempt, began by telling tobacco executives, "I'm not here to negotiate. I'm here to find out whether this can be settled."

After taking a long drag on a Viceroy cigarette, Sears asked if the industry would lobby against a bill that prohibited future suits but forced the companies to compensate states for Medicaid expenses. Later, Sears threw out a settlement figure—50 cents for each pack of cigarettes sold, or $12 billion, a year.

"A lot of money," Sharpe said.

Sears thought to himself that this was an interesting response: "He didn't say, you have to be kidding. He didn't tell us to get out of his office." Sears took that as a promising sign.

He went back to Scruggs and interpreted the meeting succinctly: "They want peace. These guys are tired of being outlaws."

Four times during the summer of 1996, Sears and Anderson returned to test ideas on the companies—such things as a compensation fund for smokers and a clearer definition of the role the FDA would have in regulating tobacco. The companies floated a proposal: The FDA would only be allowed to regulate nicotine if smoking rates among teens failed to decline 50 percent over a certain period of time.

Sears kept members of the Republican leadership informed of the progress of the talks, including House Speaker Newt Gingrich and Thomas Bliley, a U.S. congressman from Richmond, Virginia. Bliley's support for Big Tobacco prompted Democrats to nickname him the "representative from Philip Morris."

Gingrich and Bliley, along with Lott, encouraged Sears to press ahead.

Sears began faxing proposals to Scruggs, who would discuss them with Mike Moore.

In early August 1996, Sears asked Lott if he agreed it was time to write a draft bill that would outline a settlement between tobacco companies and states. Lott, sensing he had a consensus among key congressmen, state attorneys, and tobacco CEOs, said to go ahead.

Sears, Anderson, Lott, and Scruggs drafted the bill. It called for the tobacco companies to pay the states $150 billion over 15 years. In return, the cigarette companies would be freed from not only the states' cases, but also from any suits from individuals concerning the harmful effects of tobacco. Also, Big Tobacco would be spared having the Food and Drug Administration regulate nicotine as a drug.

Lott's bill never even reached Congress. The draft legislation was read to *Wall Street Journal* reporters Alix Freedman and Suein Hwang, and on August 26, 1996, the newspaper published an article that laid out details of the settlement. "Legislation Plan on Tobacco Advances," the headline said. The minute the newspaper hit the streets, the deal was dead.

Powerful opponents rose up from all sides. Health advocates like Matt Myers, executive vice president of the National Center for Tobacco-Free Kids, condemned it, calling it "a sellout," and said the plan was "too soft on the industry."

U.S. Congressman Bliley deftly tried to hide his involvement in the talks. To distance himself from the legislative proposal, he called tobacco "a question for the courts, not Congress."

RJR issued a terse denial that any talks existed: "Our tobacco subsidiary is not interested in—and has no intention of—settling the cases against it and remains confident in the strength of its defenses." Philip Morris declined to comment.

Mississippi's Mike Moore took a lot of heat from other state attorneys general, who were angry they were kept ignorant of the settlement negotiations.

At a tense meeting in a downtown Chicago hotel during the Democratic National Convention in August 1996, a dozen state attorneys general lashed into Moore for negotiating behind their backs. If he thought he could broker a settlement without getting their okay, he was mistaken, they told him.

"This is the wrong focus," said Connecticut Attorney General Richard Blumenthal. "Winning in the courtroom and coordinating our efforts is what we have to be doing."

Minnesota Attorney General Hubert Humphrey III was especially critical of the proposal. "I am very skeptical of any effort by the congressional majority to allow a group of businessmen to secure special legal immunity from the laws all other businesses must obey, simply because the industry is politically powerful," he said.

Moore, chastened, acknowledged that he had made a tactical mistake in not informing his colleagues. "If there are any more talks with the industry, you'll be the first to know," he promised.

The news report on the talks angered others with an interest in tobacco lawsuits. One was Wendell Gauthier, a silver-haired, 56-year-old attorney from the bayous of Iota, Louisiana.

Gauthier was a classic accident-victim lawyer, with a silken voice that opponents said could argue the skin off a snake, and his cases tended to be a bit more high profile than whiplash in a 10-car pileup on Interstate 10. Gauthier won $10.1 million for the victims of the 1982 crash of Pan Am flight 759 outside New Orleans. And he topped this in 1986, when he negotiated a $220 million settlement for the 96 people killed during a fire in the Dupont Plaza Hotel in San Juan, Puerto Rico.

Gauthier's best friend was Peter Castano, a 47-year-old Louisiana criminal defense attorney, who died of lung cancer in 1993 after trying to quit numerous times. At his funeral, Castano's wife asked Gauthier to sue the tobacco industry for the family. He didn't accept right away, saying the odds of success were too low.

But her plea stuck with Gauthier. In the ziggurat of lawsuits, suing Big Tobacco was always at the top of the pyramid for plaintiff attorneys—the potential payday was so huge and enticing, even if victory was elusive. And by early 1994, Gauthier decided to take the Castano case. He was just cocksure enough to think he had a new angle that would resonate with a jury. Instead of arguing that cigarettes caused illness and death, as the failed suits had done, Gauthier would focus on addiction.

Unlike Mississippi, which wanted restitution for the state's medical bills, Gauthier's clients would be a class made up of individual smokers. He would contend that tobacco was habit forming, and smokers weren't forewarned. The bold letters on cigarette packs spelled out only that tobacco can cause cancer, heart disease, or emphysema. There was nothing on the packs that said cigarettes were addictive.

Gauthier's idea was to create a class of more than 50 million smokers nationwide who would sue Big Tobacco for the costs of medical monitoring and smoking-cessation programs, compensation for being addicted to tobacco. With millions of plaintiffs, Gauthier would sue for tens of billions of dollars in damages. If he took even a fraction of the usual 25 percent in legal fees, Gauthier's compensation from a judgment would be enormous.

The Louisiana attorney lined up 65 of the nation's top trial lawyers to defray the cost of filing a class-action suit. One was John Coale, the first

American attorney on the scene after the Union Carbide disaster in Bhopal, India in 1984 in which more than 3,000 people died from exposure to a cyanide-based compound. He came to be known as "the Wizard of Bhopal" because he signed up as clients thousands of victims of that disaster and won more than $200 million for them before a federal judge dismissed the case.

Also joining Gauthier's team were Hugh Rodham Jr., President Clinton's brother-in-law; Melvin Belli, the so-called King of Torts; Ron Motley of Charleston, South Carolina; and Russ Herman, former president of the Association of Trial Lawyers of America.

Rodham had never tried any major cases in his career—he had only been an assistant public defender in Florida. But he was added to the "Castano" group, as Gauthier's team of lawyers became known, for his connection to the White House.

The Castano suit was filed in March 1994; it would become the first federal class action against the cigarette industry. In the summer of 1996, the lawsuit was thrown out by the U.S. Court of Appeals for the Fifth Circuit in New Orleans—where all three of the judges who ruled on the Castano case were appointed by Republican presidents. The judges rejected the case as unwieldy since the class-action lawsuit was trying to encompass too many different states' laws on fraud and other issues. The Castano group had seen that coming, however, and began filing new class-action lawsuits in as many states as possible. That enabled them to skirt around the appeals court's objection.

By 1996, the Castano lawyers had put two years into the class-action effort, spending thousands of hours to gather evidence. So Gauthier was annoyed to read in the *Wall Street Journal* that all his work might be for naught.

The settlement bill that Lott almost introduced in Congress would have cut out Gauthier and everyone involved in liability suits against the tobacco industry. Worse yet, the legislation would have effectively outlawed liability cases, freeing the tobacco companies from any big losses in court and ignoring plaintiffs and their attorneys.

Gauthier called two of the Castano lawyers, Mike St. Martin and Calvin Fayard, and told them to "go find out what's going on."

The two men headed for the Democratic Convention in Chicago, where they met U.S. Senator John Breaux from Louisiana. The bill wasn't going anywhere, Breaux assured the lawyers. Russ Herman, another of the Castano lawyers, cornered Mike Moore at the convention.

"No way we can go along with this," Herman told Moore. "The money isn't significant enough, there are no programs for individual smokers, and there have been no real negotiations. We're not about to drop our lawsuits for a phantom deal."

Moore apologized to Herman. "I told my colleagues, and I'll tell you, that I made a mistake," he said.

Gauthier wanted to make certain he'd be involved in any settlement talks. He could pull some strings: Tommy Boggs, a friend from Louisiana, was a top tobacco industry lobbyist. Each fall, Boggs and Gauthier went duck hunting in Maryland.

The Castano group also had other influential members, notably Hugh Rodham, who had a direct line to the White House and could be counted on to help get the president's backing for a settlement—and convince the president to reject an accord that the Castano group didn't like.

Rodham celebrated Thanksgiving 1996 at Camp David with his sister Hillary and the president. He brought up a plan he had hatched with Coale and Gauthier to have a settlement be brokered by former Senators Howard Baker and Howell Heflin, and Clinton's outgoing Chief of Staff Leon Panetta. He dubbed the group "the three wise men."

Clinton said he was interested as long as an accord would include Big Tobacco agreeing to stop marketing to kids.

After Rodham told Gauthier and other Castano attorneys about his conversation with the president, word of it filtered back to Scruggs, who was worried that this time he and the attorneys general would get squeezed out of a deal. Scruggs frantically tried to track down Rodham's colleague Gauthier, and found out that he was duck hunting with Tommy Boggs.

"I'm flying up there," Scruggs said on the phone to Gauthier, intent on breaking up what he assumed were negotiations.

"Dickie," Gauthier said, "This is a social call. You can't come up here."

Scruggs backed off only after Gauthier agreed not to cut a deal and to meet with him the next day in New Orleans.

At that meeting, Scruggs told Gauthier to drop the three-wise-men tactic.

"We're further along than you think," Scruggs told Gauthier in the Castano attorney's New Orleans office. "We've got to have a united front."

Gauthier declined to join forces with the attorneys general and instead the two men promised to keep each other informed every step of the way. They also agreed to divide up their ancillary demands on the tobacco industry: The attorneys general would fight for the FDA's objectives and Medicaid money, the Castanos would focus on addiction and treatment issues.

But the alliance was never a comfortable one. Like the prospectors in *The Treasure of the Sierra Madre,* the Castano lawyers and the attorneys general were both going for the same stash of gold. Neither side fully trusted the other to share it.

Differences between the two groups flared constantly, even up until the end of the settlement talks. At one meeting in Washington in January 1997, Mike Moore said that if they tried to include millions of dollars in attorneys' fees in a settlement package, the public would be irate, and Congress would never be able to support the bill.

"Hey, what are we supposed to be getting out of this?" said Coale. "The Wizard of Bhopal" didn't like the turn the talks were taking. His eyes fixed on Moore, Coale snapped, "It's not like we're going to run for governor."

"I'm not running for governor," Moore yelled back.

"Right," Coale responded quickly, "you want to be senator."

THE TOBACCO CEOs knew that any settlement would need to be approved by the Clinton Administration, and that posed problems for them. For one thing, the president had taken a harsh stance against the cigarette companies. His position was that they were merchants of disease, without conscience, hooking teenagers to their deadly products. Clearly, if the cigarette makers hoped to get a settlement they could approve, they needed some contact—if not a sympathetic ear—with the White House. Unfortunately, while Tommy Boggs and other tobacco lobbyists had clout in Congress, they had little access to the president.

Instead, the industry turned to allies from North Carolina's "Tobacco Road"—a name coined by author Erskine Caldwell that now describes the belt of tobacco farms extending from Virginia through both Carolinas and into Georgia. North Carolina is the second-largest tobacco growing state.

In mid-November 1996, RJR's CEO Steve Goldstone asked to meet with Jim Hunt, North Carolina's popular Democratic governor. It was an unusual request. The two rarely met formally and when they saw each other, it was only for a quick greeting at tobacco-related functions in the state. Goldstone didn't say why he wanted to see Hunt, but the governor had a hunch he knew.

So Hunt called J. Phil Carlton, a former classmate at North Carolina State University, who worked with him as a top political adviser.

"Steve Goldstone, RJR's chairman, is coming to see me tomorrow," Hunt told Carlton. "I think he might be looking for a liaison to the White House to discuss a settlement of tobacco litigation. I would suggest you, but I want to make sure you have the time."

"Sure, throw it out there," Carlton said.

Goldstone came to the state capital in Raleigh, North Carolina, the next day. As Hunt expected, Goldstone said the tobacco companies needed someone to help them get closer to the White House. In effect, they wanted an emissary they could count on.

That night, Hunt called Carlton. It was 10 days before Thanksgiving, and Phil Carlton's career, which at one time soared and then ignominiously tumbled, was about to undergo another unexpected twist.

Carlton, 59, was a polite, soft-spoken Southerner from Rocky Mount, North Carolina, where his father, J. C. Carlton, was a wealthy tobacco farmer with 200 acres of land and a huge warehouse. In college at N. C. State University, Carlton became best friends with Jim Hunt, touted by the student body to become governor some day.

They were right about Hunt; a farmer from Wilson, North Carolina, he became governor in 1976—and remained in the job for an unprecedented four terms. Carlton was also expected to succeed in Southern politics.

As it turned out, Hunt's election ensured that. Carlton was Hunt's most trusted adviser; in 1976 the governor named him his first secretary of Crime Control and Public Safety. Then in 1979, Carlton was appointed to the North Carolina Supreme Court, where he served until 1983.

But Carlton was quickly bored with reviewing lower court decisions. In 1986 he left the bench and led the merger of two established law firms, Poyner & Spruill, making it the largest practice in Raleigh.

In 1985, after two consecutive terms as Governor, by law Hunt had to leave office. Carlton got him a job at Poyner & Spruill. Then he helped Hunt get elected governor again in 1992, but he went too far in doing so.

Carlton was one of three people implicated in a political espionage operation in which a Hunt supporter, Beverly Smith, illegally listened in on phone conversations of Hunt's challenger, GOP gubernatorial candidate Jim Gardner, and fed the information to Carlton.

The cellular phone calls intercepted by Smith, who tuned in by using a police scanner, were mostly innocuous. Sometimes, Smith even eavesdropped on calls between Gardner and his family that were simply about the humdrum daily life of Rocky Mount.

Other conversations were between Gardner and his campaign staff or state GOP chairman Jack Hawke, though nothing particularly private was discussed.

Hunt won the election handily, with 53 percent of the vote. Two years later, in April 1994, Carlton, Smith, and Charlie Lane, another Hunt supporter, pleaded guilty to illegally using a police scanner to intercept phone conversations. This was essentially wiretapping.

On the day after Carlton was sentenced, the photograph of him—a close adviser to the governor, a former state supreme court justice and partner in one of the state's most prestigious law firms, standing before the judge with his hands in his pockets—was displayed on the front page of virtually every newspaper in North Carolina. Carlton paid a $5,000 civil penalty, received six months' probation, and was ordered to perform 60 hours of public service. Hunt's opponent Gardner got an undisclosed settlement from Carlton—more than $100,000, according to press reports.

"What we thought was a very casual kind of thing, sort of like in the old days when you'd pick up the telephone and hear the neighbors talking on a party line, grew into something more than that," Carlton said, explaining his actions. "There was a point in time that I wish I had realized it had grown into something more than that, but I didn't. Accidents happen."

Carlton never quite recovered. He worked for a while longer at Poyner & Spruill, then quit.

When Governor Hunt told RJR's CEO Goldstone that Carlton would be the right man to get Big Tobacco closer to the White House, Goldstone wasted no time in getting the plan in motion. He called Carlton the next day.

"I'll fly down to meet with you, or I'll send my general counsel down," Goldstone said.

Carlton replied that he and his wife were going to be in New York City, spending Thanksgiving at the Plaza Hotel.

On Tuesday afternoon, two days before the holiday, Carlton met for two hours in New York with Goldstone and Rob Sharpe, RJR's general counsel. They decided to retain Carlton on the spot.

Three weeks later, Carlton called Hunt after hearing that Clinton was going to visit Camp Lejeune, a Marine Corps base in Jacksonville, North Carolina. Carlton knew the political tradition that gives a governor 30 minutes with the commander in chief any time the president visits a state military outpost.

Carlton told Hunt he needed him to ask the president to arrange a meeting between Carlton and the president's new chief of staff, Erskine Bowles. Hunt agreed to do so.

On December 23, one month after his reelection to a second term, Clinton arrived at Camp Lejeune early in the day. The president, along with Bowles, met with Hunt in a helicopter. Hunt explained to the president who Phil Carlton was and what role he was playing for the cigarette companies. Then he gingerly passed along Carlton's request.

"Can Carlton and Erskine talk?" Hunt asked quietly.

"Absolutely," the President said without hesitation.

Clinton saw that a national settlement in which Big Tobacco paid billions of dollars and agreed to help stamp out teen smoking was something he could support. It would be an excellent part of his legacy—especially with his failure to pass a universal health care insurance plan, which the president had hoped would stamp his place in history.

The following week, a conference call was held among Carlton; RJR's Goldstone; Sharpe, the company's general counsel; and Governor Hunt, speaking from his farm in Wilson. Hunt told the men that Carlton was going to be able to meet with the White House.

"Phil, you got your foot in the door," Goldstone said. "Go for it."

Carlton was excited about the opportunity to help draft a tobacco settlement. For one thing, it could remove some of the cloud from his reputation following the Gardner wiretapping incident. Even more than that, though, Carlton was indebted to tobacco. All his father's significant wealth came from growing and distributing tobacco, and he wanted to be involved in sorting out the legal and social predicament surrounding this crop. Carlton had vivid boyhood memories of the smell of the broad leaf, and the sound of it flapping like elephant ears in the nighttime wind.

"My daddy was a tobacco man from the word go," Carlton said, his baritone drawl getting even more pronounced as he recalled the rural South of his youth. "Tobacco money educated me. To be honest, I'd like to resolve [all the lawsuits] for my daddy's sake. He didn't think he was doing anything to hurt anybody when he was growing tobacco."

Carlton became a critical negotiator in the tobacco talks over the next seven months. When the many sides in the bargaining sessions hardened their positions, and the settlement seemed doomed—which happened regularly—Carlton, working as both a mediator and attorney for the tobacco companies, would usually be the one to break the impasse and get the negotiators to try again.

At times, it was Carlton's easy sense of humor that drained the tension from the people involved in the long, nearly round-the-clock sessions.

At one point, Dick Scruggs was frustrated by an impasse in the talks and was ready to bolt them. He announced that he was going to make a private call on his cell phone and might never return. Carlton told him to be careful. "Somebody may be listening in," he told Scruggs. "I have experience in doing that."

Scruggs broke down laughing. He left the room to make his call and was back at the bargaining table within minutes.

As 1996 was coming to an end, Bruce Lindsey, one of Clinton's closest advisers, learned that Bowles would be talking with Carlton for Big Tobacco. Lindsey knew from contacts on Capitol Hill that Mike Moore and the other attorneys general were working on their own settlement. He wasn't sure how often they were in touch with the tobacco companies, but he wanted to be certain that Moore was kept informed of what Big Tobacco was telling the White House.

Lindsey called the Mississippi attorney general. He told Moore about Carlton's upcoming visit and asked Moore if he needed any help from the White House in crafting the settlement.

Moore was reluctant to bring the president into the fray, even though he knew he eventually would need Clinton's support for the plan. At this early stage of the negotiations, Moore felt that it was more workable to create a consensus among the attorneys general, the Castano group, and members of Congress, and then force Big Tobacco to accept it. Convincing the president of the merit of the agreement could come later.

Still, no one turns down the president of the United States, Moore thought. He told Lindsey that he would continue to try to get all parties to agree to a settlement. Any help the president or his staff could give would be welcome.

Moore hoped that would be the end of the talks with the White House for now.

5
PAGE ONE NEWS

If the cigarette companies are agreeing to this, it can't be good for the rest of us.

—KAREN BERTSCHI

a writer and editor of science textbooks, Portland, Oregon

P hil Carlton's secret meeting with Erskine Bowles at the White House didn't take place as quickly as Carlton had thought it would. In early January 1997, reviving tobacco settlement talks wasn't a high priority for the president and his staff. For much of the month, Clinton was preoccupied with his second inaugural address on January 20. And then after the inauguration, Bowles suddenly decided that he couldn't represent the administration's point of view in tobacco negotiations.

Bowles, Clinton's chief of staff, would have been a perfect choice. Carlton had known Bowles, a 51-year-old Charlotte, North Carolina investment banker, since Bowles was a boy. Carlton had worked for Bowles's father, Skipper, in a 1972 gubernatorial North Carolina race that the elder Bowles lost to James Holshouser, the first Republican elected to the post since Reconstruction.

But Erskine Bowles had ties to North Carolina's tobacco industry through his banking interests in the state. That, he said, disqualified him from getting involved in the settlement talks. Instead, Bowles told Carlton, the president had decided that Bruce Lindsey, deputy White House counsel, would speak for the administration in the negotiations.

"Bruce Lindsey is as close as it gets to the president," Bowles said.

The naming of Lindsey—one of Bill Clinton's closest aides and an Arkansan who'd known the president since the two worked for Senator J. William Fulbright in 1968—as White House point man for the cigarette talks showed how much the president cared about the outcome of the negotiations.

The president's ties to Lindsey were cemented in 1980 when then-Governor Bill Clinton lost a bid for reelection. Lindsey prodded the 34-year-old Clinton not to wallow in his defeat, as he was beginning to, and gave him a job at his family's law firm. Two years later, Lindsey helped plot and manage Clinton's successful attempt to retake the governor's mansion.

In Washington, the 49-year-old Lindsey—short and perpetually tan—was as softspoken as he was low profile. In a town of $1,000 suits, he preferred an old blazer. He was known at the White House as "the Minesweeper," because his job was to help the president avoid dangerous traps, and also as "Il Consigliere," for his trusted counselor role.

Lindsey's job was varied, but he always worked to make the president look and sound good. Sometimes this meant standing at the rear of the room at press conferences and signaling cosmetic advice. In Helsinki in March 1997, for instance, at the Russian-U.S. summit, as the president and Russian President Boris Yeltsin emerged from two days of meetings, Lindsey motioned for Clinton to remove a translation device from his ear that looked odd in the camera shot.

Monitoring the tobacco talks for the White House, however, was a big change for Bruce Lindsey: It would pull him out from behind the scenes and make him a highly visible figure to the press, Wall Street, health advocates, Big Tobacco, and cigarette foes.

Erskine Bowles sensed Phil Carlton's disappointment when he said he couldn't take part in the tobacco talks for the White House, but he promised to get Lindsey involved quickly. Bowles set up a meeting between Lindsey and Carlton for Saturday, February 1.

Mike Lewis conceived the plan for suing Big Tobacco while leaving Baptist Central Hospital in Memphis, Tennessee, where he visited his legal secretary's mother, Jackie Thompson, who was dying of cancer due to decades of heavy smoking.

Pauline and Mike Lewis (left) and Jackie Thompson's daughter, Alice Craven, waited several weeks before taking their lawsuit idea to Mississippi Attorney General Mike Moore, a friend of Mike Lewis's from the University of Mississippi Law School.

Don Barrett (above, left) nearly went bankrupt suing the cigarette makers before he joined forces with three fellow University of Mississippi Law School graduates (above, left to right): Mike Moore, Dick Scruggs, and Mike Lewis, shown on the state capitol steps in Jackson, Mississippi. The four lawyers filed their landmark lawsuit in May 1994.

Mike Moore's lawsuit was criticized in his home state. Later, he liked to say that few thought a lawsuit "in little old Mississippi" would ever be successful.

Merrell Williams, a troubled paralegal, stole 4,000 top secret Brown & Williamson documents—then turned them over to Mike Moore and Dick Scruggs for their use in suing the tobacco companies.

Jeffrey Wigand, the former top scientist at Brown & Williamson, also gave Moore (right) and his allies valuable information about nicotine research, becoming the highest-ranking executive to defect from Big Tobacco.

On April 14, 1994, seven tobacco company executives outraged a nation when they swore that they did not believe nicotine was addictive. From left, Donald Johnston, American Tobacco; Thomas Sandefur, Brown & Williamson; Edward Horrigan, Liggett; Andrew Tisch, Lorillard; Joseph Taddeo, UST; James Johnston, R. J. Reynolds; William Campbell, Philip Morris.

Dick Scruggs flew Mike Moore around the country in his Learjet as the two friends recruited more state attorneys general to broaden the legal assault on cigarette makers.

JOHN ABBOTT

DANNY TURNER

Wendell Gauthier, seeking revenge for the death of fellow New Orleans attorney Peter Castano, assembled 65 of the top U.S. trial attorneys to sue on behalf of addicted smokers. Gauthier's coalition filed what became the first national class-action suit against the cigarette makers.

Bennett LeBow (left), the flamboyant Miami financier who controlled tiny cigarette maker Liggett, worked with his attorney, Marc Kasowitz, to complete a staggering March 1996 settlement that called for Liggett to break with its peers and settle with five states.

Norwood "Woody" Wilner (right), a Jacksonville, Florida, trial attorney, criss-crossed Florida in his private plane, recruiting smokers to sue the cigarette makers. He convinced more than 100 people to file lawsuits, including Grady Carter (below), a retired air-traffic controller. In a stunning verdict reached in August 1996, Carter became only the second smoker to win money from a tobacco company.

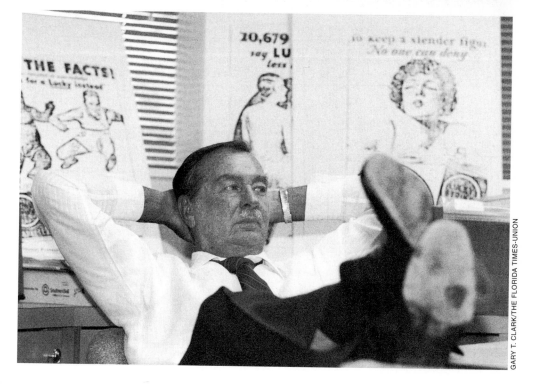

Philip Morris CEO Geoff Bible and RJR Nabisco CEO Steve Goldstone, heads of the two largest U.S. cigarette companies, began meeting in secret to plot a settlement after the Carter verdict.

Bible relied on the prosettlement advice of general counsel Murray Bring (right), promoting him to vice chairman of the Philip Morris board as the negotiations heated up.

On January 31, as a bitter wind chilled Pinetops, North Carolina, Carlton climbed into his maroon Oldsmobile Bravada and shivered until the heat warmed the four-wheel-drive truck. Heading north on Interstate 95 for the four-hour drive to Washington, D.C., Carlton rode past acres and acres of long and deep empty fields that in two months would be sprinkled with tobacco seedlings.

Inside the car, the telephone rang. An assistant to Lindsey was on the line.

"Is it okay if Mr. Lindsey wears his blue jeans at the meeting?" the assistant asked.

"That will be fine," Carlton said. He'd wear khakis and a button-down Oxford shirt along with the black New Balance walking shoes he always had on, whether dressed casually or in a suit. He needed the sneakers to ease the pain of a bad right hip.

When Carlton arrived at the White House, he was escorted to Lindsey's West Wing office on the second floor of the mansion. Carlton sat in a wing chair, and Lindsey leaned back on a sofa across from him. Carlton—who officially was representing Philip Morris, RJR, Brown & Williamson, Lorillard, and chewing tobacco giant UST, Inc.—quickly got to the point.

"My clients want to make sure our position is represented in a tobacco settlement," Carlton said. "We hear that the White House is somehow involved in discussions about a settlement, and we sure would like to be a part of it, too."

Lindsey acknowledged that he had talked with Mike Moore, but gave no details about their conversations or Moore's attempts to draft a legislative accord.

"The White House is interested only in the reduction of youth smoking," Lindsey told Carlton cagily. He quickly added he had doubts about whether a national settlement could be reached. "I'm not going to let the president get involved in an argument over lawyers' fees."

This wasn't a good sign, Carlton thought. Lindsey was being purposely noncommittal. Carlton decided to push harder, afraid to leave the meeting empty-handed and squander the industry's chance to speak directly to someone close to the president.

"Moore and his crowd haven't been willing to meet with us," Carlton told Lindsey. "Will this White House get behind an agreement if all the parties, including tobacco companies, join together and work one out?

If you say yes, I can at least use that to try to push Moore to talk to us."

Lindsey said there was a good possibility of that, but added that certain people, including public health leaders like Matt Myers of the National Center for Tobacco-Free Kids, had to be included in the talks.

Carlton sipped a Diet Coke. He took some notes on a legal pad, but he felt uncomfortable writing too much because Lindsey was sitting so close by. Carlton needed to know more, so he probed deeper.

"There are rumors that Mike Moore and Dick Scruggs are preparing a legislative draft that would be forced on the cigarette makers in Congress," Carlton said, hoping that Lindsey would reveal details of the plan, which at that time only a handful of people in Washington and Mississippi knew about.

Lindsey turned and nodded towards a file cabinet. He said he had a copy but couldn't show it to Carlton. Instead he reached for his tobacco file folder on his desk.

"Here are some people you need to know," Lindsey told Carlton. He ticked off the names: Mike Moore, the attorney general of Mississippi, who's working with Dickie Scruggs, a Pascagoula, Mississippi, attorney; Tommy Anderson and John Sears, the two Republican organizers with ties to Trent Lott, also working with Scruggs; John Coale, Hugh Rodham, and Wendell Gauthier, the Castano attorneys.

"You ought to speak to these people. I'll give them your phone number if you don't mind," Lindsey said.

In all, they talked for two hours. Lindsey was sketchy about what the White House wanted to be included in a tobacco settlement besides an end to teen smoking. But he told Carlton that the president was realistic enough to know that an accord would include some immunity from lawsuits for Big Tobacco, and that Clinton knew it was foolhardy to pressure for a complete ban on cigarettes. Lindsey also said the president wouldn't propose an excise tax on cigarettes in his State of the Union address on February 4, three days later. (While that pledge was honored in the speech, the president renewed his promise to work towards reducing teen smoking.)

For the first time, the gap had been bridged between the White House and Big Tobacco, Carlton thought. Lindsey had not been particularly forthcoming but at least he encouraged the tobacco companies to meet with attorneys opposed to them, something that to the tobacco CEOs had seemed almost impossible before. Carlton would later call this session with Lindsey one of the pivotal meetings that set the stage for real negotiations towards a settlement. The other meetings would come later that spring as both sides actually talked face-to-face.

Carlton left Washington that afternoon and headed back to North Carolina. He figured he'd need at least 24 hours to sort through his discussion with Lindsey before reporting back to the tobacco company CEOs. Instead, he was given about six hours.

On the drive home, Carlton called Rob Sharpe, RJR's general counsel, and filled Sharpe in on the meeting. Sharpe insisted on a conference call that evening to tell the tobacco executives what happened. So at 7:00 P.M., Carlton sat down in the library of his English Tudor-style house with a piece of paper on which he had hastily written the key points he intended to talk about on the call.

When the conference call began, Sharpe didn't introduce the participants, leaving Carlton in the dark about who was listening to him. The only voice Carlton recognized instantly was Philip Morris CEO Geoff Bible's; his distinctive Australian accent stood out. Bible told Sharpe to get the call moving.

"Phil," Sharpe said, "everybody is on. Report on the details."

Carlton took a deep breath and began: "A tobacco settlement is on the President's plate. The White House is definitely involved, and they've picked Bruce Lindsey to be the quarterback."

Carlton waited for reactions. He heard nothing and continued.

"The White House doesn't want to ban cigarettes, and it's amenable to some form of immunity for the companies," Carlton said. He paused again. At least eight times, Carlton broke off and asked if there were any questions. Each time he was told to keep talking.

"Our timing is great" to enter the talks, Carlton said. And the good news is, he said, President Clinton's upcoming State of the Union address would not call for a harsh excise tax on tobacco. "It will not be mentioned in the presidential speech," Carlton said, soothing concerns that a hard-line stance against tobacco would polarize any settlement talks.

Carlton said he was finished and asked if there were any questions.

"Do you sense that the administration really wants to help work out a settlement?" Carlton was asked.

"Yes, definitely."

Then, Geoff Bible, who had been quiet during the call, spoke again: "Thank you for a comprehensive report."

Carlton hung up and looked at a clock. The call had lasted 70 minutes, and Carlton had done almost all of the talking.

As PHIL CARLTON was trying to plumb the White House for the tobacco companies, Mike Moore had other things on his mind. Ever since the response to the *Wall Street Journal* article the prior summer killed the tobacco settlement legislation that he, Dick Scruggs, and Trent Lott crafted, Moore was preoccupied with writing a new bill that would be more palatable to all parties, including the Castano lawyers and public health advocates. To do this, he would have to get the groups that reacted so bitterly to last year's legislation to agree on at least a basic framework for an accord.

Piecing together a coalition of such disparate partners as plaintiff attorneys, health advocates, attorneys general, and congressmen was time consuming; Moore was on the phone or in meetings at least three hours most days trying to cajole all these special interests into agreeing with each other. In fact, Moore spent almost as much time fashioning this latest piece of legislation as working on Mississippi's case against Big Tobacco, which was scheduled to go to trial by the summer.

Moore had good reason. He was certain that if he had to actually try his case he was venturing deep into the legal unknown. Holding cigarette makers responsible for the costs of treating sick people with little money was an untested idea, with the outcome very much in doubt. Always the pragmatist, Moore knew that his best option was to settle for cash—and the public recognition—rather than risk losing out to Big Tobacco in a high-profile trial and coming away with no money and a damaged career. From this perspective, legislation—especially if it came on his terms and not Big Tobacco's—was clearly the most desirable solution.

By February 1997, Moore had come a long way. Prodded by John Sears and Tommy Anderson, who were meeting first with Scruggs and then with RJR and Philip Morris lawyers and executives, Big Tobacco was resigned to paying more than the $150 billion stipulated in the initial draft bill. That higher price, they knew, was essential if attorneys general who opposed the failed bill the previous summer were going to consider a settlement.

Health advocates were still resistant to any accord. But Wendell Gauthier's Castano group wasn't, as long as there was money for attorneys' fees included in the package and as long as his clients—smokers— got some benefit, like discounts to purchase nicotine patches or subsidized smoking-cessation programs. Support from the Food and Drug Administration and the White House would have to wait, but both were aware of the movement towards a settlement.

As the new proposal took shape, Moore had accomplished his main goal: isolating Big Tobacco and limiting its influence on a settlement. Although the CEOs had been meeting secretly among themselves for months, these sessions had turned into little more than catching each other up on industry activities, on an upcoming courtroom showdown with the FDA which was trying to regulate tobacco, and on how to keep Bennett LeBow from revealing the industry's secrets.

And while the CEO meetings dragged on to almost no purpose, Moore continued to keep the tobacco companies at arm's length from his settlement plans, making sure that they would only be informed through back channels about the thinking of the state attorneys and plaintiffs' lawyers. Go-betweens like Sears and Carlton would be the cigarette makers' pipeline for information about the legislative accord that Moore was piecing together; these men would be Big Tobacco's only means of getting its positions even considered in the agreement.

AGAINST THIS BACKDROP, on Friday evening, February 14, Carrick Mollenkamp, a 27-year-old Bloomberg News tobacco reporter, made a series of telephone calls from his 22nd-floor downtown Atlanta, Georgia, office to the homes of sources in Mississippi, Louisiana, and Florida. These weren't just routine, checking-in, casual conversations. Mollenkamp had something urgent on his mind that he wanted answered.

Since the *Wall Street Journal* article in August 1996, detailing the ill-fated $150 billion settlement, most journalists treated a tobacco accord as a dead issue. There was such vehement opposition from public health groups, many state attorneys general, and the Castano lawyers at the time that no one guessed it could be revived. The coverage of the cigarette companies in the national media—including Mollenkamp's— mainly involved reporting the news, such as LeBow's attempts to work out a second settlement and the increasing number of lawsuits against

Big Tobacco by individuals and the states. Journalists simply missed the bigger story: lots of jockeying for position as a new tobacco settlement was taking shape behind the scenes.

The tobacco CEO meetings; Mike Moore's relentless efforts to draft a new bill by finding consensus among the states, the Castano group, and health advocates; the White House's increasing interest in a settlement; and Phil Carlton's visits to Lindsey—all had gone unnoticed by the press from the summer of 1996 through the first month of 1997. The media were preoccupied with the presidential election and then the makeup of the second Clinton Administration more than anything else.

In the first two weeks of February, however, sketchy details of a prospective tobacco settlement began to emerge, as participants involved in the shaping of the accord floated trial balloons in the media to test the reaction of the public, stock market, health advocates, and Big Tobacco. And insiders responded to these press reports by giving their views about a settlement more freely.

On Sunday, February 2, the *Richmond Times-Dispatch* quoted Trent Lott as saying "There are a lot of people working" on a tobacco settlement. "It could develop."

The following week, *Business Week* magazine wrote a story suggesting that Minnesota Attorney General Hubert Humphrey had changed his position and was now behind a legislative settlement. At the same time, the *National Journal* disclosed that cigarette makers had hired top Washington lobbyists, Verner Liipfert Bernhard McPherson and Hand, to champion their positions in Congress if settlement talks got serious.

Then, on February 13, Martin Broughton, CEO of Brown & Williamson's parent company B.A.T, let drop in a televised interview in England that the company would consider paying damages to states and smokers to settle lawsuits. "They want a big payoff, and we want a peaceful life," he said.

Mollenkamp's curiosity was piqued. With these separate, but related, reports, the idea that there were serious discussions being held about a tobacco settlement didn't seem so farfetched. Mollenkamp needed to know if his hunch was right.

So, on the evening of Valentine's Day, Mollenkamp first called Mike Moore's associate Dick Scruggs. No answer. Then he tried calling two top Castano attorneys, Wendell Gauthier in New Orleans and John Coale in Washington, D.C. Neither was in.

Finally, frustrated, Mollenkamp called up one of his best-placed sources—a Mississippi lawyer who was working closely with Scruggs and Moore on the state's case against the tobacco companies. This attorney never let Mollenkamp use his name in print, but often offered guidance—especially about the plaintiffs' strategy behind the upcoming Medicaid suits against Big Tobacco; useful information that could be used as background for Mollenkamp's stories.

The lawyer's reason for being so helpful was anything but altruistic. Mainly, it ensured that the states' side in these lawsuits was well represented in Bloomberg News stories. And with the tobacco companies mostly silent on litigation issues—on or off the record—this gave the Mississippi team a leg up on its opponents, at least in the press.

After a handful of rings, the Mississippi attorney answered the phone. He sounded tired. "I'm sorry to bother you at home, but I hear something's afoot down there in Mississippi," Mollenkamp said. "I hear that Mike Moore is working on a plan for a new settlement that would end all of the states' lawsuits."

It was a bluff, and Mollenkamp was nervous. All he had was a hunch based on some cursory news reports and Broughton's comment in the televised interview.

Silence. Then a sigh. Then more silence—at least another 10 seconds. "Carrick, I can't talk about it."

"Can't talk about what? Does that mean it's true? What's going on? Your name won't be used."

"I have to go."

And the lawyer hung up.

Mollenkamp's emotions soared, then fell just as quickly. The Mississippi attorney had always been reliable; his tips always panned out. Mollenkamp was certain he would have been told he was off-base if nothing was going on. The lawyer hadn't done that; he hadn't warned him away from his hunch. Mollenkamp knew he was on the right track.

But he hadn't found out anything concrete; he wasn't much further ahead than when he started his calls that night. He still had an unverified guess and now he had an unnamed source giving him just a scant bit of encouragement.

Worst of all, knowing now that he was on to something, but uncertain what it was, only heightened Mollenkamp's fear that a dozen other reporters had the same idea; one of them, he was sure, would get it

confirmed with details. Mollenkamp dreaded walking out to his driveway on Monday morning to see the *Wall Street Journal* leading its edition with the story of a national tobacco settlement. It was midnight,
Friday, and Mollenkamp figured he'd start over the next day.

Meanwhile, with Mollenkamp's call, the Mississippi attorneys knew
that the cloud of secrecy about the settlement plan had been lifted. That
was okay with them, though. They were eager to get details of their plan
out, floating the proposal in the national media the way the $150 billion
settlement had been tested the summer before. They were confident
they had a strong consensus this time—dissidents like Hubert
Humphrey and Connecticut Attorney General Richard Blumenthal
were interested in striking a settlement.

The next morning, Saturday, Mollenkamp, more clear-headed and
determined not to get beat on this story, knew what he had to do: get
in his car, drive the 400 miles to Mississippi, and ask his source eye-to-
eye what he meant on the call—giving him no opportunity to hang up
or hide the truth behind a phone line. Though Mollenkamp was
unaware of it, it was a fortuitous strategy. The Mississippi lawyers—
after months of stonewalling the press—were now willing to leak the
story of the settlement.

At around 1:00 P.M., Mollenkamp got in his green 1996 Ford
Explorer and headed west on Interstate 20 out of Atlanta towards
Tuscaloosa, Alabama. It was a cold February day, though the sky was
clear and the sun was shining brightly.

Mollenkamp looked forward to the drive across the South. Born in
Atlanta, he loved the region, its people, its traditions. One of the reasons
he'd left a job at the *Raleigh* (North Carolina) *News and Observer* to
work at Bloomberg News was the opportunity to travel the South.

It took about three hours to reach Tuscaloosa, where the University of
Alabama has its largest campus. From there, Mollenkamp drove west on
Highway 82 toward Reform, Alabama, and the Mississippi state line. It's
a four-lane road lined with strip malls, motels, and fast-food restaurants
like Johnny Ray's Barbecue—a hard-to-miss big, pink cardboard pig at its
entrance—catering mostly to the college crowd and the employees at the
new Mercedes plant which had sprung up outside of town.

After about 30 miles, Highway 82 cuts away from the clutter of sub-
urban Tuscaloosa into the Bible Belt of rural Alabama. Towns fly by in
split-second, half-mile consistency. Small sharecropper shacks, many of

them vacant now—the Sun Belt industrial miracle erasing the feudal, farm-worn South—dotted the roadside, overgrown with wild-colored lilies and sedges spreading untouched toward ramshackle front porches. On the hillocks, one tiny Baptist church after another—white-shingled, wooden worship centers with names like Open Door, Faith, and Emanuel—sat quietly, unused, parking lots empty except for a lone car or two on this Saturday afternoon.

Mollenkamp called Dick Scruggs from his cellular phone. He hoped to pry at least some small details of a settlement out of Scruggs so he wouldn't walk into his source's house without any information for building an interview.

Scruggs's wife, Diane, answered the phone and said her husband was parking the car and would return in a second. Scruggs soon picked up the phone.

"Mr. Scruggs, I hear y'all are working on something. A settlement. What's going on?" Mollenkamp asked.

"Carrick, I can't talk about it," Scruggs said.

For the second time in 24 hours, an attorney had told Mollenkamp that he couldn't talk—a good sign that something was happening, but there was still no hard information.

"I can't talk about it," Scruggs repeated. "It's something big."

Mollenkamp knew there wasn't much use in trying to squeeze answers out of Scruggs, who was usually eager to talk. He thanked the attorney and turned off the phone.

Mollenkamp arrived at his source's house at about 8:30 P.M. He parked the car in a grassy strip at the end of a long drive that swept up past a row of trees to a red brick mansion with white columns.

For Mollenkamp, studying the house in minute detail from the car was easier than getting up the nerve to walk towards it. He felt embarrassed about showing up unannounced—and suddenly realized that he had never even met this source before. That made him feel even more foolish. What possessed me to take this drive? Mollenkamp thought. This is a rude visit.

After a few minutes, with the chill of the February night beginning to suffuse the car, Mollenkamp remembered why he came and knew he couldn't turn back. After months of working the tobacco beat, he was hell-bent on getting this story first. He slowly walked up the asphalt driveway toward the house.

The lights were on in the downstairs rooms—the parlor, the dining room, the den, and the kitchen—and as Mollenkamp got closer, he heard voices talking, others laughing, and the sounds of glasses and silverware. There were about six cars parked in front of the house. The lawyer had company.

Mollenkamp knocked at the front door. Nobody heard him. He knocked again. Still no answer. After about three minutes, he walked around to the side door in the carport. Mollenkamp rang the bell.

Dogs started barking, and the outside light over the porch came on. The Mississippi lawyer opened the door—while two dogs dashed past Mollenkamp—and he stepped out of his darkened foyer to where Mollenkamp was standing. The attorney looked perplexed to see this young man, one hand holding a business card and the other extended to shake his hand.

"Can I help you?" the lawyer said.

"I'm Carrick Mollenkamp, a reporter for Bloomberg News. We spoke last night. I'm really sorry to show up at your house, but I wanted to follow up on what we discussed."

The lawyer shook his head and a smile curled on his face. "You didn't drive all the way from Atlanta to see me?"

"Yes sir, I did," Mollenkamp said.

"Well, come on in," the attorney said. The time had come for the Mississippi lawyers. If it weren't for this visit, it was likely only a matter of weeks before the *New York Times* or *Wall Street Journal* would be fed the story.

There were five people sitting around the table, steaks half eaten, wine glasses half full. They stopped talking as Mollenkamp and the lawyer entered the room.

"This is Carrick Mollenkamp, a reporter from Bloomberg— Bloomberg? Is that how you say it? He's come all the way from Atlanta to talk to me."

Everyone stared at Mollenkamp, bewildered by his presence. The attorney asked Mollenkamp if he wanted to join them for dinner. Mollenkamp declined. He preferred to speak privately with the attorney.

"Okay, we're going to go into the sitting room and talk. Do you want a drink? Wine or beer?" Mollenkamp asked for a glass of wine.

Mollenkamp sat in a chair, the lawyer across from him on a sofa. Stacked books and a TV were on shelves against the wall of the room.

"What do you want to know?" the attorney asked, fully aware of what Mollenkamp was about to ask.

"Well, are y'all working on something? What is Scruggs working on?"

The lawyer leaned back on the sofa and smiled. "Well," he began, "it's pretty ambitious." And for the next two hours, the attorney spoke almost nonstop, describing every detail of Mike Moore's attempts to draft a tobacco settlement that could be introduced in Congress, the likely makeup of the agreement, and what was at stake.

The proposed settlement was stunning. The tobacco companies would pay $250 billion over 25 years and get immunity from all lawsuits; the legislation would be sponsored by Trent Lott, who had met with Moore and Scruggs in Washington, D.C.; the White House knew about the talks; Big Tobacco had been told about the plan through back channels and was agreeing informally to most of it; the Castano group had also been informed, mostly at sessions with the attorneys general at the Peabody Hotel in Memphis, Tennessee.

Mollenkamp listened wide eyed but kept his notebook in his jacket pocket, afraid to stop the attorney from talking. His heart was beating wildly; this was an incredible story, the biggest of his life. No one to this point had reported direct White House involvement in the settlement talks. More important, there had been no reports of even indirect contact between the two sides.

By 11:00 P.M., Mollenkamp was leaving. He thanked the attorney repeatedly. "No problem," the attorney said, wondering to himself what would happen when the story hit the wires.

The night had gotten colder, but even the stiff wind didn't stop Mollenkamp from sweating as he ran down the driveway. In the car, he quickly took his pad out and jotted down notes from memory:

1. $10 bln x 25.
2. Immunity.
3. Scruggs/Lott meeting. @ Wash. Hotel ANA?
4. W. House knows.
5. AGs/Castano Peabody Hotel.
6. FDA not involved yet.

Mollenkamp needed to get to a motel, to call Bloomberg News editors and tell them the remarkable story he'd heard. About a half hour later, he stopped at a Super 8 Motel, a single-story structure with 30 rooms, and asked at the front desk for a place to stay.

"Can't you see the sign?" the clerk said. "We're full."

"Maybe in an hour?"

"We're not that kind of motel," the clerk said, looking at Mollenkamp suspiciously.

An hour later, Mollenkamp found a room at a Comfort Inn.

He called bureau chiefs in Atlanta and Princeton, New Jersey, Bloomberg's main hub for business news, and excitedly told them word for word what the lawyer had said.

"Are you sure your source can be trusted?" the national news editor asked.

"Absolutely. He's always on the money, he's well placed," Mollenkamp said quickly, frustrated by the questioning.

"We'll have to get some confirmation," the editor said. "Someone on the record—or no story."

Ten Bloomberg News reporters and editors were immediately assigned to the story—to confirm, write, and get it ready for publication. "This is a big story," they were told. "Don't let anybody know about it."

By late afternoon Monday it was done. A Louisiana official in the attorney general's office who was briefed on the settlement said the story was accurate, but the official demanded to remain anonymous.

Then a big break: Michigan Attorney General spokesman Chris de Witt went on the record and corroborated the details of the agreement. "There have been discussions as far as settlement," he said. "Members of the staff have been involved."

Now the reporters had two separate people verifying a story that had been told by a reliable, well-placed source in the first place. Tobacco companies and the White House didn't want to talk about it, but they didn't deny it either.

The story ran on Bloomberg News at 5:40 P.M. on Monday: "U.S. Tobacco Companies Hold Talks to Settle Suits."

The story began: "U.S. cigarette companies are in talks with antitobacco lawyers and states' officials to settle all health-related lawsuits for as much as $250 billion, people involved in the negotiations said.

"The talks, held at hotels in Washington and Memphis, Tennessee, and by telephone in the last few months, may settle suits by 21 states to recoup billions of dollars spent treating smoking-related illnesses, the people said."

The 1,000-word story was carried the next morning on the front pages of a half dozen U.S. newspapers, from the *Arizona Republic,* to the *Atlanta Journal-Constitution,* to the *Philadelphia Inquirer.*

THE NEWS WAS out, but the reaction, at least from the media and tobacco industry analysts at Wall Street brokerages, was nothing but skepticism. After the aborted $150 billion settlement reported by the *Wall Street Journal* the prior summer, it seemed that everyone was keeping his distance from this report.

At first, the *Wall Street Journal* and the *New York Times* didn't even acknowledge the story; neither published a follow-up article. Then, two weeks after the Bloomberg News article, the *Journal's* widely read "Heard on the Street" column tiptoed in by saying that the odds were against a sweeping settlement and the White House didn't appear to be in a rush to compromise either. In its next issue, *Time* magazine wrote that the reported $10 billion annual payment for 25 years was a red herring, and any actual payments would be for only a few billion dollars a year.

Even stock market analysts who followed the tobacco industry largely downplayed the report.

"We suspect there is more smoke than fire regarding any meaningful discussions among the interested parties. Don't hold your breath; it doesn't appear to be a likely settlement," said Emanuel Goldman at PaineWebber.

Smith Barney's Martin Feldman agreed: "I don't see it in the cards."

Sanford C. Bernstein & Co.'s Gary Black echoed these sentiments, telling his clients that the report was probably "more hype than fact."

Investors, though, looking for any positive news to spur the stock of Big Tobacco, ignored the analysts. Cigarette stocks were trading at surprisingly low levels given their consistently strong profits—the shares were weighed down by the stream of lawsuits that threatened future earnings.

On Tuesday, the first trading day after the Bloomberg News article about the settlement was published, Philip Morris's stock rose $6 to $131.50. RJR Nabisco's shares rose $1.88 to $37.38, its highest close in three years. Investors surmised that if the report was true, the cost of the settlement could be passed on to smokers, and the agreement would remove the concern that a verdict could force cigarette companies into bankruptcy.

And this wasn't a one-day aberration. Within three weeks, Philip Morris's shares reached close to $140, adding more than $10 billion to its stock-market value—or the combined worth of Delta Air Lines and United Airlines' parent UAL Corp.

"Even the news of a possible settlement was like the lifting of this incredible dark cloud that was hanging over the industry for as long as anyone could remember," said Donald Yacktman, a major holder of Philip Morris stock through Yacktman Asset Management. "All of a sudden, life without this endless stream of litigation was an alternative."

The smarter investors, looking at the dynamics of a settlement and the people and companies involved, knew that everyone would benefit from an accord. States and smokers who sued the tobacco companies would get billions of dollars in damages. The attorneys general who spearheaded the talks would be able to stoke their political ambitions by taking credit for bringing Big Tobacco down. After all, by this point Mississippi's Mike Moore had told associates that he wanted to run for governor in 1999 or the Senate in 2002. And Scott Harshbarger, Massachusetts's attorney general, who also filed suit, had already announced he would run for governor in 1998.

Plaintiffs' lawyers, too, had a powerful incentive to settle: money. The Castano group had spent upwards of $25 million just getting its lawsuits filed in 17 state courts. None had won a dime in its fight against Big Tobacco.

Hard-to-get cash was also on the minds of the public health groups. They'd been losing the battle to curb smoking especially among teens, and sorely needed money to fund antismoking campaigns. And both President Clinton and Congress would want to take credit for tackling Big Tobacco during their watch and hammering out an agreement that made few compromises with the industry.

ON FEBRUARY 20, three days after the Bloomberg News story, White House spokesman Mike McCurry confirmed that the Clinton Administration was monitoring the talks, although the president didn't intend to get actively involved until an agreement or some legislation was produced. That was the stance the White House would take throughout most of the negotiations.

Publicly, the cigarette makers refused to verify that settlement talks were going on. Just a day before McCurry announced the White House was watching the negotiations, RJR Chief Executive Steve Goldstone at a February 19 analysts' conference in Naples, Florida, had downplayed Big Tobacco's involvement. "I can tell you that I'm not interested in having these kinds of discussions, and I don't know anybody who is," Goldstone told reporters.

He was lying. Months earlier—while the CEOs were holding their own meetings to decide whether they would back an accord—Goldstone had asked Phil Carlton to be the industry's go-between in settlement talks and help broker a deal. In addition, by this point, Lott lieutenants Tommy Anderson and John Sears had been shuttling back and forth between the tobacco companies and Scruggs and Lott for a year.

By the end of February—just as Goldstone was debunking the news of a possible agreement—Carlton had already had his initial meeting with Bruce Lindsey in the White House; a critical first step for Big Tobacco, Carlton felt, because even if the administration was taking a hands-off posture on the talks, Carlton wanted tobacco company positions represented inside the administration as the president put his stamp on the accord.

On March 10, barely two weeks after Goldstone's statement, Carlton met with former U.S. Senator George Mitchell, the Maine Democrat who was working for Verner Liipfert, the firm hired by Big Tobacco to lobby lawmakers. Carlton updated Mitchell on his meeting with Lindsey in a brief session. Then, the two men went to the White House for a 2:30 P.M. appointment with Bruce Lindsey, whom Carlton kept informed about every detail of every critical meeting he had. Later that day, Carlton filled in Goldstone and Philip Morris's CEO Geoff Bible on the substance of the discussion with Lindsey.

Bible was clearly encouraged by what he heard. On March 11, Philip Morris filed a 10-K report with the U.S. Securities and Exchange Commission, acknowledging publicly for the first time that a settlement was possible.

Philip Morris "may enter into discussions with appropriate parties" about settling lawsuits, the cigarette maker wrote in the filing. "Were that to happen, the company would not contemplate making any further comment as to the existence or progress of any such discussions."

Two days later, the incentive to settle grew even greater for Big Tobacco when the industry lost one of its last remaining chances to quash Mike Moore's lawsuit in Mississippi.

Urged on by the tobacco companies, Mississippi Governor Kirk Fordice, a Republican, asked the court to rule that Moore didn't have the right to sue the cigarette makers to recover public money spent treating people with smoking-related illnesses.

On March 13, at 1:00 P.M. in Jackson, Mississippi, the state supreme court rejected Fordice's claims. The way was clear now for Moore to proceed with his case, which was slated to go to trial in the summer. This decision was not only damaging to Big Tobacco in Mississippi: It might be used as a precedent to stop anyone from trying to stand in the way of the 21 other states that by this time had filed look-alike suits against the cigarette companies.

Big Tobacco was running out of time and options. A settlement was becoming more and more desirable. It was less than three months before the scheduled start of Mississippi's lawsuit, and Bible and Goldstone wanted to strike a settlement before that trial began.

Frustrated that even with better access to the White House, Big Tobacco still wasn't able to meet face-to-face with Mike Moore and the other attorneys general—Moore was purposely keeping the industry at arm's length—Bible told his top outside legal advisers at Wachtell, Lipton, Rosen & Katz to try to arrange a sit-down with the attorneys general.

Meyer Koplow, a partner at Wachtell Lipton, had a plan to make this happen. Koplow—a 46-year-old, soft-spoken Brandeis University graduate—knew a Charleston, South Carolina, lawyer, Joe Rice, who was working with Mike Moore and Dick Scruggs in Mississippi's suit. Koplow and Rice had been on opposite sides of a landmark asbestos case in Texas. In that case, Koplow's client, Fibreboard, which made asbestos insulation from 1928 to 1971, agreed to pay $3.1 billion to settle a class-action lawsuit by Rice-represented consumers exposed to the cancer-causing product. It was a wrenching settlement, and Koplow and Rice gained mutual respect for each other squaring off at the negotiating table.

In mid-March, Rice was in Durham, North Carolina, teaching a mediation class at Duke University School of Law, an institution built from tobacco money. The largesse had come from Buck Duke, whose

American Tobacco Company had manufactured Lucky Strike and Pall Mall cigarettes and was the predecessor of B.A.T. Rice was using Bennett LeBow's first Liggett settlement with the five states as his mediation case study in the course.

After his final lecture, on his way to Raleigh-Durham International Airport to fly back to Charleston, Rice checked his office and was told that Meyer Koplow had left a message. Rice returned the call on his cellular phone. Koplow told Rice to get to a secure landline telephone that couldn't be intercepted by people eavesdropping on a scanner.

"What do you want to talk about?" Rice asked.

"Tobacco," Koplow said.

"I'll get right back to you."

Rice parked at a Waffle House and called Koplow.

The conversation was brief. They agreed to meet in Charlotte, North Carolina, on March 18. Koplow said he'd bring some of Big Tobacco's top attorneys.

"I'll bring either Dickie Scruggs or Mike Moore," Rice countered. "Maybe both."

Rice and his partner, Ron Motley, 52, at the Charleston law firm of Ness, Motley, Loadholt, Richardson & Poole, made their name—and millions of dollars—in the 1980s by winning or settling dozens of asbestos litigation cases that eventually bankrupted the Manville Corp. On one case, in Pascagoula, Rice and Motley had worked with Dick Scruggs.

Rice and Motley had perfected a remarkably effective attorneys' version of the good cop/bad cop strategy. Motley, who would crop his long, burnt-red hair before trials and counter his slight Carolina drawl by waving his hands wildly to make a point, was the courtroom genius, using theatrics to sway a jury. In one case that he won, Motley donned a white gown and toy stethoscope to ridicule the medical expertise of an opposing expert witness.

Rice, meanwhile, some 10 years younger with shoulder-length hair, Hawaiian-print open-necked shirts, and a quick grin, hardly ever set foot in the courtroom. He gave the impression of not caring particularly much about money and even less about the minutiae of litigation. But in reality, Rice was a cold, hard numbers man who fought tenaciously and often brilliantly for every last dollar when opponents were willing to talk about a settlement.

So, in lawsuits, Motley would lead the charge, ripping through adversaries with damaging discovery and withering cross-examinations. Then, when the defendant was ready to deal, Rice was the attorney who swept in to squeeze out how much the defendant would have to pay.

Rice and Motley began working with Mike Moore and Dick Scruggs shortly before the Mississippi attorneys filed their state's Medicaid tobacco lawsuit in 1994. Using that connection, Rice and Motley had helped sign up several other states to file similar suits, including Florida and Arizona.

After his conversation with Meyer Koplow, Rice called up Scruggs and Moore and told them about the upcoming meeting.

The Mississippi lawyers were focused on drafting the tobacco settlement legislation and didn't want to meet directly with the industry. They were more interested in brokering an agreement among the tobacco foes and then getting the industry involved after the accord was announced. That would force the cigarette makers—under public and congressional pressure—to accept the agreement without too many compromises.

Still, Moore and Scruggs were curious to see what the tobacco companies were offering. After staring down this enemy for so many months without ever seeing it face-to-face, being in the same room with Big Tobacco had a certain perverse allure. And Moore and Scruggs wanted to be courteous to Rice as well. Although hesitant to do so, they agreed to join the meeting.

The cigarette makers chose their top outside attorneys to attend the March 18 session: Koplow and Herb Wachtell for Philip Morris and Arthur Golden for both RJR and B.A.T. Phil Carlton would also be there.

Wachtell, known as a "pit bull in pinstripes," led Philip Morris's $10 billion libel suit against ABC in 1994 after the network aired a segment on its *Day One* news program that said the tobacco industry spiked cigarettes with extra nicotine. ABC ended up paying about $15 million in attorneys fees and issuing an apology.

A 65-year-old native New Yorker and New York University law graduate, Wachtell had a thin build and wavy, salt-and-pepper hair and always wore blue pinstripe shirts. An assistant U.S. attorney in Manhattan for three years in the mid-1950s, he wrote a book on civil procedure that was still in use more than 30 years later. In the 1950s he joined the firm that later bore his name, Wachtell, Lipton, Rosen & Katz.

In the tobacco settlement talks, Wachtell was best known to his counterparts for his salty language. He shouted, cursed, and questioned the professionalism of lawyers who opposed him. During one point in the negotiations, which were usually fairly civil, Wachtell used variations of the word "fuck" three times in the same sentence.

The contrast with Wachtell's associate, Koplow, couldn't have been more stark. Koplow was deeply religious and typically nonconfrontational. He was a highly regarded defense attorney, an expert on protecting corporate officers and directors, and he avoided the spotlight.

Arthur Golden, a partner at the New York firm Davis Polk & Wardwell, was vacationing at Sea Island, Georgia, the week the meeting was scheduled to take place. He cut his holiday short, flying to Charlotte for the session on one of the few RJR corporate jets to survive the debt-ridden company's recent austerity.

The 51-year-old Golden had earned a reputation for making the best of bad situations. In 1995, for example, he was hired by ICI Explosives USA Inc. to save it from a $490 million antitrust judgment. Golden convinced a less-than-receptive audience of attorneys for Thermex Energy Corp., the company that ICI had driven out of business, that ICI couldn't afford to pay the judgment. Thermex settled for $36 million.

Golden and RJR CEO Steve Goldstone were especially close, after spending 26 years together at Davis Polk before Goldstone was tapped to the No. 1 job at RJR. During that time, their two families lived near each other in Connecticut, and Golden chose Goldstone to be the godfather of one of his three children.

On the night before the March 18 meeting, Mike Moore and Dick Scruggs suddenly changed their minds about attending the session. Scruggs called Joe Rice, and said he and Moore had decided they couldn't trust Big Tobacco. Scruggs and Moore wanted to work on their legislative agreement, hoping to win congressional and White House support. They didn't want to compromise that plan, and they definitely didn't want to be in a position where they might slip and reveal any of its details to the cigarette companies.

Rice tried to change Scruggs's mind. "Dickie, what makes you think that even with the White House, we can get a bill through Congress without support from the tobacco companies?" Rice asked.

Scruggs wouldn't relent. "I may be wrong," he told Rice. "Go if you want to. I'm not going."

At 12:30 P.M. on March 18, Herb Wachtell, Meyer Koplow, Arthur Golden, Phil Carlton, and Joe Rice began their meeting in a sparse conference room at the Sheraton Airport Plaza on Billy Graham Parkway in Charlotte. Rice sat alone on one side of the glass-topped mahogany table; the tobacco attorneys sat across the table.

Carlton was furious that Scruggs and Moore had canceled.

At first the meeting consisted mostly of small talk. Chatting about their backgrounds, Carlton told Rice that he had worked for Erskine Bowles's father Skipper in the 1970s when Bowles ran for governor of North Carolina and lost. That broke the ice between Rice and Carlton. As it turned out, in that election Rice was one of Bowles's youth campaign coordinators.

But Rice knew why Carlton had told him that story—and it had nothing to do with nostalgia. Carlton wanted Rice to understand that his long ties to Erskine Bowles gave him and his tobacco clients access to the White House.

As the meeting got serious, Rice told the attorneys that they had to be sincere about seeking a settlement. There could be no more tricks. The attorneys general wanted to reduce youth access to tobacco. They wanted Big Tobacco to turn over internal documents such as the ones that Merrell Williams had stolen. Rice said the tobacco industry would have to make an initial payment to a settlement pool to be followed by annual payments.

"You're only going to have one shot at a deal," Rice said, knowing that might be promising too much, since he couldn't even get Scruggs and Moore in the same room as these attorneys.

Golden and Wachtell said their clients were serious. The rising tide of litigation wasn't helping anybody, and the tobacco companies wanted it off their shoulders.

"We want some way to end all these suits," Golden said. But he added that the companies would settle only if the agreement included the cessation of all litigation—not just from the states and their Medicaid cases, but also from the private lawyers, like the Castano group, who were representing smokers.

"If we can work out a settlement like that, the companies are willing to put money into a fund to be divvied up among the plaintiffs at the government's discretion," Golden said.

Koplow emphasized that the companies were willing to compromise—even to offer previously unheard-of concessions. Among them,
banning outside cigarette advertising completely and restricting cigarette vending machines.

"In return, though," Koplow said. "Any settlement must be embod-
ied not just in a court filing but in a federal law."

The tobacco lawyers spoke for more than an hour. They felt that their
performance was convincing, offering a picture of Big Tobacco as anxious and willing to give on key points—to change its stance as it never
had before—and unwavering only on one: All litigation had to be erased
now and forever.

When they were finished, the tobacco attorneys leaned back in their
chairs, all four giving a sigh of relief in unison, as if choreographed. They
stared at Rice, who looked back, going from one face to the next.

"So what do you think?" Golden finally said.

"Well," Rice answered. "I'm glad you're not asking for anything complicated."

6

THE FDA AND THE WHISTLE-BLOWER

They have a provision for a cessation program for addicted smokers in the settlement; that's fine and dandy, but do they have a cessation program for the tobacco grower? There is no one more addicted to tobacco than a grower, and many have never inhaled.

—J. T. DAVIS

a federal crop agent, who wanted the settlement
to include subsidies for tobacco farmers

Both sides felt that the Charlotte, North Carolina, meeting was productive, but there was one issue that no one dared discuss at the Sheraton that day: what the Food and Drug Administration's role should be in regulating tobacco. This was a tricky subject; to bring it up would only have made the session, which was supposed to be informal and introductory, rancorous and contentious.

Limiting the FDA's power to control cigarettes was critical to Big Tobacco—and a prime reason why the companies were willing to be flexible on the amount they would have to pay in a settlement. The tobacco companies feared that if the FDA were allowed to regulate cigarettes, eventually tobacco products would be banned. Or if the agency didn't go that far, it might at least reduce or eliminate the amount of nicotine allowed in cigarettes, in effect weaning the smoking public from the habit.

Big Tobacco would be willing to exchange higher payments in a set-tlement for curtailing the FDA. And the industry intended to take a firm stance on this position if the negotiations got serious.

All of which made an agreement that much more important to the cigarette makers, because in March 1997, the tobacco companies weren't confident that they could keep the FDA at bay without an accord. The FDA's chairman, David Kessler, had waged a three-year crusade against the tobacco industry, and it was finally beginning to pro-duce results.

Kessler, a Phi Beta Kappa graduate from Amherst College in Massachusetts, also had a medical degree from Harvard and a law degree from the University of Chicago. In 1990, he had been medical director of New York's Albert Einstein College of Medicine for six years when George Bush tapped the then 39-year-old to head the FDA.

Bearded, blond, his eyes almost lost behind thick lenses, Kessler talked in bursts and rarely finished sentences. To Bush, what stood out most about him was his impressive resume; in terms of accomplishments, he outshone most of his predecessors at the agency. He was considered an excellent choice for a thankless job.

Kessler inherited an agency that was in disarray. A decade of cutbacks under Ronald Reagan had left it understaffed, underfunded, and drowning in applications for approval of new medicines. Critics com-plained that it took the FDA an unacceptable 33 months to okay poten-tially life-saving drugs like those for treating AIDS—a tough charge to fight. At the same time, the agency was embroiled in a scandal involving FDA chemists who were accused of accepting bribes for approving generic drugs. Vice President Dan Quayle had even spearheaded a failed effort to strip the agency of its powers, proposing to let drug mak-ers, for example, hire private companies to perform pharmaceutical studies and approve drugs for the open market.

With all of that, Kessler spent his first months on the job trying to restore the FDA's credibility with the public and Congress and raising morale inside the agency. One method was to restructure the FDA into specialized teams to better manage day-to-day crises and set priorities.

"Otherwise," Kessler said, "it was like playing soccer with eight-year-olds. Everybody goes where the ball is."

As Kessler worked on this reorganization, he also kept himself in the public eye, sending the message that the FDA was taking enforcement seriously. He was nicknamed Eliot Knessler, after Eliot Ness, the government special agent who doggedly pursued Al Capone.

Kessler seized 40,000 gallons of Citrus Hill orange juice after Procter & Gamble ignored warnings to remove the word "fresh" from cartons when the juice was from concentrate.

"That action had nothing to do with the word 'fresh,' or with orange juice," Kessler said. "It had to do with the way we were going to enforce the law."

A short while later, Kessler forced the drug company Syntex to pay tens of millions of dollars to retract misleading ads for Naprosyn, which Syntex claimed could prevent joint deterioration from arthritis. The problem was, there were no clinical studies to back that up, and the FDA had okayed the drug only for treating pain, inflammation, and fever in arthritis patients.

Kessler's activism buoyed FDA staffers and encouraged them to take on issues that they had ignored during the tightfisted Reagan Administration, when the agency was headed by Frank Young.

Like smoking.

In April 1991, Jeffrey Nesbit—an FDA spokesman whose father, a heavy cigarette smoker, had recently died of cancer—led a strategy session of FDA staffers attended by the new commissioner. He showed Kessler many years' worth of petitions containing hundreds of thousands of signatures calling for the agency to regulate tobacco products as drugs—much as the agency controls other substances, from over-the-counter antihistamines to medical cocaine hydrochloride.

"Here's this product that cuts short the lives of millions of Americans, and it's totally unregulated," Nesbit said. "The FDA is the premier consumer protection agency in the world. Why isn't it doing its job?"

The meeting was emotional. Some staffers were vehemently opposed to the agency regulating tobacco and reversing a decades-long policy of all but leaving the cigarette makers alone.

"It's a fool's mission," said one veteran staffer. Kessler agreed.

"We'll get to it," he promised the group. "But I'm not going to get to it now."

Kessler's hesitance was two-pronged. For one thing, the man who hired him, President Bush, was protobacco, and Kessler didn't want to buck up against his backer. For another, the FDA simply didn't have enough scientific evidence to support a claim that cigarettes were essentially a drug delivery device that disperses nicotine—and thus should be regulated by the agency.

Still, Kessler felt strongly about the issue and said it was far too important to ignore. He assigned several dozen FDA scientists, lawyers, and other staffers to collect data that eventually could be used to buttress a recommendation that the agency be allowed to regulate tobacco products.

In March 1994, the FDA investigators finally latched onto a piece of information that made Kessler much more willing to challenge Big Tobacco. Kessler still thought that the cigarette makers were going to be difficult to tame—especially with the legal talent they always assembled to fend off attempts to regulate them. But he finally had the right political environment to at least increase the pressure on Big Tobacco. Bill Clinton, avowedly antismoking, had defeated George Bush for the presidency. And the new president's own health team was less distracted after spending a wrenching year in a failed effort to pass the Administration's overhaul of the nation's medical insurance system.

It was thus good timing that in March 1994, the agency received an anonymous telephone tip to look at Brown & Williamson's patents, especially those dealing with the development of a new breed of tobacco carrying extremely high levels of nicotine.

Following the lead, an FDA investigator began to sift through patent records and grew curious when he discovered a document written in Portuguese. Unable to speak the language, the only lettering that he could read was "Y-1" and "6 percent"—although he didn't understand what those cryptic items stood for. But the document contained the names of two scientists who worked for DNA Plant Technology, a small company in New Jersey.

The investigator tracked down one of DNA's researchers, Janice Bravo, and asked her to translate the document. She said it showed that 15 pounds of tobacco seeds were shipped to Brazil by Brown & Williamson. The seeds were for a strain of tobacco that had a 6 percent level of nicotine, more than double the amount that under quality control rules could be grown in the United States.

The investigators were flabbergasted. The 15 pounds of tobacco seeds were enough to yield, at minimum, a million pounds of tobacco. They went back and combed through agricultural import records, where they found an invoice from a Brazilian company, Souza Cruz, to Brown

& Williamson for half a million pounds of Y-1, the high-nicotine tobacco plant. It seemed that using Brown & Williamson's seeds, Souza Cruz was growing a new strain of tobacco—and selling it back to Brown & Williamson.

Then they approached Brown & Williamson, whose chief product developer told the FDA that the company was creating the breed to be able to mix it with tobacco that had lower levels of tar. In other words, Brown & Williamson was attempting to maintain or increase the level of nicotine in cigarettes even as it lowered the amount of tar.

It was a fantastic discovery. The investigators had uncovered evidence that a major tobacco producer was so concerned about keeping the nicotine level in cigarettes up that it was breeding a whole new plant. "It flies in the face of everything they [the industry] have said," said one senior FDA official. "They have said over and over that nicotine is not set [by the cigarette companies], but it follows the tar levels. Now we have a top product developer . . . telling us what they said in public is not true."

Kessler called the information a turning point, concrete evidence of manipulation and control of nicotine. "You don't insert nicotine without the intent to control it," he said. One month later, Kessler would get his second big break.

Jeffrey Wigand, Brown & Williamson's research chief, was home watching C-SPAN in the den of his Louisville, Kentucky, home. He heard Andrew Tisch, chairman of Lorillard, testify to Congress that nicotine was not addictive. Then he heard Tommy Sandefur, Brown & Williamson's CEO, say the same thing.

Like Grady Carter, the Jacksonville, Florida, smoker who sued Brown & Williamson after seeing clips of the hearing on Capitol Hill, Wigand was taken aback by the obvious hypocrisy—and knew he had to act. "I realized they were all liars. They lied with a straight face. Sandefur was arrogant, and that really irked me," Wigand said. "When that TV image replayed in my mind, I realized that, by my silence, I was not that far removed from the men on my screen."

Jeffrey Wigand, the son of a mechanical engineer, grew up in a strict Catholic household in the Bronx. He had coarse, silver hair and wore silver-rimmed aviator glasses, which he frequently took off to rub his eyes.

For most of his life, Wigand defined himself as a man of science. He worked in the corporate development department at the drug company

Pfizer, then as a marketing director at Union Carbide in Japan, and later as a senior vice president at Technicon Instruments, where he marketed blood-testing equipment. In 1989, he was fired along with several other senior managers in an executive shake-up. A headhunter asked if he'd consider working for Brown & Williamson.

He was 46 years old when he accepted the job as head of research at Brown & Williamson in Louisville. Wigand, a black belt in judo and a sparring partner for members of the U.S. Olympic teams, wasn't a smoker and didn't particularly like the tobacco companies. But he took the $300,000-a-year job with a $30 million budget and a staff of 243 anyway, because he was told he would lead a research team in developing a safer cigarette to compete with Premier, a low-nicotine, low-tar, smokeless product made by rival RJR.

That never happened. Three months after Wigand was hired, RJR withdrew Premier from the market because the taste was unpleasant. When that happened, Wigand sensed that Brown & Williamson was quickly losing enthusiasm for his pet project. He decided to confront his boss, Tommy Sandefur, who was then Brown & Williamson's president. The reply was harsh.

"I don't want to hear any more discussion about a safer cigarette," Sandefur said. "It would put us at extreme exposure with every other product."

For the next year and a half, Wigand felt isolated. He asked pointed questions about the nature of his job and executives shunned him. He grew increasingly vocal at work. He had "difficulty in communication," according to his 1991 company evaluation. He was sounding off at meetings, asking probing questions about why there wasn't documentation for research reports. He asked Sandefur to remove coumarin, a tobacco additive linked to high rates of cancer in rats, from cigarettes. Sandefur refused. In January 1993, Sandefur was named CEO of Brown & Williamson. Two months later on March 24, Wigand was fired and promptly escorted from the building.

Wigand groused about his severance plan. Several months later he learned Brown & Williamson was suing him for breach of contract for disclosing to a colleague details of his separation agreement and wanted to take away his medical benefits. He reluctantly settled, signing a lifelong confidentiality agreement so stringent that he could be in violation if he publicly discussed anything about the corporation. In exchange, he got his medical coverage back. That was of particular concern to Wigand, whose older daughter Rachel had a deformity of the spine that required costly surgery and medical care. He felt trapped. "If Brown & Williamson had just left me alone," he later said, "I would have probably gone away."

Wigand got in touch with Lowell Bergman, a senior producer for CBS's influential investigative news show, *60 Minutes*. Bergman, who worked almost exclusively with veteran reporter Mike Wallace, hired Wigand as a $1,000-a-day tobacco consultant.

Word filtered out in antitobacco circles that Wigand was telling CBS secrets about Brown & Williamson. That's when an FDA investigator called him up and asked him if he would brief the agency about activities at the tobacco company. Wigand wanted to cooperate but was hamstrung; he had the threat of a lawsuit hanging over his head if he talked. Wigand felt that speaking to the FDA could lead to a subpoena to testify in court or at hearings, and if he did, he'd be exposed for breaching his confidentiality agreement and lose his medical insurance.

Two weeks later, Wigand saw Sandefur and the other tobacco chiefs testify on Capitol Hill. That convinced him to start talking to the FDA— though he was still concerned about the risks. He proceeded with caution. Wigand said he'd help the FDA under two conditions: He'd meet only with Kessler, and his name had to be kept confidential.

In late April, a man known only by his code name, "Research," snuck in through a side entrance at the FDA's headquarters in Rockville, Maryland, to meet with Kessler for the first time. Research was skittish, but full of information. In a series of sessions that extended for weeks, Research tutored Kessler on ammonia additives, which cigarette companies had used to make nicotine more potent.

On May 18, at a conference-room table piled high with documents that the FDA had obtained under subpoena, Kessler was combing through a list of names of Brown & Williamson executives.

"Who's Jeff Wigand?" Kessler said. "I'm Jeff Wigand," the informant revealed.

By the end of the summer, with the help of Wigand, the FDA had thousands of pages of explicit evidence of what the major tobacco companies were doing to make cigarettes stronger and more addictive.

Wigand helped the FDA preempt the industry's tactic of document dumping—answering a subpoena for documents related to nicotine studies by unloading a tractor-trailer with 10 tons of files—by telling Kessler exactly which ones to request.

Kessler formed two groups at the FDA. One was to continue working on the scientific investigation and to write the findings into a legal paper that could form the basis for legislation regulating tobacco. The other group would try to come up with regulatory policies that might be included in the law. The work was painstaking. It took months to pore through legal precedents and analyze the U.S. code governing the FDA, which was written in the 1930s. Investigators talked to tobacco control experts around the world and studied established programs.

In early August 1995, some five years after arriving at the FDA, Kessler was ready to go to the White House to seek backing for his proposal.

His plan had already been leaked to the *Wall Street Journal* and *New York Times,* which reported that the FDA wanted to declare nicotine a drug and propose stiff regulations on it—banning vending machines, which give children easy access to cigarettes; prohibiting advertising in the media; and requiring Big Tobacco to pay for public education campaigns, among others. Additional measures would be taken in states where teen smoking didn't decline by 50 percent in seven years. These would be the first substantive rules for the regulation of Big Tobacco ever proposed by the government. The decision on whether to push forward on Kessler's plan rested in the hands of Bill Clinton.

Kessler and Health and Human Services Secretary Donna Shalala went to the White House to meet with Clinton and Vice President Al Gore. They entered the building through a back entrance so they wouldn't be spotted by reporters and went directly into the Clinton family quarters.

Clinton said he was familiar with the gist of Kessler's plan but asked him to lay out the agency's proposal more specifically. Kessler opened a brown book filled with his agency's findings and began to read some of the industry's own comments on nicotine and tobacco.

"These are their words?" Clinton asked. Vice President Gore read aloud a 1972 memo by RJR Assistant Chief of Research Charles Teague quoted in a newspaper article: "In a sense the tobacco industry may be thought of as being a specialized, highly ritualized, and stylized segment of the pharmaceutical industry. Tobacco products uniquely contain and deliver nicotine, a drug."

Kessler stared into Clinton's eyes, "Mr. President, it would not be credible for us not to proceed."

Clinton was up for reelection in the fall and was worried that even the mildest antitobacco move would mean election defeat in five southern tobacco states—Virginia, North Carolina, Georgia, Tennessee, and Kentucky. But Dick Morris, the presidential adviser who had also counseled Senate Majority Leader Trent Lott, told Clinton that even in those protobacco states, polls indicated that voters would support some kind of tobacco regulation, especially if it was aimed at protecting children.

On August 10, 1995, Clinton publicly ordered Kessler to proceed. "It is time," the president said in a televised news conference from the White House, at which he surrounded himself with children, "to free our teenagers from addiction and dependency. When Joe Camel tells our children that smoking is cool, when billboards tell teens that smoking will lead to true romance, when Virginia Slims tells adolescents that cigarettes will make them thin and glamorous, then our children need our wisdom, our guidance, and our experience."

In the election, Clinton won two of the five southern tobacco states—Tennessee and Kentucky—and lost Georgia by a bare 1 percent margin.

In Congress, the reaction was predictable, especially among Republicans who were the largest beneficiaries of Big Tobacco's campaign contributions. Newt Gingrich, for example, said simply that Kessler was "out of his mind."

Big Tobacco blasted Kessler, too: "Kessler's action can only be described as a Trojan horse, set forward under the guise of preventing youth smoking," said Philip Morris's senior vice president, Steve Parrish. "Make no mistake: The real hidden agenda here is prohibition."

Hours after Clinton ended his press conference, Big Tobacco raced to file a lawsuit to prevent the FDA from taking any action to regulate cigarettes and to discard the proposed regulations because they were illegal. The companies could have filed their suit anywhere, but chose the U.S. District Court in Greensboro, North Carolina.

Greensboro, in north central North Carolina, is 26 miles due east of Winston-Salem, in the heart of tobacco country. R. J. Reynolds built his first, small tobacco factory in 1875 on a lot the size of a tennis court, in Winston-Salem. In time, RJR became the world's largest tobacco company and the city's biggest benefactor. There's an oft-repeated story in

Winston-Salem of a state highway commissioner who visited the city in the 1930s to discuss some road plans with city leaders. The commissioner pulled out a pack of cigarettes not made in the area. A hush settled on the room and somebody slid him a pack of Camels, an RJR product. The commissioner was told he would be expected to smoke them while in town.

Winston-Salem benefited greatly from RJR's presence. Downtown sprang up around the company's headquarters, a magnificent scaled-down version of New York's Empire State Building. Bowman Gray/Baptist Hospital, the largest employer in town, was built with tobacco money donated by Bowman Gray, the former president of R. J. Reynolds.

The influence of Big Tobacco on this softly rolling North Carolina hill country is more evident in the dozens of little towns surrounding Winston-Salem and Greensboro than in the cities themselves. In places like Tobaccoville, Kernersville, and Walnut Cove, leathery-skinned second- and third-generation tobacco farmers put down tobacco plugs and nurture the fragile plant until it's time to cure the golden leaf in sheds in the fall. Then the smell of tobacco wafts through the countryside.

For generations the people of the area lived off Big Tobacco. Even now, when the region is losing jobs in the cigarette industry to overseas factories, and workers are forced to switch to making furniture and machine parts in plants built during the Depression, there are constant reminders everywhere of the importance of tobacco.

For example, in Smithfield, North Carolina, two hours east of Greensboro on US-70, Shirley's Grill, a popular downtown restaurant, doesn't have a nonsmoking section. Dried tobacco leaves drape shelves like icons, and a portrait of a tobacco farmer—standing in worn clothes in a lush, green field, clutching a bunch of tobacco leaves—hangs on the back wall. "This town was built on tobacco," said Shirley Johnson in her smoke-filled diner. "Our churches are built from tobacco money, and so many of our families have lived from the crop. Next to God and family, it's really most of what we got."

With sentiments like that, the cigarette companies at least knew they were in sympathetic territory in Greensboro, as they spent 1996 preparing to ask the court to block Kessler and the FDA from taking any action to regulate cigarettes. Their confidence was bolstered by the fact that U.S. District Judge William Osteen, who was set to hear the suit, had ties to the tobacco industry.

A Republican appointee and former state legislator, in 1974 Osteen was a lobbyist for tobacco farmers, who paid him a couple thousand dollars to urge Earl Butz, then U.S. secretary of agriculture under President Nixon, not to proceed with a plan to eliminate the federal price-support program for tobacco.

Twenty years later, Osteen refused to throw out a lawsuit in which tobacco companies attacked the U.S. Environmental Protection Agency for releasing a report that said secondhand smoke caused cancer.

The tobacco industry had a well-connected attorney heading up its case: Richard Cooper, who had been the chief counsel at the FDA from 1977 to 1979, a former Supreme Court justice law clerk, and a senior policy adviser to President Jimmy Carter. Representing Kessler and the FDA would be George Phillips, Douglas Letter, and Gerald Kell, three attorneys from the U.S. Justice Department.

On February 9, 1997, the night before the hearing in Judge Osteen's court, David Kessler flew into Greensboro at about 9:00 P.M. and took a cab to the Hilton Hotel in the downtown quad. The hotel was packed with executives and public relations staff from the tobacco companies— which also rented a suite of rooms for the media, complete with fax machines, telephones, and communications lines—as well as reporters from the national press, and sightseers.

By the time Kessler arrived, there were few rooms available. "I'm sorry, sir," the desk clerk said. "All I have is a smoking room." This isn't a good omen, Kessler thought.

The hearing began promptly at 9:30 A.M. In a chilly, dimly lit courtroom, Kessler took a seat in the front row. Across the aisle, 60 tobacco company attorneys sat on the wood benches.

Big Tobacco attorney Richard Cooper started off the hearing, telling Judge Osteen that no matter what the FDA said, the agency was actually taking a step toward banning cigarettes.

"Before us today is an extraordinary exertion of power by a federal agency," Cooper said. "The FDA wants to exert its jurisdiction over the entire tobacco industry. Tobacco products have no medical use, and the FDA says they're dangerous. Products that the FDA finds unsafe and dangerous are removed from the market."

Cooper argued that over the last 28 years, Congress had refused to grant the FDA authority over tobacco. He cited two bills that were voted down that would have given the agency the power to regulate cigarettes. But Judge Osteen was skeptical of that argument and cautioned the industry that failed bills weren't a good indication of what Congress wanted. "There's a lot of reasons things don't pass," Osteen said. "It's hard to give much credence to that."

Often, Judge Osteen seemed sympathetic to the FDA's efforts to curb teen smoking. "I guess this is beside—I know it is beside—my authority or jurisdiction, and has nothing to do with this case," Osteen told Kell, the Justice Department lawyer, "but . . . why doesn't Congress or somebody simply outlaw smoking by minors?"

He echoed those concerns later when industry attorney Dan Troy argued that the problem of children smoking called for drastic but carefully specific measures, and that the restrictions sought by the FDA were too vague and overreaching. "You can't really use precision in this area," Osteen countered.

At times, though, Osteen was equally hard on the FDA. When Kell argued that the agency's power to regulate tobacco stemmed from the 1938 Food, Drug, and Cosmetic Act, Osteen said: "There is some question about the statue."

The hearing wrapped up by 3:00 P.M., and both sides held press conferences. Judge Osteen promised a decision within 10 weeks. He'd spend the spring studying the law's definition of drugs and drug delivery devices and poring through rulings by the Supreme Court and other courts in regulatory disputes. A rare, late-winter snow fell on Greensboro that day, and everyone wanted to get home. Kessler issued just a few words. He praised his agency's lawyers for "the eloquent way the government argued." Then he added, "The president stands firmly behind the regulations to try in a commonsense way to reduce the number of children who will become addicted. What is at stake here is the future health of our children."

Big Tobacco was confident it had made a convincing argument and the judge would rule that the FDA would overstep its authority if its proposal to regulate tobacco was implemented. "We don't feel we'll need to appeal," said Charles Blixt, general counsel of RJR's tobacco unit.

BY MARCH 1997, Bennett LeBow, his request for more financial help for Liggett rebuffed by Philip Morris, was getting desperate to cut a deal with the 17 states with which he still didn't have an agreement. As Liggett continued to lose money every month, LeBow knew that the cigarette maker would likely go out of business if it didn't get out from under the pile of lawsuits.

The states were certain they weren't going to get a lot of money from LeBow, but they had much more important demands for this second settlement with him that they wouldn't compromise on. For one thing, they wanted LeBow to admit that the nicotine in his cigarettes, brands such as L&M, Chesterfield, and Eve, was addictive. That could be powerful testimony in the states' as well as the Castano group's suits against the tobacco companies.

For another, they wanted Liggett to turn over confidential tobacco industry documents. These papers detailed meetings among tobacco company attorneys discussing how to dodge federal subpoenas by destroying documents, thus showing that Liggett and the rest of the cigarette makers conspired to cover up internal activities from investigators. The documents also revealed that the industry talked about ways to hide research that proved smoking was unhealthy.

LeBow at first was reluctant to admit the addictive nature of cigarettes. No tobacco executive had ever conceded that before. And in a meeting the previous fall, at the start of his negotiations with the states, LeBow proposed only to acknowledge that the U.S. surgeon general said nicotine was addictive.

"Anybody could admit that," Arizona Attorney General Grant Woods said. "This does nothing for me."

But by March 1997, as LeBow grew increasingly restive about his company's future, he agreed to acknowledge that cigarettes are addictive and turn over to the attorneys thousands of pages of internal Liggett documents.

In return, though, LeBow tossed in what he called a nonnegotiable demand of his own. The agreement had to settle all outstanding lawsuits against Liggett—not only the state Medicaid cases, but the Castano group litigation on behalf of individual smokers.

That posed a problem. The Castano attorneys, led by Wendell Gauthier and John Coale, didn't want to participate in the settlement. Considering Liggett's dire financial situation, there just couldn't be enough money in a settlement with the cigarette maker, they felt, and they might as well continue with their lawsuits.

So, Marc Kasowitz, LeBow's attorney, and Mississippi lawyer Don Barrett came up with a legal gambit to include cases brought by individual smokers in the settlement without expressly getting an okay from the Castano lawyers. With the help of private attorneys in Alabama, they cobbled together a group of individual smokers who would agree to the settlement with LeBow. Liggett could then argue this accord encompassed all of its smokers. (Courts later rejected this idea.)

With this scheme, LeBow dropped his nonnegotiable demand to include all cases brought by individual smokers in the settlement. Everything else fell into place quickly, and on March 20, at 3:00 P.M., the second agreement with LeBow was announced.

Liggett agreed to pay 25 percent of its annual pretax income over the next 25 years to the states that had sued for Medicaid reimbursements. Based on 1996 performance, that amounted to nothing per year, because that year Liggett had a pretax loss of $14.6 million.

In addition, Liggett would turn over the documents that showed Big Tobacco covering up research into the health risks of smoking and scheming to prevent investigators from obtaining data.

Most important, Liggett made a significant admission in the settlement: Tobacco is addictive and causes cancer. Liggett agreed to label all its cigarette packages with a warning that "smoking is addictive." With this concession, Liggett rejected the sworn denials of the seven industry leaders, including Liggett's now-retired chief executive, Edward Horrigan, made before Congress on April 14, 1994.

In return, Liggett was removed as a defendant in the 22 state Medicaid cases and (at least, so the settlement said) in the lawsuits, class action or otherwise, that had been filed—or would be filed in the future—by individual smokers.

The reaction from investors was chilling. Cigarette company stocks plunged immediately on the news; Liggett's unprecedented concessions had seriously wounded Big Tobacco's ability to beat the opposition in court. Philip Morris shares fell 5 percent to $115.88, down $6.12. RJR dropped 75 cents to end the day at $31.50.

The most revealing of the documents that LeBow had agreed to turn over concerned communications between Liggett lawyers and attorneys from the other cigarette makers—the memos that showed conspiracy to hide damaging research. Big Tobacco struck early to make sure these papers wouldn't be released.

On the morning before the settlement was announced, the other cigarette makers—Philip Morris, RJR, Brown & Williamson, and

Lorillard—raced into state court in Winston-Salem and argued that disclosure of those documents violated *their* attorney-client privileges. That's because, they claimed, the papers described communications between *their* lawyers and executives, as well as Liggett's. That argument prevailed. The cigarette makers won an emergency order temporarily barring Liggett from releasing any documents.

This was more than a minor victory for Big Tobacco. It would be months—well after the landmark tobacco settlement between the cigarette companies and the states—before any of these papers were made public by the courts. By the time a few dribbled out, it was decidedly anticlimactic.

The industry also wasted little time in casting the settlement a selfish act by LeBow, orchestrated to attract RJR as a suitor. "We suspect he is simply brokering this deal in a desperate attempt to force one of the other cigarette manufacturers to take over his financially troubled and failing tobacco interests," Big Tobacco said in a joint news release.

The attorneys general who struck the accord with Liggett were delighted with the agreement. They got what they wanted: Liggett's testimony against the other tobacco companies. For the state attorneys, the settlement was akin to a low-level drug dealer pleading to lesser charges in exchange for cooperation in fighting big drug cartels.

"We got the least important culprit to turn state's evidence and give testimony against the really bad guys," said Frank Kelley, Michigan's attorney general.

Tobacco foes hailed the Liggett settlement as a monumental event. "It's an historic victory," said Vice President Al Gore, speaking for the White House. "It's about time the tobacco companies told the American people the truth."

Though Moore led the press conference announcing the settlement, he had stepped out of the spotlight during the Liggett negotiations. Now he knew the tide was turning in his favor. He thought to himself, "I don't see how the industry can recover from a setback like this."

7

MEET THE CHAIRMEN

Sometimes I'll have to pass by four or five smokers at the building's entrance. I feel like I've taken a couple of puffs myself. It's disgusting.

—JOHN FRANKLIN

an Atlanta, Georgia, documents courier

On the night of Thursday, March 27, 1997, Phil Carlton was busy fielding a series of phone calls from the library in his Pinetops, North Carolina, home. The airport hotel meeting on March 18 between South Carolina antitobacco attorney Joe Rice and the top ciga-rette company lawyers in Charlotte, North Carolina, should have been the start of serious negotiations between the two sides towards an omnibus settlement. But without Mississippi Attorney General Mike Moore and his associate Dick Scruggs there—both had decided at the last minute not to attend—little could be accomplished. Carlton, who by this time had developed a good working relationship with point man Bruce Lindsey in the White House, knew it was critical to get Moore and Scruggs face-to-face with Big Tobacco—to deflect them from crafting a legislative tobacco settlement without the involvement of the cigarette companies.

At 7:00 P.M., Tommy Anderson, Trent Lott's back channel between the tobacco CEOs and Dick Scruggs, called Carlton.

"Dickie Scruggs is getting pressured by Bruce Lindsey and [North Carolina Attorney General] Mike Easley to meet with you," Anderson said. "I've told Scruggs to give you a call."

Carlton barely had time to let Anderson's call sink in. At 8:17 P.M., Mike Easley phoned. "I done good today," said Easley.

For days Easley had been working to broker a meeting between Mike Moore and Carlton, at Carlton's request. Now he was about to deliver the next-best thing. "Judge, you can expect a call from Dickie Scruggs," Easley said.

Easley promised he'd still continue to press Moore to meet with Carlton.

At 9:30 P.M., Carlton's phone rang again.

"Judge Carlton, I've heard a lot about you, and I'd like to meet," said Dick Scruggs. "We need to talk right away."

Scruggs said that if the meeting went well, he'd have Carlton meet with Moore, figuring that getting the Mississippi attorney general to attend this first session would be just about impossible.

"Let's set the meeting for eleven o'clock Monday morning," he told Scruggs. "Why don't you fly into Greenville, North Carolina, which isn't too far from Pinetops? There's a private airstrip. I'll pick you up."

The next morning, Friday, March 28, Bruce Lindsey called Carlton. Lindsey, as he had told Carlton in their White House meeting, wanted all sides represented in the settlement talks—even the tobacco companies. This way everything would be agreed upon before a bill was sent to Congress; otherwise, lobbyists could tack on provisions that would make it unrecognizable and acceptable to no one.

"Phil, listen. I'll come to a meeting if it is absolutely essential to get everybody together," Lindsey said.

Carlton thanked him but said that wouldn't be necessary. He told Lindsey about the call he'd received the night before and Monday's planned meeting with Scruggs.

Later that morning, Lindsey met at the White House with John Coale and Hugh Rodham, two leading Castano attorneys. Lindsey told the attorneys about the upcoming meeting between Carlton and Scruggs.

"Should we be there?" Rodham asked.

"Yes," Lindsey replied. "The president wants everyone involved or he won't sign on."

Coale and Rodham called up lead Castano attorney Wendell Gauthier to inform him of Monday's meeting, and the three agreed that Coale should attend.

At 12:30 P.M., Gauthier called up Carlton: "John Coale will be there when you meet with Scruggs."

Carlton was amused. Carlton told Gauthier it was fine with him, but with a wry smile he thought to himself that Coale was in effect crashing the session.

THAT NIGHT, NORTH Carolina Attorney General Mike Easley was driving home from Raleigh-Durham International Airport when he dialed Mike Moore from his car phone. Easley had finally convinced Scruggs to meet with Carlton, but he knew that Big Tobacco really wanted to meet with Moore himself.

Even though Moore had approved Scruggs's meeting with Carlton, the Mississippi attorney general still didn't trust the cigarette executives. Their tactics disturbed him as much as their products. Moore had learned recently that Big Tobacco had hired private investigators to uncover scandalous tidbits that could be used against him. And Moore still didn't want the views of Big Tobacco obstructing his single-minded efforts to craft a legislative settlement that he could force the cigarette makers to accept.

Still, Moore was becoming less hesitant to meet with his foes. Though he and Scruggs had decided not to attend the March 18 meeting with the tobacco attorneys, instead letting Joe Rice handle the session, Moore liked what Rice had to say about it afterward.

"They were upset that you guys didn't come," Rice had told him. "But you probably ought to meet with them. They seem like they're serious."

Moore smiled to himself, knowing that if Rice was saying this, Big Tobacco must be earnestly seeking a settlement. "Joe could smell money a mile away," Moore would say later.

Now Easley was on the phone, hoping to convince Moore to meet Carlton.

The 47-year-old Easley, like Carlton, was the son of a tobacco farmer and warehouseman in Rocky Mount, North Carolina, in the flatlands of the state's tobacco belt. Easley, whose smartly combed black hair had a touch of gray over the ears, was a star defensive back at the same local high school and went to the same college—North Carolina State—as Governor Jim Hunt and Phil Carlton.

After college, Easley went to law school at North Carolina Central. In his third year, 1972, he worked for a law firm in Wilson, North Carolina, thirty miles east of Raleigh, and argued a case before then-state judge, Phil Carlton.

In 1992, Easley was elected attorney general. Though he represented a protobacco state, he and Moore got along well. About the same age, they had made their reputations as drug-busting prosecutors, and both were Catholic. Moore and Easley had become friends during national meetings of the state attorneys general; their sons, about the same age, were a common bond between them.

When Easley reached Moore from his car phone, it was nearly 10:00 P.M.

"Hey, Mike," Easley said, trying to sound casual. "I need you to talk to Phil Carlton."

Moore knew that Carlton wanted to meet with him about a possible settlement and didn't have to think about an answer.

"I can't, Mike," Moore said. "I don't trust him."

Easley backed off. Moore's stubbornness was unyielding, focused, like tunnel vision. He knew trying to change Moore's mind at that point was useless.

"Let me give you a call tomorrow. We'll talk about it again."

Easley couldn't let it die that simply. Coming from a protobacco state, Easley was convinced that a settlement was absolutely necessary if the cigarette companies were to stop being perceived as corporate America's embodiment of evil. It was time for Big Tobacco to get on with the business of making money instead of fighting lawsuits, Easley thought. And a settlement would also alleviate the concerns of North Carolina tobacco farmers that one day their crop, their livelihood, might be banned.

Considering this, Easley knew he had to persuade Moore to speak to Carlton and hear directly from Big Tobacco what it was willing to accept in a settlement. Moore was being foolhardy to continue to draft a legislative accord without the tobacco industry's input, Easley felt; given Big Tobacco's lobbying clout, any bill that didn't have its support would never make it through Congress. Easley's national political allies from protobacco states would make sure of that.

Easley decided to stop using logic to convince the Mississippi attorney general to take the call from Carlton and instead decided to offer it as a political IOU that Easley would one day have to return.

On Saturday morning, March 29, Easley telephoned Moore at home. It was about 10:00 A.M.

"Hey, Mike, I'm really sorry to bother you again, but I've been thinking about our conversation last night, and—"

Moore cut Easley off. "I already told you, I don't want to talk to the tobacco people. I don't trust them. I won't believe what they promise. And I want to work out an agreement, a bill, without them."

"No, this is different," Easley said. Gone was the caution in his voice, replaced by a more demanding, unwavering tone. "This is a major problem, and I need you to do this for me—as a favor. I'll owe you one."

Moore was silent. He was balancing Easley's request—its political and personal weight—against his own carefully calculated stance not to speak to the tobacco companies. Moore didn't say anything for at least a couple of minutes. Hoping Moore's silence meant he was giving in a bit and to ease the tension, Easley continued, more lightly: "Look, if Carlton or tobacco ever lie to you, I'll file a lawsuit against the cigarette companies in North Carolina. It would be a shot heard around the world."

Moore, seeing a tactical opportunity, relented. Not only had Easley convinced him that it now made sense to meet with the cigarette makers, but Moore knew that Bruce Lindsey at the White House wanted all sides to participate in the talks. Moore couldn't ignore Lindsey's desires. The president's backing was crucial for any pact, both to help it gain support in Congress and because it involved government agencies such as the FDA. To dismiss the White House would be a mistake.

And by now Moore had grown tired of negotiations with Big Tobacco taking place in the shadows, with messages passed back and forth by go-betweens John Sears and Tommy Anderson.

Moore, pocketing Easley's IOU, said he'd attend the meeting that Dick Scruggs had already set up for Monday.

"But I have one condition," Moore said, thinking quickly. "If I meet with the industry, I want at least one chief executive present. Either they deal directly, or I'm not going to deal."

"Mike, I think that can happen."

THE NEXT DAY, March 30, Easter Sunday, Scruggs called Carlton to say that they needed to change the site for Monday's meeting, partially because John Coale, who was based in Washington, D.C., had decided to attend.

"Can you come to Washington on Monday, instead?" Scruggs asked Carlton.

Carlton booked a flight on USAir. The meeting was set for March 31 at the offices of the National Center for Tobacco-Free Kids. Attending for the tobacco foes would be Moore; Scruggs; Matt Myers, who ran the center; and John Coale, the "Bhopal" lawyer for the Castano group of attorneys suing on behalf of smokers over tobacco addiction. Few besides the attendees knew about it.

Carlton would be the sole representative of Big Tobacco. Despite Easley's assurance to Moore a couple of days earlier, no CEOs were coming to this session. Moore swallowed that rebuff, assuming that the meeting was a prelude to sitting down with the tobacco executives.

The next morning, a USAir representative called Carlton at his office in Pinetops and told him his flight to Washington had been canceled. Frantic, Carlton quickly gathered his notes and rushed down the steps of the two-story office building. He hopped in his car, hoping that he would hit little traffic and could make the drive in the usual four hours or so. Otherwise, he'd be late for the meeting.

The session was slated for 4:00 P.M.; the tobacco foes showed up at Myers's office on L Street an hour early to discuss strategy before Carlton arrived. Sitting in a cramped conference room, Scruggs, Moore, and Coale were nervous and tense. This could be a fatal misstep, like bringing a cat burglar into your home to show him how well you hid your valuables. They had to be careful not to disclose any still-secret details about the settlement package they were working on or the strategy they planned to use to get it passed. They knew that's what Carlton would be listening for, useful information that he could bring back to the tobacco companies. They agreed that they were there to listen and not reciprocate.

Then Coale brought up a touchy subject. "You know, we really ought to be having the first meeting in New Orleans," Coale said. "After all, Wendell Gauthier (the Castano group leader, who was undergoing treatment for colon cancer) started this whole thing."

Scruggs stared at Coale angrily. This tug-of-war between the Castano group and the attorneys general over who was preeminent in the settlement was tiresome, Scruggs thought. "No, John, you're wrong," Scruggs said adamantly. "Washington is where a settlement would have to be approved by Congress. And anyway, the states are more important than the Castano lawsuits."

Scruggs's message was clear. He and Moore would lead any discussions with Big Tobacco. Coale backed down; he knew that Scruggs was right. Big Tobacco wouldn't settle just with the Castano attorneys; if they had to go it alone. To the cigarette companies, the states were pivotal.

"We'll keep this private," Coale said. "We can't have fights in front of Carlton."

Carlton arrived at about 3:45 P.M. The moment he walked in he knew he was in enemy territory. Facing him on the walls was a series of anti-smoking posters, including one that showed an ashtray brimming with snuffed out cigarettes and the words: "You Smoke, You Die."

Matt Myers led Carlton into the conference room where Coale, Scruggs, and Moore were waiting for him.

The introductions were formal. Scruggs referred to Carlton as "Judge." Carlton was surprised to see a cordial look on Mike Moore's face. The Mississippian's hatred for Big Tobacco always seemed so unyielding.

Carlton wasted little time.

"Let me put it plainly: Tobacco wants to negotiate," Carlton said. "We want peace."

Myers told Carlton that his words were welcome, but nobody in the room really believed the cigarette makers, no matter how earnest they tried to sound.

"The products that the tobacco industry makes kill thousands of people," Myers said. "You have a bad credibility problem."

Carlton nodded his head. He wanted to remain polite—yet tough. "That's all very interesting, but I can't cure 40 years of acrimony instantly."

The room got silent.

"We need a 15-minute break," Moore said as he led Myers, Scruggs, and Coale out of the room.

Moore told the others that Carlton sounded sincere. But since Carlton was just an intermediary, they'd need to speak directly with Big

Tobacco. Coale said the group should demand nothing less than the CEOs. After all, he said, that's who would make the decision to settle.

When they came back in, Carlton was waiting, reading notes from his yellow legal pad.

"I want to see the whites of their eyes—the tobacco CEOs—I want you to produce them," Moore said. "If you can bring the CEOs of Philip Morris and RJR to a meeting, and they say the industry is sincere in wanting peace, we'll take it from there."

"I think that's a real good idea," Carlton said. "I'll see what I can do."

Carlton said he was on his way to New York and promised to pass this message to the chief executives the next day.

Scruggs handed his business card to Carlton, who stuck it in his shirt pocket. For the next three months, as the tobacco settlement talks heated up, Carlton put that card in his shirt pocket when he got dressed every morning, afraid that without it he would lose his daily lifeline to Scruggs.

At 7:30 A.M., April 1, Phil Carlton sat down to eat breakfast at the Waldorf Astoria Hotel in New York City with Murray Bring and Rob Sharpe, the top in-house lawyers at Philip Morris and RJR, respectively. Carlton was there to brief the two men on his meeting with Moore and Scruggs in advance of a bigger meeting scheduled for 2:00 P.M. at Philip Morris headquarters.

The three men had barely been seated when Bring looked around the room. "Let's change tables," Bring said. "I don't want to be overheard." They moved to an out-of-the-way corner and ordered breakfast.

They decided to set up a meeting with Moore and the tobacco CEOs for April 3, two days later. Philip Morris head Geoff Bible and RJR CEO Steve Goldstone would be there to make brief comments. Then the conversation turned to which attorney at the meeting would speak most for Big Tobacco.

Carlton said he didn't want a tenacious lawyer like Herb Wachtell to do the talking; he might antagonize the attorneys general. "Murray, we need the mildest attorney to speak for the industry," Carlton said. "[RJR outside counsel] Arthur Golden might be the best person."

At 2:00 P.M. that afternoon, Carlton walked into the 24th-floor conference room at Philip Morris headquarters. Sharpe and Bring were there, along with Arthur Golden and Geoff Bible. They were seated around a mahogany-veneer conference table, coffee cups and yellow legal pads in front of them, talking about the incredible late-season storm that would dump more than two feet of snow on New York City before the day was through. Bible seemed anxious, wanting to get on with the session. He cut through the chatter in the room: "Phil, give us a report."

"Gentlemen, you're in," Carlton said. "Mike Moore wants to meet with you."

Bible leaned back in his chair and sighed.

"We need to make a big gesture, something that says we're serious," Bring said. He suggested they offer to take down all the outdoor billboards and remove cigarette vending machines.

"You'll blow their minds with that," Carlton said.

Bible agreed. "That will get their attention."

Then the men began hammering out the outline of what the CEOs would say, relying on a two-page list of settlement objectives that the attorneys general had drawn up during the Liggett negotiations.

They decided to respond to each objective. When the topic of the extent of the FDA's regulatory authority came up, Bring suggested changing the name of the agency to the Food, Drug, and Tobacco Administration. The FDTA wouldn't be allowed to reduce tar or nicotine levels, but it would be able to inspect Big Tobacco's manufacturing plants and determine the ingredients listed on packages. The companies would agree to fund antismoking campaigns, add tougher warning labels to cigarette packages, and disclose much of their health-related research.

The biggest negotiating concession, though, would be in the area of advertising. Bring was confident that the tobacco companies would win their challenge to the FDA's authority to restrict billboards near schools—part of the ruling that was soon expected from Judge William Osteen in Greensboro, North Carolina. But, Bring said, giving up near-school advertising could be used as a counterweight for Big Tobacco's key demands: relief from FDA authority that would include the power to reduce nicotine levels and protection from future lawsuits from smokers and states.

The men nodded and the meeting adjourned.

Bring pulled Golden aside.

"Arthur, I want you to be the main speaker," Bring said. "A shouting match isn't going to get us anywhere, especially with Geoff and Steve present."

Golden agreed.

The tobacco attorneys chose the Sheraton Hotel in Crystal City, Virginia, a suburb of Washington, as the meeting place.

As THE CIGARETTE executives were meeting with Carlton, the tobacco foes were being briefed by Dick Scruggs, who was calling key attorneys one by one. Scruggs reached Steve Berman, the Seattle, Washington-based lawyer who was working on several state Medicaid lawsuits, including the state of Washington's case. Berman was one of Scruggs's closest confidants.

"We're going to meet with the tobacco executives to talk about a settlement," Scruggs said. "I want you there."

He told Berman that Moore felt Big Tobacco was sincere about settling, enough to send its top executives to meet with them.

"I'll be there," Berman said. Scruggs told Berman that the more conciliatory attorneys general, like Grant Woods of Arizona and Bob Butterworth of Florida, would also be invited.

While Scruggs was lining up the private attorneys, Moore was on the phone to Grant Woods, the Arizona attorney general who had played a pivotal role in leading the Liggett negotiations.

"I want you to be at this meeting," Moore told Woods. "We need to figure out who all should be there. I know one person should be Bob Butterworth because his case is the next one to go to trial after mine. Is that enough, or somebody else?"

To avoid internal rifts, Moore and Woods decided to invite one of the attorneys general—Christine Gregoire of Washington, Skip Humphrey of Minnesota, or Tom Miller of Iowa—who had been skeptical about the Liggett pact and were not convinced that any tobacco settlement was in their interest.

Later that day, Moore called Gregoire, who was in Washington, D.C., on other business.

"We've been asked to go to the table with tobacco," Moore said. "What do you think? Do you want to come?"

Gregoire was unsure. "I think it will be a waste of time. This industry would never agree to anything that would be remotely sufficient."

The 49-year-old Gregoire, elected attorney general in 1992, had spent a year weighing the decision to join eight other states in suing Big Tobacco. She decided to go ahead after her 12-year-old daughter told her that she thought an ad in *Rolling Stone* magazine was cool. It was a two-page spread that had a three-dimensional Joe Camel popping out of the magazine with mock concert tickets and an application for free goods emblazoned with RJR logos. Gregoire finally filed the suit in June 1996.

Gregoire told Moore she'd go for one day, out of respect for him.

The meeting was slated for 3:00 P.M. on April 3. Both sides knew that a face-to-face encounter between antitobacco attorneys and CEOs from the companies they were suing could just as easily turn into a shouting match as produce the first steps toward a compromise settlement. So they made sure the media didn't learn about this session. No one could predict the outcome, and neither side wanted to be embarrassed in the press if they failed. The only indication that this meeting was even going on was a notation on the events board in the Crystal City Sheraton's lobby: Phil Carlton. None of the tourists in town for cherry blossom season took notice.

Inside the conference room in the minutes before the meeting, it was like a scene from *West Side Story*. Off to one side were Geoff Bible and Steve Goldstone and their general counsels, Murray Bring and Robert Sharpe; Marc Firestone and Steve Parrish, two Philip Morris senior vice presidents; Jane Hickie and former Senate Majority Leader George Mitchell, lobbyists for Big Tobacco; and the industry's attorneys Herb Wachtell, Meyer Koplow, Arthur Golden, and Phil Carlton, all four of whom had also attended the session with Joe Rice in Charlotte two weeks earlier. Lott go-betweens John Sears and Tommy Anderson were there, too.

Bible whispered to Carlton.

"Are these people going to be businesslike, or are they going to be rude?"

"Based on my first meeting with Mike Moore," Carlton answered, "I'm confident you'll be treated with respect."

On the other side of the conference room, eyeing their counterparts nervously, were Mike Moore and Dick Scruggs from Mississippi; Grant Woods from Arizona; Christine Gregoire from Washington state; Bob Butterworth from Florida; and Matt Myers, executive vice president of the National Center for Tobacco-Free Kids. The Castano coalition was represented by John Coale, Stan Chesley, and Hugh Rodham, who in order to hammer home his relationship to the president, sported a White House pass around his neck.

It was eerily quiet. There were only self-conscious whispers; no one was comfortable enough to joke, even among themselves. At precisely 3:00 P.M., all of the participants edged toward the square table in the middle of the room, and the two groups took seats on opposite sides.

The room was anything but elaborate or well kept. The cloth chairs were stiff and poorly upholstered, the carpet was dingy, and there were stains on the white drapes. Bob Butterworth thought that history was made in the most unlikely places.

Phil Carlton started the session by welcoming everyone and restating his role in the talks.

"Thanks for coming. My name is Carlton, but no relation to the Carlton cigarette." The joke failed. The people in the room were too tense, and no one laughed. Carlton then introduced George Mitchell.

Mitchell spoke briefly. "I've come to believe that the industry is making an act of good faith," he said. "This is a very historic meeting. We're all interested in doing the right thing."

Few of the tobacco foes listened too intently to Mitchell. The headliners were Bible and Goldstone; what they would say was really all that mattered. Moore stared at Bible. He had seen his picture many times and often thought how defiant and arrogant he looked in newspaper and magazine clippings. In person, though, Bible—short, with his hair slicked back and wearing metal-rimmed glasses—seemed much less threatening. Bible knew Moore was watching, but refused to look back; instead, he slowly thumbed through a stack of index cards in front of him.

"I know the attorneys general here are skeptical," Mitchell said. "But as a personal favor, please hear the executives out."

Woods, though a Republican, was disappointed that Mitchell, a Democrat and once the nation's highest-ranking senator, had stooped to becoming a servant of Big Tobacco.

Bible nodded at Mitchell and then looked across the table to the tobacco foes. As Bible spoke, he referred to notes on the index cards. "The industry is united in its desire to find a fair and comprehensive solution," Bible began stiffly, each word staccato and leaden.

This was corporate perestroika, and it was no easier to swallow than the political kind. Bible, the headstrong and steady spokesman for Big Tobacco—the protector (some would say apologist) of its values—never thought he'd be in this spot, putting a positive spin on surrender to people who wanted nothing more than the destruction of the cigarette industry. But Bible knew as well as anyone that survival in business depends simply on the ability to make money—and more of it each year. All of the litigation had jeopardized that for Big Tobacco.

"We come with the utmost good faith," Bible continued, his voice flat. "We want fundamental change. Philip Morris does not want kids to smoke, and we are prepared to find effective and sensible ways to accomplish that. We want to get out of confrontation and into cooperation."

Steven Goldstone spoke next. He told the group that he and Bible were authorized to speak for the chief executives of B.A.T Industries, the London-based parent of Brown & Williamson; Loews Corp., parent of Lorillard; and UST Inc., a smokeless-tobacco maker.

"I ask you to think about something else: the enormous role tobacco plays in the U.S. economy, and the jobs that are at stake today," Goldstone said. "As long as you realize that this is a legitimate product for adults, we are willing to reform. Please hear us out."

Mike Moore followed. "Don't waste our time," Moore told the executives. "We want a reduction in teen smoking. We want the public health to change. We want you to tell the truth."

Then, under an agreement Carlton had struck earlier with Moore and Scruggs, Bible and Goldstone were allowed to leave without taking any questions. Carlton was worried that given the chance, the tobacco foes would cross-examine the CEOs harshly or make inflammatory statements, perhaps even call them murderers, as they had so many times before. That, he was certain, would cripple the talks before they got moving.

Before he and Bible left, Goldstone sent a final message across the table. "We will be available personally. We won't be in the negotiating room, but we are ready to help."

Hearing these formerly implacable opponents concede that their longtime foes might actually have some valid concerns, Steve Berman leaned over to Christine Gregoire and whispered: "Jesus. This is history. Whether we fail or succeed, this is history."

After a short break, everybody except the two CEOs and their general counsels were back at the table. Carlton told the attendees that he would serve as the industry's liaison, meaning that when the attorneys general wanted to float a proposal, Carlton was the person they should contact.

Then Carlton introduced RJR lawyer Arthur Golden. To the surprise of the attorneys general, who expected this to be a session to hear each other's voices, test resolve and willingness to compromise, and nothing else, Golden began to negotiate in earnest. He said Big Tobacco was ready to tear down its billboards and end sports sponsorships. In return, the industry wanted immunity from civil lawsuits and criminal prosecution.

The attorneys general weren't prepared to respond, yet. But Mike Moore wanted to see how far he could push Golden.

"Are you going to get rid of [RJR's] Joe Camel?"

"We're willing to talk about that, too," said Golden. Not wanting Philip Morris to get the upper hand, he added: "But the Marlboro Man has to go as well."

Florida's Bob Butterworth decided not to let the issue drop. He looked directly at Herb Wachtell, who was representing Philip Morris.

"How about it?" Butterworth asked. "Are you ready to put the Marlboro Man on the table?"

Wachtell said he didn't know. "Let me talk to my client tonight."

Both sides agreed this was a good place to break for the day—after three hours. More had been accomplished than was expected. Both sides had shown that they were capable of compromise and good will. They decided to reconvene the next day.

That night, Mike Moore, Christine Gregoire, Grant Woods, Bob Butterworth, and others ate at a seafood restaurant. Moore took a bite of fish and sat back to relax. Today was his 45th birthday, and he hadn't given the occasion any thought; he'd been too busy. He was still skeptical that the talks would lead anywhere, but he was energized by how well the meeting had gone.

Even Gregoire—who found Big Tobacco so odious and evil that Moore almost didn't invite her to the meeting for fear that she'd jackhammer the road to a settlement—was swayed.

"Maybe I'm wrong," Gregoire said. "Maybe they're serious."

When she made her travel arrangements for the D.C. meeting, Gregoire had planned to return home after one day. Now she changed her mind. "By the way, Mike," she told Moore. "I'll be there tomorrow. I enjoyed watching this."

Over coffee, the tobacco foes decided that the next day they would focus mainly on teenage smoking and health issues and leave the more ticklish matter of how much money Big Tobacco would have to pay for later sessions.

While the cigarette foes ate lobster and Maryland crab cakes, Carlton and the tobacco lawyers retreated to the Ritz Carlton Hotel, where they met with Bring and Sharpe, the general counsels of Philip Morris and RJR.

During a buffet dinner, the lawyers held a conference call with Bible and Goldstone to brief them on what happened after they left. Golden said that by all measures, the first day was extremely successful.

"I'm glad we've got it started," Goldstone said. "It's going to be a long road."

Bring got right to the point with Bible.

"Geoff, they want Joe Camel gone, and RJR will only agree if the Marlboro Man goes, too," he said. "Are you willing to do that?"

These characters were household names and the centerpieces of two of the most successful and best-recognized ad campaigns ever. Still, Geoff Bible didn't shrink back.

"Tell them," Bible said forcefully, "that we'll stop using all human and cartoon figures."

Bible figured that a sharp reduction in advertising would essentially lock in Philip Morris brands at their record share of the market, close to half the cigarettes sold in America. That's because without extensive advertising new and second-tier brands wouldn't be able to be marketed to the public, so they couldn't cut into Philip Morris's sales. Furthermore, Bible knew that the United States was of diminishing importance to his company. In the United States, the 483 billion cigarettes sold in 1996 represented a 1 percent drop from 1995's sales. By comparison, eastern and central Europe consumed some 660 billion cigarettes in 1996, 37 percent more than the United States—and that number was still going up.

The Friday, April 4, meeting at the Crystal City Sheraton began at 9:00 A.M., an hour late.

Arthur Golden opened the session by telling his counterparts that the cigarette companies were willing to drop Joe Camel and the Marlboro Man.

Mike Moore looked at Dick Scruggs and shrugged, as if to say, "I don't have a clue what these guys are up to. They're giving in way too easily."

The tobacco foes said they wanted to talk about some of the public health issues, to stake out areas of agreement. President Clinton had indicated that his goal was to cut teenage smoking in half. "We want to put in the accord that if this goal isn't met by a predetermined number of years, the cigarette makers would have to pay a steep financial penalty," said Matt Myers, of the National Center for Tobacco-Free Kids. "That could mean billions of dollars."

"We can live with that," said Golden. "But we are not going to give you a blank check."

Golden added that he was impressed with the progress that had been made. "Before we break, I have something to ask the four attorneys general at this table," he said. "What are your thoughts on how well we're progressing?"

Moore, Grant Woods, and Bob Butterworth said they were hopeful—but skeptical.

Then, Gregoire, who sat silently for most of the two days, spoke. As soon as he heard the tautness in her voice—the unmistakable bitterness that she wasn't even trying to mask—Moore knew why his first inclination had been not to have her at the talks.

"You say you want peace?" she said, looking at Wachtell. "You may get that, in terms of the cases the states and Castano are filing. But if you mean peace at the price of taking away the rights of my citizens to sue, it isn't going to happen. Your industry sells death."

The tobacco attorneys winced. The negotiations they were used to weren't so emotional. In the early 1990s, Wachtell, for instance, had represented media entrepreneur Barry Diller in his hostile attempt to buy Paramount Communications. It was a bitter, ugly fight with lawsuits in numerous states, months of negotiations, tendentious press conferences, and half a dozen angry executives who could barely look at each other before it was over. And at the end, Diller's QVC Networks lost Paramount to Sumner Redstone's Viacom. But at least nobody called anyone a death merchant or a murderer.

Before breaking, the tobacco foes asked their counterparts for their positions on specific issues for the next meeting: What was the industry's view as to the regulatory role of the FDA? What would be the dollar penalty for the failure to reduce teen smoking? How would sick smokers be able to collect money from the companies in the future? Would there be any limits on how much they could win?

The two sides agreed to resume talks in Chicago the next week.

Before the antitobacco lawyers departed for their homes and the weekend, Castano attorney Stan Chesley told Mike Moore that he wanted to discuss one thing with the group. It was clear, when he started talking, that there was a deep rift among the tobacco foes that would have to be worked out.

"What about the money for the plaintiffs and their attorneys," Chesley said. "We haven't even discussed that among ourselves or come to some agreement on what percentage we'll get out of a settlement."

Moore blanched. He knew, as he had told Gauthier and Coale many times, that Congress—and the public, for that matter—wasn't going to accept a lot of money—even from an accord—going into lawyers' pockets. It would make the tobacco foes look as greedy as the cigarette makers.

"The attorneys general are first interested in reducing youth smoking and increasing the power of the FDA," Moore said firmly. "Then we'll get to money."

That, of course, didn't bury the issue. The blockbuster movie *Jerry Maguire,* starring Tom Cruise as an aggressive sports agent, was playing at that time, and the attorneys general borrowed its popular line, "Show me the money," to use in the weeks to come when snickering about Chesley behind his back.

THE SECRET TALKS resumed Tuesday, April 8, in Chicago.

The tobacco company executives and attorneys stayed at the Drake Hotel, the giant, landmark building at the foot of Chicago's "Magnificent Mile" upscale shopping district. The attorneys general were booked in the Ritz Carlton. They met halfway in between at the Westin Hotel.

Moore, Woods, Butterworth, and Gregoire along with Scruggs, Rice, and Berman were representing the states. Coale, Chesley, and Rodham were there on behalf of the Castanos. Joining Wachtell, Koplow, Carlton, and Golden on Big Tobacco's team was Robert Fiske, the former Whitewater independent counsel, who was working for Philip Morris.

The tobacco industry had not complied with the attorneys general's request to respond to their questions in writing, citing fears that their answers would be leaked to the press. Fiske spoke first, demanding that the executives receive immunity from criminal charges.

To the attorneys general this was out of the question. They were the top law-enforcement officials in their states. Granting criminal immunity so easily went against their instincts as prosecutors. Besides, the attorneys general didn't have the right to offer immunity from a federal investigation; the U.S. Justice Department alone has that power.

"If someone has committed a crime, they shouldn't get out of it by settling a simple lawsuit," Gregoire said.

Philip Morris's pugnacious outside counsel Herb Wachtell was incensed. "We're giving at every turn, and you keep asking for more," he snapped, staring angrily at Mike Moore. "When something that we want finally gets mentioned, you just reject it. There's no give-and-take at this table. You call this negotiations?"

Meyer Koplow, Wachtell's partner at Wachtell, Lipton, Rosen & Katz, cut in quickly before the older attorney's contentiousness derailed the session.

"Let's just take that off the table for now," Koplow said. "There's no point in trying to hash out something that complicated in a short time."

For Wachtell, that outburst was part of a pattern that would play out throughout the tobacco settlement negotiations. Put simply, Herb Wachtell wasn't a calming influence at the talks; being placid just wasn't his style.

During depositions of ABC producers in 1994 after Philip Morris sued the network for libeling the company on its *Day One* program, Wachtell yelled and badgered witnesses. So much so that one of the producers complained for the record that Wachtell was rude and made it difficult for him to answer questions.

Wachtell didn't apologize for his approach. "Sometimes it's necessary to litigate," he said.

Perhaps, but that's a far cry from making peace, especially among fractious enemies like the two sides sitting at the table in the Westin Hotel that day. As the talks progressed, it became clear that his role would have to be limited. "Having Wachtell involved was like having General Patton help set up the U.N.," said Castano group attorney John Coale.

Thereafter, Meyer Koplow took a much more prominent place at the talks, and Wachtell appeared less often. A quiet, intense, deeply religious Jewish lawyer, Koplow displayed none of Wachtell's pyrotechnics. His style was to look for areas of agreement in each issue rather than point out the distance between the two sides.

The tobacco companies proceeded. They wanted to bar future smokers from suing until they had tried a program to help them quit. The states agreed to the idea—at least for now.

Both sides decided to split up into smaller groups to start hashing out details of each of the major issues in the talks—such as advertising, labeling, and FDA control.

By mid-week at the Westin, the amount of money the cigarette companies would pay was broached in a serious way for the first time.

"The industry needs to know how much the settlement is going to cost," Wachtell said.

The attorneys general, citing studies of the states' medical expenses, said it would be at least $500 billion, which would include a whopping fund to compensate smokers—the key Castano demand—and *not* include fees to the Castano lawyers.

The amount was more than triple the $150 billion payment that had been floated the summer before in the legislative settlement that died after it was leaked to the *Wall Street Journal.* It was more than twice the amount that Bloomberg News reported just six weeks earlier.

"That's not even in the ballpark," Golden said. "It's way too much, and you know it."

Big Tobacco countered with $1 billion up front, increasing eventually to $10 billion a year—all of this over 25 years. The total price tag: $230 billion.

The state attorneys said that was unacceptable.

Coale whispered to Scruggs, "Well, we made history today. When the fuck has any attorney turned down $230 billion?"

Indeed, that amount would have dwarfed by more than $200 billion any prior litigation settlement.

The second week ended with both sides feeling optimistic. They had reached a preliminary agreement on a provision that would require the cigarette companies to pay a penalty if teen smoking isn't curtailed. Strict curbs on advertising and marketing were also assented to. They were still far apart on the amount of money that the tobacco companies would have to pay. And, at the very least, both sides knew there was work to be done on the two toughest issues: the extent of FDA control of tobacco and the industry's demand to receive immunity from all lawsuits and criminal proceedings.

Considering how compelling the notion of a tobacco settlement was to the public and the media, the negotiators had done a remarkably good job of keeping the face-to-face talks between Big Tobacco and its foes quiet. For two solid weeks, they negotiated in secret with no leaks. The national media were focused on Woody Wilner's second tobacco trial in Jacksonville, Florida, not on the settlement talks.

During the third week of talks, though, which began at the Doubletree Hotel in the Washington suburb of Tyson's Corner, Virginia, the veil was lifted.

By Tuesday, April 15, Alix Freedman, a *Wall Street Journal* tobacco reporter who had won a Pulitzer Prize for her day-to-day coverage of the industry two years earlier, learned that Big Tobacco and its opponents had been meeting steadily for the past two weeks. Some speculate the tip came from RJR, while others think the leak emanated from Hubert Humphrey III, who was complaining that he wasn't given a big-enough role at the negotiating table. Both deny tipping Freedman off.

On Wednesday, April 16, the *Wall Street Journal* ran a front-page story in its prominent right-hand column, written by Freedman and Suein Hwang: "Peace Pipe—Philip Morris, RJR, and Tobacco Plaintiffs Discuss a Settlement. Up to $300 Billion Would Go into a Fund for Claims; Ads Would Be Curbed." The 2,100-word article said state attorneys general and tobacco company negotiators were in talks to settle pending lawsuits for as much as $300 billion—$50 billion more than the figure in the Bloomberg News story—citing people familiar with the negotiations. The article disclosed that the CEOs of America's two largest cigarette makers—Philip Morris's Bible and RJR's Goldstone—attended the first day of the talks. The article also said that the industry would ban ads, including the Marlboro Man, and would set up a system similar to the workers' compensation fund, from which smokers could seek payments. Philip Morris and RJR declined comment.

The *Wall Street Journal* article was stunning because it showed for the first time the extraordinary shift that had taken place in the tobacco industry. Earlier reports had indicated that a settlement package was being written for congressional approval, but that Big Tobacco was not included, except tangentially, in the discussions. Instead, the bill would represent a consensus of the views of state and private attorneys as well as antismoking advocates. Now, with the *Journal* story, it became clear that even the CEOs of the cigarette companies were motivated to settle, that they and their representatives were compromising on key points—more FDA regulation, banning billboards and advertising characters—in order to be freed from the torrent of litigation.

The morning of the *Wall Street Journal* story, Moore and Scruggs, who were staying at the Doubletree, rose at dawn to work out at a Gold's Gym. They hadn't yet seen or heard about the *Journal* article. During the talks, the pair usually started the day lifting weights and jogging. Then they cooled down with a fruit shake, while planning their responses to issues that would likely be brought up in the negotiations.

There would no time for a shake this day. Moore was on a Nautilus machine when his beeper went off. He called the number back, and a *New York Times* reporter answered the phone. The *Times* reporter briefed Moore on the story. Moore grimaced. When he got off the phone, he turned to Scruggs.

"Here we go again," Moore said, his mind flashing back to the previous summer, when a leak about their efforts to put together a legislative package had scotched the plan. "Somebody has leaked the talks in order to kill the deal."

In New York, top Wall Street tobacco analyst Gary Black had already read the *Wall Street Journal* story by the time he got to his office at 6:30 A.M. He called up his sources inside Philip Morris and RJR, expecting them—as they had with the Bloomberg News article—to deny the accuracy of the story. He was astounded by the response he got from his sources. The story is true, they said, every bit of it—even how much a settlement might cost.

"It's almost as if the industry has put out a trial balloon on how much money it would spend," Black scrawled on the blue paper used only for in-house communications at his firm, Sanford Bernstein. In this handwritten memo, which he would distribute to the company's stock and bond traders, Black noted that the chances of a settlement were sky-high—as much as 95 percent—and that the industry would pay for its staggering cost by raising cigarette prices, maybe a quarter or fifty cents a pack. Meanwhile, the industry would save hundreds of millions of dollars on marketing and legal fees; the deal looked like a winner for tobacco, Black wrote.

Black added that an agreement could be struck within four to eight weeks. He was off by two days.

Traders placed a blizzard of "buy" orders for tobacco shares. Philip Morris's stock didn't even trade for almost half an hour as buyers couldn't find enough holders willing to sell their shares.

By day's end, Philip Morris's shares soared $4.13 to $43.13, up 11 percent, as more than 18 million shares changed hands. That increased the value of the company's stock market worth by $10 billion—a one-day jump greater than the entire market value of Federal Express. RJR's stock also shot up 11 percent, or $3.25.

"It was the best news for the industry since matches were invented," said Marc Perkins, a money manager in Jupiter, Florida.

With the chaos surrounding the *Wall Street Journal* article, the talks fell apart for the day. Both sides agreed to meet the following week, in Chicago again. Moore, chased by TV cameras at the Doubletree Hotel, met with Christine Gregoire and Bob Butterworth to decide how to respond to the *Journal's* story. In a press release, Moore acknowledged the talks, pointing out that he and 21 other attorneys were working to shield kids from the dangers of smoking. "To date, we have made substantial progress—especially toward achieving our No. 1 goal of protecting our children from tobacco. But we still have a long way to go." There was no mention of the billions of dollars at stake.

Late that morning, RJR's Steve Goldstone was at the podium in Winston-Salem, North Carolina, at the city's downtown M. C. Benton Jr. Convention Center to address shareholders at the company's annual meeting. With the *Journal* story breaking that day, Goldstone—who had been appointed CEO after Charles Harper retired at the age of 68 and was presiding over his first session with investors—decided that he was both blessed and cursed by the timing of the annual meeting. With a media storm swirling around the company, Goldstone would have his biggest stage yet to showcase RJR's recent successes under his leadership. But he'd also be asked questions about the settlement talks, and as a lawyer, it went against his instincts to speak publicly about continuing negotiations. He would have no choice, he knew, but to sidestep.

Standing before a packed house of hundreds of shareholders and reporters, Goldstone began by declaring victory over Bennett LeBow and Carl Icahn, who had failed in their effort to wrest control of the company. "We beat off some pretty miserable people," he said.

Goldstone then ticked off other accomplishments to scattered applause. "Reynolds International has been growing fantastically over the years. Yet we only have 4 percent of the world market."

Andrew Schindler, head of RJR's tobacco unit, next gave a presentation about the strength of the company's tobacco business. Camel cigarettes had reached their highest U.S. market share—5.1 percent—in 24 years, he said. "We seem to be doing quite well." The audience applauded.

When Goldstone returned to the podium, things got contentious. Tobacco foes and political activists who owned small amounts of shares—usually just one or two, so they could attend the annual meeting—protested loudly about the way cigarettes were developed and marketed. "This company is staying the course of absolute denial," charged Edward Sweda, a senior attorney with Northeastern University's nonprofit Tobacco Control Resource Center. "It's bad public policy, and it's bad for the shareholders."

Goldstone grimaced noticeably as the cigarette foes attacked. But he held his tongue and thanked each speaker for his comments.

Shareholders defeated a slate of antismoking proposals—to test the ingredients that RJR was putting in its cigarettes, to do more to warn pregnant woman of the dangers of smoking, to scuttle its controversial Joe Camel ad campaign.

"He was thrown a lot of curveballs which I thought he handled extremely well," said Mel Stocks, a retired North Carolina schoolteacher who owns a couple hundred RJR shares. "Cigarettes may not be good for you, but a lot of things aren't."

On the most pressing issue—the settlement talks—Goldstone was closemouthed. "I won't comment on those discussions," he said, adding pragmatically that he'd continue to talk to all kinds of people. "A resolution to this issue is important to our shareholders, our customers, and our country. But it has to be fair, and it has to be reasonable."

The audience was silent, waiting for Goldstone to continue. Then the 51-year-old attorney vowed to forge ahead in courtrooms across the country. "We're going to do it the old-fashioned way, by continuing to win cases," he said before ducking out of the meeting.

MEANWHILE, IN WASHINGTON, Moore was worried by the reception on Wall Street to the article. He knew that if the cigarette companies saw that shareholders were firmly behind a settlement, they would be much more motivated to give in and not disappoint their investors. Yet he couldn't forget what had happened the last time the *Wall Street Journal* wrote about a settlement. Except for his press release, Moore said little to the media, only that both sides were "making tremendous progress" towards a settlement. Moore added that he would brief Congress on the status of the talks the following week.

White House spokesman Mike McCurry, in his morning meeting with reporters, also said the talks were going well. He wasn't aware of any objections from the cigarette companies to the Clinton Administration's main requirement for a deal: a reduction in teen smoking.

"They are fully aware of the standards we have set," McCurry said. "I don't think they would be proceeding with the conversations they are having unless they understood at the end of the day that they have to meet our requirements."

In the face of all this optimism, settlement opponents from among the attorneys general and tobacco foes attacked the negotiations.

"Everything the tobacco companies have discussed to date falls short of the mark," said Minnesota Attorney General Hubert Humphrey. "While I'm willing to listen, I have insisted from the beginning that any resolution of the tobacco lawsuit require the industry to change the way it does business, pay for the tremendous harm its illegal conduct has caused, and disclose the truth."

And Stanton Glantz, the University of California at San Francisco professor of cardiology who disseminated Merrell Williams's stolen documents over the Internet, also blasted the settlement as "a complete sellout. The tobacco companies should not have the right to kill people."

On Sunday, April 20, the negotiators were in Chicago ready to resume the talks.

At about 1:00 P.M., Moore and Scruggs led a contingent of about 20 attorneys general and private attorneys from their rooms at the Marriott Hotel and took a chartered bus three blocks to the 80-story Amoco headquarters, the third-tallest building in the city. The skyscraper housed the law firm of Kirkland & Ellis, which represented Brown & Williamson in some litigation matters but had no role in the talks.

They walked over to the guard's desk to sign in.

"Your name, please," she said.

Grant Woods spoke first: "Joe Camel, Phoenix, Arizona."

Without blinking, the guard jotted the name down in the notebook.

The talks in Chicago lasted two days, focused mainly on the critical issue of immunity. Big Tobacco wanted to be completely relieved from all future and current lawsuits—whether by the states, the Castano group, or some other class or individual smokers. The state attorneys were dead set against granting that. Prohibiting Americans from filing lawsuits just wasn't acceptable to them and would, they argued, be squelched by Congress or the public.

"We can't settle this and limit your liability," said Richard Blumenthal, the Connecticut attorney general.

John Sears couldn't believe how illogical that was. "This is great," Sears told Scruggs. "We'll end up with a settlement where the industry pays no money and gets no protection." The talks broke at noon Monday, to allow some participants, such as Koplow and Myers, to observe the Jewish holiday of Passover. No new date for a meeting was set.

At the White House, Bruce Lindsey wasn't happy to hear that the talks had snagged on liability for lawsuits. He spoke to Phil Carlton and Mike Moore separately. Lindsey suggested a compromise: U.S. tobacco companies would get limited immunity from health-related lawsuits if they slashed teenage smoking in half over seven years. Moore embraced the White House's plan as a way to break the impasse.

"If we can come up with a formulation like that, I think the attorneys general would agree," Lindsey told Carlton.

Two days later, in New York, more than 100 tobacco investors and analysts went to the Grand Hyatt Hotel in midtown Manhattan—a block from Philip Morris's headquarters—to listen to a presentation by RJR's top in-house tobacco lawyer, Charles Blixt.

Blixt spoke for two hours and frustrated the audience by avoiding the subject most of them came to hear about—the settlement talks. Instead, the attorney talked mostly about the upcoming decision in Judge William Osteen's U.S. district court in North Carolina on whether the Food and Drug Administration had the power to regulate tobacco as a drug and thus the authority to reduce or even eliminate the amount of nicotine in cigarettes. This ruling—which would follow from the hearing two months earlier when Big Tobacco and its opponents argued the legality of a Clinton Administration plan to give the FDA control over cigarettes—was expected any day.

Blixt said that considering Osteen's tough questioning of the FDA lawyers and the soft-pedaling he did with tobacco attorneys, the industry's odds of winning the case were high. It doesn't hurt, he added, that the case is being tried in North Carolina—tobacco country.

"It looks pretty good for us," Blixt concluded.

8

OSTEEN'S RULING

*What happened to personal responsibility in the U.S.? Must we as
a society blame every mistake we make on someone else? As an
ex-smoker, I realize the health risks involved in smoking and would
never dream of asking for compensation for something that is a
personal choice.*

—JULIE BYRD
an ex-smoker from Akron, Ohio

R JR's Steve Goldstone may have been mute on the subject of
settlement talks at his company's annual meeting, but Geoffrey
Bible wasn't about to take the same approach.

The Philip Morris CEO didn't enjoy being coy. Directness always
worked well for Bible. It ensured that everyone—employees, rivals,
shareholders, whomever—knew what he was thinking and what he
wanted from them. Usually that meant, Bible learned, that others would
try to live up to his expectations—giving him a position of control that
he enjoyed and found advantageous.

Bible had been on the job only a few months in 1995 when his top
managers discovered how straightforward the Australian-born CEO
could be. It was the day before a meeting with the company's biggest
stockholders, and Bible asked his senior managers to run through the
presentations they would be delivering. Then Bible critiqued and

graded each executive as they finished. The highest mark: D.

The Philip Morris managers got the message. Many of them stayed up late that night rewriting their copy and polishing their performances to better fit what Bible wanted. As it turned out, the meeting that year was a huge success, and Bible sent each executive who had spoken a handwritten thank-you note and a bottle of wine.

PHILIP MORRIS'S 1997 annual meeting was held on April 24 in Richmond, Virginia. The settlement talks had recessed three days earlier and still had not started up again. So far, Big Tobacco hadn't even admitted that the talks existed, publicly remaining noncommittal. Meanwhile, Judge Osteen in Greensboro, North Carolina, had already said that on April 25, the next day, he would rule on whether the FDA had the inherent right to regulate cigarettes—including how they are made and to whom they're distributed—on the basis that they were essentially delivery systems to dispense the drug, nicotine.

If the tobacco companies lost that case, it would weaken them further in the talks; in effect, any issues regarding the FDA's role would have already been decided by the courts, and the cigarette makers would have no leverage to trade an expanded FDA role for a compromise from the attorneys general on some other issue.

With all of this as background, Geoff Bible relished the notion that he would have the spotlight and TV cameras when he made the first public confirmation by a cigarette executive that there were settlement negotiations going on and stated Big Tobacco's positions on the talks, the FDA, and its opponents.

The annual meeting was held in the auditorium at Philip Morris's sprawling manufacturing center on Commerce Road in Richmond, which houses the company's U.S. cigarette headquarters. Outside the building, which spans over 200 acres, a brick statue of a cigarette towers 100 feet high, emblazoned with the logos of many of the company's brands. A Richmond icon, the brick cigarette is visible to the millions of cars that drive past the city each year on Interstate 95.

"Uncle Phil," as the company is called in the region, employs 8,000 people and pays among the top salaries in the area. Philip Morris factory workers earn more than $40,000 per year; skilled mechanics and electricians take in $50,000 or more; and senior managers sometimes break $100,000.

Every job at Philip Morris in Richmond creates two jobs in the region's private sector—some 17,500 in all—at companies that supply the cigarette maker with paper, tobacco, computers, and transportation.

The ties that bind Philip Morris to the area extend all the way down to small businesses like Tammy's Auto Body & Paint Shop on Hull Street Road in the southwestern, industrial part of town. Pat Guthrie started Tammy's in 1994 with more than $60,000 in profit sharing she received from Philip Morris after she was laid off. Then, as she struggled to turn a profit at the body shop, Philip Morris called her temporarily back to work in 1996. That paycheck helped to keep the business open and to avert laying off two employees.

"If it weren't for Philip Morris," said the 38-year-old Guthrie, "I wouldn't be able to have my own business."

There's no city in the United States more rooted to tobacco than Richmond. It became the site of America's first mass farming of tobacco as an exportable product after 1612, when a British settler named John Rolfe, who would marry Indian princess Pocahontas two years later, mimicked the local tribe and began cultivating the plant, which he then shipped to London.

The English were instantly entranced by the green gold, and quickly became addicted to smoking tobacco, mostly in pipes. The rest of Europe followed suit, and money poured into Richmond, which became the first commercial boomtown in the New World. Huge tobacco farms sprung up—manned by slaves and sentried by massive nouveau riche plantation homes—along the James River, where the crop was loaded on barges to be towed to the Atlantic and its trip across the ocean.

In 1929, Philip Morris, which had begun as a British company nearly 100 years earlier, opened its first factory in the United States, choosing Richmond as its location because of the town's rich tobacco tradition. Today, the Richmond Philip Morris facility cranks out 400 billion-plus cigarettes a year, enough to supply every man, woman, and child on Earth with about four packs annually.

The annual meeting was slated to begin at 9:00 A.M. At dawn that morning, TV trucks from CNN, Richmond network affiliates, and other local stations began pulling into the factory's parking lot, identifiable by the satellite dishes on their roofs and the beefy, disheveled cameramen driving them. Dozens of print and electronic newspaper reporters—from the *Wall Street Journal* and the *Washington Post* to Bloomberg News and

Reuters—showed up at around 8:00 A.M., mingling around the media buffet tent set up outside, which even provided matzo ball soup for the Jewish journalists observing Passover. Soon, thousands of investors arrived, plus dozens of Philip Morris retirees—many in seersucker pants and white shoes, often with canes or in wheelchairs—who still thought of the tobacco giant as *their* company and were keenly interested in its activities.

Many of them remembered Geoff Bible's incendiary appearance at the annual meeting in 1996, when he compared Philip Morris's struggle against the tobacco foes to the fight waged by Winston Churchill and Franklin Roosevelt in World War II. "It took them [more than five years] to prevail, to get these bad guys and others who tried to prevail against the Allies. It took a lot of smart thinking. We shall fight, fight, fight. When you are right, and you fight, you win."

Then Bible took on Big Tobacco's opponents even more directly: "The other side is engaging in a reckless campaign of propaganda, mistruths, half-truths, innuendo, false piety, and downright deceit."

No one, except Bible and his closest advisers, knew what he would say at the 1997 annual meeting, but since he had never been conciliatory towards the industry's foes in public before, curiosity was palpable in the auditorium.

Minutes before the meeting started it was clear that Bible was softening his hard-line attitude towards company critics this year. Under orders from the CEO, antitobacco activists—even those without shares in the company—were allowed to participate in the session, and Philip Morris employees ushered them to their reserved seats.

Finally, at a little after 9:00 A.M., Bible walked onto the stage to a rousing ovation. By almost every measure, this had been a stellar year for the company. Philip Morris's net income in 1996 had shot up 15 percent to $6.3 billion, sales gained 8 percent to $68.9 billion, and the company's stock by the end of 1996 had risen 23 percent to more than $37.50 a share. (In February 1997, Philip Morris's stock split three-for-one: investors received three shares for each they held and to make up for this, the value of these new shares were set at about one-third of the old stock.)

Around the world, 154,000 Philip Morris employees watched via video. Bible, wearing a dark suit, beamed and waved at the crowd. Plumes of smoke filled the room as shareholders and employees lit up Philip Morris cigarettes.

Bible soon answered the question on everyone's mind. "We are prepared to work with responsible government representatives and others to develop a consensus about a regulatory system that would be balanced, reasonable, and effective."

If Bible had stopped there, it would have been a standout moment in Philip Morris's history, especially coming from a blood-and-guts CEO who seemed to actually enjoy the fight against tobacco's opponents. But he was set on accomplishing much more than that—the corporate perestroika gambit: He wanted to send a broad message of conciliation, one that would help propel the negotiators at the table toward an agreement that he could accept.

In that vein, Bible said that he was willing to submit to stiffer federal regulations in exchange for legal protections for the tobacco industry.

The room was quiet as Bible continued. "With a little trust and a spirit of cooperation there can be a change for the better. Many people have good ideas. We will listen and explore all reasonable measures that make sense."

Bible indicated that the industry would make concessions on central demands of its opponents, including reducing teen smoking, an issue that the Clinton Administration had said must be a key part of any accord.

"We do not want kids to have access to cigarettes. We do not want kids to smoke," said Bible, who started smoking at age 14. A handful of spectators applauded.

In all, the speech was vintage Bible in its directness and clarity. There was no ambiguity, and everything was said for a purpose: to ensure that both his expectations, and what he was offering to have those expectations met, were understood.

Only the Food and Drug Administration came in for Bible's venom. With Judge Osteen's ruling on whether the FDA had the right to regulate cigarettes just 24 hours away, Bible called the agency's actions "unlawful and unreasonable."

After Bible spoke, the meeting continued with questions from the floor. A few investors asked about the settlement, but Bible said he felt he had explained it about as well as he could. He had told them whatever he knew, he said. Then, the tobacco foes streamed toward the microphone, one after another accusing Philip Morris of everything from undermining American democracy with excessive campaign donations to both parties to endangering the public health both in the United States and the world. Hoots of derision greeted their statements. Bible was stolid at the podium.

"This company has killed more people than the Holocaust," said Anne Morrow Donley, cofounder of Virginia Group to Alleviate Smoking in Public (GASP).

Donley was drowned out by boos. "Sit down," someone hollered.

Another antitobacco activist took the microphone and lambasted the company for selling illegal products.

Bible cut him off. "Everything we do is legal."

There were more hisses and catcalls. "Get out of here, you don't belong here," someone yelled.

Bob Luecke, a shareholder from Chicago, stood up and pleaded with Bible: "Don't let these people dominate the meeting. They shouldn't be at the meeting."

Bible motioned for him to sit down. Then, looking over at the tobacco foes, he went on, his voice patient but stern, like a parent lecturing an unruly child. "Everything we do is legal," he repeated. "We are committed to the rights of adults to make informed decisions to use, or not use, our products."

Applause thundered from the company's shareholders.

Bible knew that allowing tobacco opponents to attend the meeting was anything but a mistake. It gave him a chance to show that Philip Morris welcomed opinions from all sides. It also gave him a natural foil that he could shut down with a high-road statement—after all, it was his audience, not theirs. Either way, he won. After two hours and nine minutes the meeting adjourned.

The next morning, company-owned jets ferried Philip Morris's senior executives, including Bible, Murray Bring, and Steve Parrish, to the Cloister on Georgia's Sea Island, a five-star, rambling resort of bungalows and beach houses with five miles of private oceanfront. There they would plan the future of the company in day-long sessions and await Judge Osteen's ruling on the issue of the FDA's right to regulate cigarettes.

EVER SINCE AUGUST 10, 1995, when Big Tobacco sued the FDA to block the agency's efforts to regulate nicotine as a drug, the spotlight had been turned on Greensboro U.S. District Judge William Osteen Sr.

This was a tough case for the 67-year-old judge. The FDA, led by David Kessler, had asserted that it had the authority to regulate tobacco. That position had a lot of public support and the backing of President Clinton, of health advocates like Matt Myers of the National Center for Tobacco-Free Kids, and of C. Everett Koop, the former U.S. surgeon general.

Still, Osteen had to rule on the merits of the case—if the FDA was overstepping its bounds in asking to regulate cigarettes as a drug delivery device for nicotine—and not on public sentiment. But if he decided for Big Tobacco, he knew he would be lambasted widely as being a pawn of the cigarette makers. He'd be seen as a regionally biased, tobacco-country judge who caved in under pressure from people like U.S. Senator Jesse Helms of North Carolina, Geoff Bible, and Steve Goldstone.

Osteen was already hearing that charge, even before he ruled. Tobacco foes said he was handpicked by the industry. His past clearly showed a prejudice towards the golden leaf, they complained.

Osteen was born during the Depression. His family owned an old tobacco farm just outside the town of Greensboro. The Osteens hired tenant farmers and sharecroppers to grow and pick the tobacco. Some of young Bill's earliest memories were of watching the fires stoked to cure tobacco in late summer, the pungent odor of the leaf filling the still, hot, nighttime air as the crackling cinders rose like fireflies toward the black sky.

In 1974, Osteen, who had a degree from the University of North Carolina at Chapel Hill and had just opened his own private law office, lobbied Congress to not eliminate the price-support program that was a benefit to his state's tobacco growers. Five years later, he defended an heir to the R. J. Reynolds tobacco fortune who was facing stock manipulation charges. Then, in 1994 as a judge, Osteen refused to throw out a lawsuit in which Big Tobacco was suing the U.S. Environmental Protection Agency for releasing a report that said secondhand smoke caused cancer.

But those who knew Osteen best said the tobacco foes underestimated him. The judge had always acted on his conscience and not his biases—even if it meant taking an unpopular position. They cited one instance when Osteen and one of his partners were interviewing a client in a jailhouse conference room. The accused man told the attorneys that he could find someone to lie for him on the witness stand. Osteen got up and left the room; he declined to represent the client.

And in 1962, as Republican minority leader of the North Carolina General Assembly, Osteen incurred the anger of political and corporate powers in his region by proposing a tax on cigarettes to replace a food tax. "He definitely calls it as he sees it," said Wallace Harelson, Guilford County's public defender, who had tried several cases before the judge.

The FDA ruling was expected at 11:00 A.M. on April 25. Before dawn, reporters from national wire services and runners hired by Wall Street analysts and investors to get the decision lined up at the U.S. district court building in downtown Greensboro.

At 8:00 A.M., when the clerk's office opened on the third floor, the reporters and runners jostled for position to prepay for the 65-page ruling. The first to pay would later be the first to be handed the decision.

At the same time, Osteen let 10 attorneys from both Big Tobacco and the FDA read the ruling in two vacant jury rooms away from reporters. The lawyers had a three-hour head start on the public and the media but were not permitted to take their cellular phones into the room. They were given copies of the ruling to digest so they could draft statements, decide whether or not to appeal on the spot, and prepare to brief their employers. The antitobacco lawyers—including Walter Dellinger, the acting U.S. solicitor general, and Frank Hunger, the assistant U.S. attorney general in charge of the Justice Department's civil division—worked in tense silence, barely speaking. In another room, tobacco attorneys—including lawyers Peter Grossi and Richard Cooper, the former FDA counsel—were equally quiet as they read the judge's ruling.

In the cramped clerk's office upstairs, more than 20 reporters and runners armed with cell phones stood shoulder to shoulder. At two minutes after 11:00 A.M., they were given copies of the decision. The reporters and runners sprinted out of the room, literally tearing pages as they ran, looking frantically through the ruling for the decision.

Desperate to be the first to report the news, the reporters found Osteen's words frustrating. In page after page, he weighed the arguments at great length, packing legal precedent, meanings, and outcomes into long paragraphs and footnotes. Skipping to the end didn't work either, because Osteen didn't summarize his findings there. Instead, he discussed and then ruled on each of the three main arguments in sequence.

PUT SIMPLY, BIG Tobacco lost.

Osteen gave the Food and Drug Administration authority to regulate tobacco, dealing Big Tobacco its biggest-ever legal blow and adding another setback in the courts to the once invincible industry.

The judge upheld the FDA's 1996 claim of expanded authority to regulate tobacco. In so doing, Osteen rejected two of the industry's main arguments—that the FDA lacked congressional authorization to regulate cigarettes, and that tobacco did not fit the agency's definition of a "drug" or "medical device."

On the first point, Osteen said that Congress never expressly excluded the agency from controlling nicotine or cigarettes, making that issue moot.

As for the second argument, that tobacco shouldn't be categorized as a drug, Osteen found that nicotine alters bodily functions just as other drugs do: It quickens the heart rate and triggers the release of chemicals in the brain, for example. Moreover, Osteen said, cigarettes deliver nicotine, so they are a drug-delivery device, something that the FDA is empowered to regulate under its charter, even though the companies said they didn't advertise their products as drug devices or intend for them to be used that way.

In giving the FDA the right to regulate cigarettes as a drug, the judge also upheld some of the agency's rules for how and when tobacco products could be sold and distributed. The FDA now could freely ban cigarette vending machines in places not restricted to adults. In addition, the agency could prohibit cigarette companies from giving out free samples and selling cigarettes to people under 18. And retailers could be forced to check for proof of age before selling cigarettes.

Also, the FDA could compel tobacco companies to print on cigarette packs: "Nicotine delivery device for persons 18 years or older," Osteen ruled.

"The fact that Congress has up to this date allowed the manufacture and sale of cigarettes to carry the [existing] required warning does not clearly demonstrate that no other requirements may be imposed," Osteen wrote.

Big Tobacco won on one point, though: Judge Osteen ruled that the agency had exceeded its power when it ordered the tobacco industry to curtail advertising intended for minors, a rule that was to take effect in August.

"Although the FDA has the authority . . . to impose access restrictions and labeling requirements on tobacco products, FDA lacks the authority to restrict their advertising and promotion," Osteen said in the ruling.

With this, Osteen struck down several FDA-imposed limitations: Cigarette makers could continue to sponsor sporting events like NASCAR racing and print color ads in magazines with youth readership. The FDA was also stripped of its ability to ban billboards within 1,000 feet of schools.

Minutes after Osteen's ruling, President Clinton issued a statement praising it. "This is a historic and landmark day for the nation's health and children," the president said. "With this ruling we can regulate tobacco products and protect our children from a lifetime of addiction."

The administration, though, was dismayed that Osteen had given Big Tobacco free rein in how and where cigarettes could be advertised and promoted. The FDA was told to appeal this part of the decision to the U.S. Court of Appeals for the Fourth Circuit in Richmond. That court had twice upheld a ban in Baltimore, Maryland, on most cigarette billboard advertising in areas frequented by children.

For David Kessler, the ruling was especially sweet, validating his crusade against cigarette makers. "The way we view tobacco products has changed forever," Kessler said. "It is indisputable that these drugs fall within the purview of the federal Food, Drug, and Cosmetic Act. It is an enormous victory. It is historic."

Reporters had such a difficult time figuring out what Osteen's decision actually was at first that conflicting wire-service headlines were sent out. Dow Jones, for example, incorrectly flashed the news, across thousands of its computer terminals on Wall Street traders' desks, that Big Tobacco had won. Philip Morris shares rose instantly. However, the next headlines sent out, by Bloomberg News, were different: "Federal Judge Rules That FDA Can Regulate Tobacco Products."

After it was sorted out, Big Tobacco took a hit on Wall Street. Philip Morris's stock dropped $2.13 a share, or 5 percent, to $39.50. Shares of RJR were hurt even more, slipping $2.75, or 8.7 percent, to end the day at $28.88.

Perhaps more important, it was evident that the defeat in Osteen's court meant that the tobacco foes had gained more leverage in the negotiations. Without FDA regulation to barter, the cigarette makers lost a key giveback that they could offer in return for an equally strong concession from their opponents. "This means the industry will have to shed some more blood," said Merrill Lynch & Co. analyst Allan Kaplan.

The antitobacco negotiators agreed.

The ruling "puts into law much of what the tobacco industry has been dangling as a bargaining chip in its settlement efforts," said Minnesota Attorney General Hubert Humphrey. "The tobacco industry came to the table, but this cuts the legs off their chairs."

John Coale, the Castano attorney, was even more blunt. The cigarette companies can "be regulated out of existence. They better come back to the table with a bunch of big concessions."

Big Tobacco's response was muted. Charles Blixt, RJR's lawyer who earlier that week at the session with analysts and shareholders in New York predicted that the industry would prevail in Osteen's court, said the cigarette makers were "very pleased the court struck down restrictions on advertising and promotion of tobacco products." He added that the companies would appeal the other parts of the decision.

Geoff Bible learned of Osteen's ruling at the post-annual-meeting Sea Island retreat that he and the other executives attended. As Bible led a planning session with the company's board of directors and other top executives, Philip Morris General Counsel Murray Bring and Senior Vice President Steve Parrish stood by fax machines and TV monitors in another building, awaiting Osteen's decision.

At a little after 11:00 A.M., Peter Grossi, one of Philip Morris's outside attorneys, phoned Bring. Up to that moment, Bring wasn't particularly nervous about the call. He, like so many other attorneys on the tobacco side, expected to win; this should be easy. But when the phone rang, Bring jumped. Suddenly he realized this was a make-or-break moment for his team.

"You got good news?" Bring said, picking up the phone after one ring.

"No. We lost. Nicotine's a drug and the FDA can regulate it and cigarettes," said Grossi. "But we won on marketing. They can't tell you how to advertise."

"Fax it to me," Bring said. He hung up and read the ruling page by page as it came over the fax machine.

Taking the fax with him, Bring walked downstairs toward another building, a 70-year-old stucco structure, where Bible and the other executives were sitting in a conference room.

Without knocking, Bring entered. He paused, and then looked at Bible. "On the core issue of jurisdiction, we have lost," Bring said. He said that the industry had kept the right to advertise without government restraint, and that both sides would appeal. The directors nodded grimly.

Bible looked down. How did we get this so wrong? he wondered. "We'll win on appeal, right?" he asked.

MOMENTS BEFORE OSTEEN'S ruling was disseminated, RJR's corporate jet carrying Arthur Golden touched down in eastern North Carolina, where Golden picked up Phil Carlton. The men then headed southwest to Jackson, Mississippi, for a secret meeting with Mike Moore, Dick Scruggs, Joe Rice, and Wendell Gauthier. Robert Fiske, the former independent counsel for the Whitewater investigation, was flying into Jackson separately to represent Philip Morris.

For all of the participants, the meeting provided an opportunity to avoid the press horde that had chased them in Washington, D.C. And Moore, Scruggs, and Rice saw the session as a chance to negotiate without other attorneys general interfering in the talks.

While flying to Jackson, Golden and Carlton called the R. J. Reynolds headquarters in Winston-Salem, North Carolina, and asked that Osteen's ruling be read to them. The phone connection was poor, but the two men heard enough through the static to know the impact.

Carlton shook his head, turning to Golden. "We'll hear the heart of a lion," Carlton said, referring to the boastful glee he expected to come from the attorneys general. Before landing at Jackson International Airport, Carlton and Golden asked that the Osteen decision be faxed to their homes, where they could read it during the weekend.

The two tobacco attorneys went directly to a conference room at the airport that Moore had reserved. Moore, Scruggs, and Rice were already sitting in chairs that looked out a window onto the tarmac. Robert Fiske was seated next to them. Wendell Gauthier, despite his ongoing treatments for colon cancer, also was there; Carlton was glad to see the boss of the Castano attorneys.

"I always thought he was their best leader," Carlton recalled. "After he dropped out of the talks because of his illness, I wasn't sure who their boss was."

For several hours, the negotiators worked on the issue of civil liability.

"Complete immunity is completely out of the question," Moore said, leaning across the table. "My attorneys general will never approve it and neither will Congress."

A waitress walked into the room carrying a pitcher of iced tea. She looked at the men assembled around the table, then her gaze alighted on Moore. She smiled.

"You're Mike Moore," she said. Moore grinned sheepishly.

Scruggs jumped in: "Look, we can't protect you from individual lawsuits but we're agreeable to shielding you from future class actions."

Golden was pleased that Scruggs said this. It was at least some movement, a concession, by the tobacco foes that they were willing to offer limited protection from liability.

But Robert Fiske, representing Philip Morris, wasn't quite so sanguine. Frustrated, he asked why his client wasn't getting more legal protection. "Tell us why the industry should do this deal if we're not getting any closure," he asked.

Rice stared at Fiske. "You've got an alternative. We'll go to trial."

Scruggs, though, had a better alternative, one that had been accepted by Gauthier, the lead Castano attorney.

"What we can do," Scruggs said, "is cap the amount of damages y'all would have to pay individual smokers—say at $250,000 a smoker."

Golden immediately objected. "That's not good. The industry could still end up paying tens of billions of dollars to smokers."

"We could get around that," Scruggs said, "if we ban class-action lawsuits and punitive damage awards."

"And," Moore said, jumping in, "we could require that any smokers who sue at least try to quit first."

Carlton and Golden looked at each other and both raised their eyebrows. This was an interesting proposal, they both thought. Capping the amount that an individual could win would reduce the number of smokers who would take on costly lawsuits against the industry. Banning class-action lawsuits, which spread the costs of filing suits among hundreds or thousands of smokers, also would cut down Big Tobacco's exposure to litigation.

"We'll get back to you, gentlemen," Carlton said, as he and the other tobacco attorneys stood to leave.

ON APRIL 28, three days after the Osteen ruling, 24 attorneys general suing the tobacco industry met at a Marriott Hotel near Chicago's O'Hare International Airport. Also in attendance were a dozen state attorneys who had yet to file a lawsuit, including Ohio's Betty Montgomery and North Dakota's Heidi Heitkamp. Frustrated by getting reports mostly from newspapers, they were all there to get an update on the settlement talks from Mike Moore.

In a morning meeting in a small conference room, Moore first briefed the attorneys general who had yet to file lawsuits.

"We're making progress," he said. "Already they've agreed to get rid of vending machines, Joe Camel, and the outdoor ads. We're still negotiating other points. We're hopeful that the cigarette makers will declare that nicotine is addictive much like Liggett did. That issue is still on the table."

Moore shifted to money. "We're still a long way from reaching an agreement on the amount the companies will pay. Those states that have sued may receive some favor."

After a short break, Moore and the 24 attorneys general who had filed Medicaid suits met in a larger conference room over sandwiches and soda.

First, Christine Gregoire, Washington state's attorney general, at Moore's request, handed out a memo giving specific attorneys general responsibility over each of the four areas that the negotiations covered. The memo, dated April 23, earmarked Gregoire to lead discussions about reducing teen access to cigarettes, the role of the FDA, and the corporate culture of the tobacco companies. She also would investigate the provision in the settlement that would penalize cigarette makers if they didn't reduce teen smoking.

Connecticut Attorney General Dick Blumenthal would head the civil liability section, meaning that he'd be in charge of the persisting problem of whether to grant Big Tobacco immunity from past and future lawsuits; Florida Attorney General Bob Butterworth would be in charge of the "money" provisions; and Grant Woods of Arizona would head the discussions of civil and criminal enforcement, the part of the settlement that would ensure that the rules agreed upon were followed.

Moore gave an overview of the talks, then asked for others to comment.

"I'm not in agreement on this settlement," Hubert Humphrey III,

Minnesota's attorney general, said. "I want that made clear. It's too early. We can fight first in court. Any settlement should be years away."

Moore was angry at Humphrey for being so divisive. He hoped some of the state attorneys that he recruited to join his fight against Big Tobacco would support him. That happened. Texas Attorney General Dan Morales and Indiana's Jeff Modisett said they backed the talks. Then others followed them.

"Why are we arguing about this?" asked Darrell McGraw, West Virginia's state attorney, whose own Medicaid lawsuit was gutted two months before when a judge tossed out most of his claims. "There is only one enemy, and that enemy is Big Tobacco."

Moore was relieved to hear how much support the settlement had among the attorneys general. He called for a vote: "Do y'all want to proceed with the talks? Who votes, yea?"

Twenty-three hands rose.

"And nay?"

One hand rose. It was Humphrey's.

The meeting broke at 5:00 in the afternoon, six hours after it had begun.

ON MAY 2, at a little past 5:00 P.M., the case of *Raulerson v. R .J. Reynolds,* presided over by Judge Bernard Nachman, went to a Jacksonville, Florida, jury of five women and one man.

This case, a wrongful death lawsuit filed by the family of Jean Connor who had died of lung cancer, was the first to go to trial since Grady Carter the summer before, in the same city, had won a stunning $750,000 verdict against Brown & Williamson. Before Carter, no smoker had defeated Big Tobacco in court. In light of that and the Osteen FDA ruling a few days earlier, the Connor case was being closely watched as yet another signpost in tobacco's increasingly difficult road in the courts.

Connor smoked Salem cigarettes for much of her life. In a deposition, Connor testified, "Anytime anything happened—you get stressed out, nervous, you finished eating, the minute you get out of bed, after you had sex, the first thing I reached for was a cigarette. You get this craving where you need to smoke a cigarette."

She was 49 years old when she died in 1995. Just before dying, she hired Woody Wilner, Grady Carter's attorney, and Ron Motley, the firebrand Charleston, South Carolina, trial attorney with a ruddy face and stirring courtroom style, to argue her case.

Motley's partner was Joe Rice—Dick Scruggs's associate and the lawyer who met with Carlton, Koplow, and other Big Tobacco representatives in Charlotte on March 18.

The Connor case against RJR was a grueling, three-week trial, with a less than perfect plaintiff. For one thing, Jean Connor only quit smoking because her doctor told her if she didn't, he wouldn't give her a tummy tuck. She never had any real health concerns about cigarettes until she got lung cancer. It's hard to elicit much sympathy from jurors for a vain woman wanting plastic surgery.

The strategy by Wilner and Motley was simple: Show the six-person jury that R. J. Reynolds sold a product that the company knew was dangerous. Two weeks into the trial, Motley called a company researcher to the stand, and the scientist testified that in the 1970s, R. J. Reynolds shut down a so-called Mouse House, where tests found that animals exposed to cigarette smoke developed cancer. At times, Motley turned dramatic, telling the jury they had the power to "indict" R. J. Reynolds, with the word "indict" echoing through the courtroom.

Far less emotional in his defense of RJR, attorney Paul Crist of the Cleveland, Ohio, office of Jones, Day, Reavis & Pogue argued that plenty of public information was available to Connor, who should have known the dangers of smoking and went ahead anyway. RJR couldn't be blamed for that.

In his closing statement, Motley was typically compelling. He told the jury that Jean Connor, as a young girl, used to preen in front of the mirror with a pencil in her mouth, mimicking a smoker, thinking this is what movie stars looked like.

"Jean Connor as a young girl imitated that which would take her life," Motley said, continuing, "You are going to be asked in this case to have the courage to speak the truth. This national health disaster called the cigarette epidemic can be stopped."

After a 10-minute break, Crist, RJR's attorney, gave his closing statement with little flair. It was solid and straightforward, detailing decades of information that warned of the health risks. "She made the decision in the face of that information and then she continued to smoke for 27 years after the warnings appeared on the cigarette packages. And then ladies and gentlemen of the jury, she chose to quit, and she quit in May

1993, the first and only time she ever tried, and she quit because she had sufficient motivation and sufficient self-efficacy. The motivation was to get a tummy tuck."

Crist also reminded the jury of pop-culture warnings of the danger of smoking. "You heard the song, 'Smoke, smoke, smoke that cigarette, till you smoke yourself half to death.'"

Motley strode back over to the jury for a final summation. Think about "Salem" country, he told the six people in the box.

"Form a picture in your mind of a young girl on the swing in Salem country. Where she swings through the air, what if they had interrupted that swing and flashed up there '. . . warning: 35,000 people have died from cigarette smoking.'"

He paused and stood silently, staring at the jurors, one by one. "This case is resting in your hands. Thank you. God bless."

Minutes later, at 5:15 P.M., after Judge Nachman's instructions, the jurors left to decide the verdict. They deliberated for two hours, then returned to the courtroom. They hadn't reached a decision yet and wanted to tell the court.

"When I sent you out, I said we'd keep you until about seven o'clock unless you felt that you were so close to the decision," Judge Nachman said. "Do you want to go home now or do you want to stay."

"Go home," one juror said. And the five others nodded in agreement.

9

TOO MANY LAWYERS

The big companies are looking for peace, the lawyers are going to get money and I'm going to get nothing.

—DANNY SAPP

a fourth-generation tobacco farmer in Toombs County, Georgia

On Monday, May 5, at 9:00 A.M., the Jacksonville, Florida jurors in *Raulerson v. R. J. Reynolds* returned to their deliberations. Six hours later, they had reached a verdict.

Word spread quickly, and Judge Nachman's court filled up. Dozens of journalists crammed into the spectator seating area, already packed with curious retirees and courthouse junkies in sneakers, carrying crumpled legal pads with notes on the case. Reporters who couldn't find seats were in a media room where they watched the proceedings over a live television feed.

The plaintiff, Jean Connor, died in 1995 of lung cancer at the age of 49. She had never attracted this much attention in life. But by the time of her trial, deceased or dying cancer victims had become Big Tobacco's unwelcome poster children, their fame tied to their addiction. Suddenly, it was everybody's business whether Jean Connor won or lost.

Ron Motley and Woody Wilner, the cocounsels on this case, were at the plaintiffs' table, absentmindedly shuffling their documents. Their work was done; only the result was unknown.

RJR's lawyer, Paul Crist, sat opposite them, surrounded by associates. This trial was big—for Crist and for RJR. The cigarette companies, in the midst of settlement negotiations, couldn't afford another defeat in court.

At 3:47 P.M., Nachman asked for the jurors. Everyone turned toward the door that led from the jury box to the deliberation room. For Motley, Wilner, and Crist it seemed as if that door would never open. Finally, a half minute later, the jurors filed in and stood facing the judge.

"Members of the jury, I understand that you have reached a verdict in this case," Nachman said.

The jurors nodded in unison.

"Which one of you is the foreman?" Nachtman asked.

Laura Barrow, 26 years old with shoulder-length brown hair, raised her hand.

"Mrs. Barrow, would you hand the verdict to the bailiff?"

Barrow's hands were shaking as she gave the bailiff the folded piece of paper. This was the most high-profile and serious event the CSX Corp. marketing analyst had ever been part of—leading a jury to a decision on an emotional case that intertwined with the aspirations of billion-dollar corporations, local and national politicians, and the family of a smoker in this Florida town. The case taught Barrow a lesson she was sure she'd never forget: The distance between yes and no, she found out, is often minute.

Nachman took the verdict from the bailiff and glanced at it before handing it to the court clerk. Barrow thought she saw a slight flicker of surprise on the judge's face.

Ron Motley looked first at the jurors' faces and then at Nachman for a clue to the verdict. He saw none. After all the theatrics during the trial—many of them his own—this quiet ritual of silently passing the verdict always seemed anticlimactic to Motley; ironic, since it was, at the same time, so final.

"In the Circuit Court, Fourth Judicial Circuit, Duval County, Florida," the clerk began, "We the jury return the following verdict:

"One: Was there negligence on the part of the defendant, R. J. Reynolds Tobacco Co., which was the legal cause of the death of the decedent, Jean Connor?

"No.

"Two: Were the cigarettes manufactured by the defendant, R. J. Reynolds Tobacco Co., unreasonably dangerous and defective and a legal cause of the death of the decedent, Jean Connor?

"No."

R. J. Reynolds had won.

The nine hours of deliberations were intense and emotional for the jury. At first, they were nearly unanimous—five to one—*against* RJR. The jurors were so biased against the tobacco company that, as one put it: "We wanted to fine Reynolds a lot of money and give it to a charity like the American Cancer Society."

Slowly, though, the jury switched positions. Each member of the panel began to see that no matter what his or her predilection was, RJR couldn't be blamed for the death of Jean Connor. Yes, the cigarette company disregarded its moral responsibility and failed to disclose adequately the dangers of smoking. But Connor was, indeed, a flawed plaintiff, as Ron Motley had presumed: She knew the risks of cigarettes all along, had been cautioned by her doctors—and never quit. Stronger warnings wouldn't have made her stop smoking. Only a tummy tuck did.

As the jurors realized that they had no choice but to decide in favor of Big Tobacco, the deliberation room had momentarily been blanketed with something like an emotional sandstorm. Some cried, others stared languidly into space. Everyone felt numb.

After the verdict was read, Motley slumped in his chair. Every losing trial was a personal embarrassment to him. It was impossible to get used to. Motley took a sip of Diet Coke, his eyes darting around the courtroom.

Connor's sister, seated between Motley and Wilner, stared straight ahead, tears in her eyes, her face a mask of disappointment.

Paul Crist was elated. Beaming, he jumped out of his seat and shook hands with the other attorneys on RJR's team. This was perfect, he thought, just what his client needed after the recent courtroom defeats.

The tobacco companies bellowed that even in light of all the negative publicity cigarette makers get, the people had spoken honestly.

"Our faith in the jury system is reaffirmed," said Daniel Donahue, R. J. Reynolds's senior vice president and deputy general counsel, standing on the courtroom stairs. "Despite anyone's feelings about this verdict, it should be reassuring that our American system of justice works—

that a jury of peers can hear all the facts for what they are, rejecting the unsubstantiated allegations of our critics."

Of course, even the cigarette companies knew that this was just one day in court—albeit an extremely satisfying one. Woody Wilner alone had 200 more lawsuits lined up against cigarette companies. There were also the Castano group class actions, not to mention the 25 states that had by then filed lawsuits seeking to recoup the money they spent treating sick smokers.

Wilner strode from the courtroom, with reporters close behind him. "You want a statement?" Wilner said, walking quickly. "We're disappointed. But we'll be back in August."

THE SAME DAY as the Connor verdict, May 5, the cigarette companies and the antitobacco attorneys met in Dallas, Texas, for a new round of settlement talks—the first since April 21.

The four weeks of meetings between the two sides in March and April had led to several points of agreement.

Big Tobacco had done most of the compromising. The tobacco companies had agreed to tear down and ban all billboard advertisements and cigarette vending machines and to run only black-and-white ads in magazines that weren't read almost entirely by adults. The industry also said it was willing to implement a plan to curb teen smoking. Now the attention of the negotiators turned to three main unresolved problems.

First, Big Tobacco wanted protection from smokers who might decide in the future to file lawsuits against the industry. The tobacco foes were divided on how much immunity the industry should receive. A proposal to compensate smokers based on their injuries—much like the workers' compensation system—was shot down in a Chicago meeting. Connecticut Attorney General Richard Blumenthal, for one, didn't want to give the industry any protection at all. Others, like Dick Scruggs, backed a plan to bar smokers from banding together in class-action lawsuits and from seeking punitive damage awards. In addition, Scruggs proposed setting an annual cap of a quarter of a million dollars on the amount an individual could collect from Big Tobacco. Blumenthal and other attorneys general—Hubert Humphrey III among them—wouldn't agree to that, though.

Second, both sides still remained far apart on money. Big Tobacco had offered $230 billion as its settlement payment and the attorneys general wanted $500 billion. Florida's Bob Butterworth, the attorney general in charge of the money part of the negotiations for the states, said hammering out the dollars and cents of the pact would be the easy part.

"Once everything else is done, we'll turn to the money," he said.

The potentially thorniest problem at this point in the talks was a disagreement over the extent of the FDA's authority over cigarette ingredients. Judge William Osteen's ruling had given the FDA authority to regulate cigarettes as drug devices. But tobacco companies had appealed that ruling and were likely to tie it up in court for years.

There was a lot to do in Dallas.

The tobacco attorneys stayed at the Adolphus, a luxurious, rococo hotel in the city's financial district, built in 1912 by beer baron Adolphus Busch. This rambling mansion is best known for its objets d'art from virtually every era in history, displayed in quiet alcoves and huge, great rooms—all of this imbuing the hotel with a dusty patina of plushness and wealth.

The tobacco foes' headquarters, the four-star Fairmont a few blocks away, was more modest. Located in the Dallas arts district, the Fairmont featured a European-style open lobby where corporate executives clad in suits and cowboy boots did business. On the third floor, a rooftop, Olympic-sized pool and patio sported chaise-longue chairs that overlooked the Dallas skyline.

The number of antitobacco attorneys attending the talks had swelled considerably since the last session in April. The regulars were there—attorneys general Mike Moore of Mississippi, Grant Woods of Arizona, Christine Gregoire of Washington, and Bob Butterworth of Florida, and private attorneys like Joe Rice, Dick Scruggs, and John Coale.

And now there was an array of newcomers: attorneys general Tom Miller of Iowa, Dennis Vacco of New York, Jeff Modisett of Indiana, and Dan Morales of Texas. More private attorneys also came, including Woody Wilner, Charles Zimmerman of Minnesota, and Peter Angelos, the bald, diminutive attorney from Baltimore, Maryland, who owned the Orioles baseball team and represented Maryland in its suit against the tobacco companies.

The antitobacco lawyers fell roughly into two camps. The first was the state attorneys general, who above all else wanted to recoup state money spent on treating sick smokers and to reduce teen smoking (a goal shared with the Clinton Administration). The other group was made up of private trial lawyers, headed by the attorneys involved in the Castano class action, who wanted cessation programs for their clients while pushing for a big payout for themselves.

During the two days before the negotiations with the tobacco companies resumed, these two groups and other lawyers for cigarette foes packed into the Fairmont's Patio Room to plan strategy.

It quickly became clear that there were too many people at the table. The talks had become a victim of their perceived success; with everybody beginning to believe the negotiations would succeed, they all wanted a piece of the settlement. Moreover, they didn't trust the other attorneys enough to believe that they'd get their share if they didn't show up. So they all came.

It was impossible to accomplish anything with so many lawyers representing individual positions. Every time someone spoke, there were a half dozen opinions aired in response.

Joe Rice, Ron Motley's partner from South Carolina, couldn't stand it. He was used to private, one-on-one negotiations: just he, his opponent, and a legal pad. "This is a zoo," he said in frustration.

The pressure of planning strategy was exacerbated by the presence of a dozen print and TV reporters, who sat in an anteroom outside the meeting, reading newspapers and drinking coffee and soft drinks that actually had been set up for the attorneys general—hoping the door would open and a lawyer would emerge so they could pounce.

Sometimes the reporters didn't wait for the session to break. At one point during the meeting, Christine Gregoire was walking around the room, building an argument, when she absentmindedly looked out the hotel window to see a boom microphone outside at eye level trying to pick up her words.

Faced with such media attention, the antitobacco attorneys agreed that no one would talk to the press individually. At some point, they would make a group statement, but only when they all felt ready.

That resolution lasted until the first break. As soon as the attorneys started walking out of the Patio Room, Connecticut's Richard Blumenthal, a patrician-looking, 51-year-old lawyer with slick-backed reddish hair and degrees from Harvard College and Yale Law School, made a beeline for the cameras. Reporters jumped out of their seats to surround him. With no reluctance, the ambitious Blumenthal began to give his opinion of how the strategy session was going.

Following Blumenthal out the door, Moore and Gregoire grimaced. Incidents like this one earned Blumenthal the nickname the "Hawk," because he always spotted the nearest reporter and swooped in for publicity.

With all of these distractions and the number of attorneys competing for speaking time, the tobacco foes weren't able to achieve much during their two days of discussions before negotiations with the cigarette makers resumed.

One area they did make some progress on, though, was how much money they would ask from Big Tobacco. Ignoring the Jean Connor courtroom defeat in Florida and emboldened by Judge Osteen's ruling in North Carolina that gave the FDA power to regulate cigarettes, the attorneys were convinced that the tobacco companies had lost much of their leverage.

Even a $300 billion settlement—the figure that first surfaced in the *Wall Street Journal* article on April 16—seemed too low now. They discussed what number was feasible and bandied about dozens of amounts. Mike Moore listened for consensus. The attorneys general wanted the tobacco companies to make annual payments over a period of 15 to 25 years. One scenario called for the payment the first year to be $7.5 billion, an amount that would cost the companies an additional 31 cents for each pack of cigarettes sold. The second year, the companies would pay $8 billion. By year 25, the companies would be paying $19.3 billion. The total was $302.3 billion.

One attorney general scribbled on the back of a paper drink coaster: 25 x 15 = 375: $375 billion to be paid over 25 years.

The antitobacco officials agreed that for now they'd stick with the $300 billion request because that amount would not bankrupt the companies. The attorneys then tested their plan's viability by analyzing the tobacco companies' finances and ability to pay. As one guidepost they used an April 13 memo prepared by Steve Berman, the Washington private attorney who was helping Christine Gregoire with her state's case.

The three-page memo, entitled "Tobacco Industry Preliminary Financial Analysis," outlined the portion each company would have to pay—based on market share. Philip Morris, with a 49.4 percent market share, "will bear half of the costs associated with this settlement," including a $1 billion up-front cash payment, the document said. "Philip

Morris does not have enough cash to make a $1 billion up-front payment, but could easily raise this sum from borrowing or capital injections [selling bonds or stock] into the market."

RJR, however, with a 28 percent market share, had high debt costs, the memo said. While Philip Morris's strong financial position afforded it the ability to make the annual payments, RJR's debt burden meant that not only would it have to sell debt or stock to pay its up-front amount, it also would have to repeat the process to make the annual payments.

Loews Corp., the parent of Lorillard, would have few problems, the memo said. With its broad array of holdings—life insurance, hotels, oil-drilling operations, Bulova watches—and an 8.4 percent share of the U.S. market, Loews could easily stomach its small (less than 10 percent) portion of the payments.

ON THE MORNING of May 5, the talks resumed at the Dallas offices of Jones, Day, Reavis & Pogue, a tobacco industry law firm. Because the number of antitobacco lawyers attending had grown so vast, the meeting took place in a conference room that spanned an entire side of the building on the 18th floor.

Mike Moore took his customary seat at the center of one side of the table. Next to him were Dick Scruggs, Bob Butterworth, Christine Gregoire, Grant Woods, and Joe Rice. Sitting behind them were the Castano attorneys, the other attorneys general, and almost a dozen private attorneys. Across from them, representing Big Tobacco, were Phil Carlton, Herb Wachtell, Meyer Koplow, Arthur Golden, and Steve Parrish.

The tobacco lawyers—sophisticated corporate attorneys with years of experience litigating and negotiating legal matters from complex contracts to product liability—were perplexed when they saw the sizeable retinue that filed in to sit opposite them. A couple of them shook their heads in disbelief.

Mike Moore knew what his opponents were thinking—and, anxious to forge a settlement and not slip backwards, had sympathy for how they felt. To veteran negotiators like Herb Wachtell and Arthur Golden, this was amateur hour. They knew how difficult it was to come to an agreement on complicated issues, especially those burdened by years of enmity. The only way to do it was to gradually chip away at the other side's positions and compromise when an opening emerged.

But when there were too many attorneys in the room, the process became cumbersome, if not impossible. Facing a sea of attorneys—all primed to stand up for their own particular bent against the cigarette companies—Big Tobacco's lawyers were frustrated and disappointed even before the session began. What previously seemed like serious negotiations had turned into something akin to the stateroom scene in the Marx Brothers' *A Night at the Opera.*

The negotiators made very little headway on the first of the three major issues facing them: punitive damages, which is the amount of money awarded to a plaintiff by a judge or jury to punish a company sued for misconduct. Punitive damages are rarely awarded at trial. But because they often can be as large as a jury wants, they are a sensitive topic for both corporate America, which is always lobbying for more restrictions on punitive awards, and for plaintiffs' lawyers, who often indulge in elaborate fantasies about spending their one-third cut of a potential billion-dollar verdict.

Private lawyers said that the prospect of such awards is a powerful deterrent for corporate wrongdoing. Exxon, for example, had to pay $5 billion in punitive damages after the 11-million-gallon *Exxon Valdez* oil spill. Sometimes onerous punitive damages are decided upon for less catastrophic events. In 1990 an Alabama jury awarded $4,000 in compensatory damages and $4 million in punitive damages to a doctor unhappy with the paint job on his BMW. (Eventually, the punitive judgment was reduced, but only after costly appeals.)

In the April negotiations in Chicago, the cigarette companies had asked for protection from all lawsuits. Antitobacco attorneys refused to agree to that, partly from the fear of appearing to be too cozy with Big Tobacco and anticipating problems getting the required congressional and presidential approval for the settlement, neither of which was certain. The tobacco companies then asked for a ban on punitive damages, which were so unpredictable that a jury could wipe out a company. Besides, punitive damages weren't tax deductible, the way compensatory awards were.

So, Big Tobacco came back to the negotiations in May embracing a new plan that Scruggs had proposed at the secret meeting in the Jackson, Mississippi, airport: limiting the amount of damages any individual could collect up to a quarter of a million dollars.

RJR's attorney Arthur Golden told the antitobacco lawyers that the industry liked Scruggs's plan and that it was willing to back down from its demands to be shielded from all punitive damages from future actions.

Then Golden listed other industry demands. No punitive damages for past misconduct. A ban on class-action lawsuits. And no smokers could sue unless they'd proved they tried to quit first.

"We're tired of being vilified," Golden said.

Scruggs sat at the table thinking the two sides were about to make real progress toward an agreement. That's when several attorneys general began shouting.

Florida's Bob Butterworth objected to all the hurdles smokers would have to clear in order for them to sue and win. "That dog is not going to hunt!" he bellowed.

The tobacco lawyers were nonplussed. After all, this is what Moore, Scruggs, Rice, and Gauthier had brought up as a compromise in the Jackson meeting.

Meyer Koplow, the lawyer for Philip Morris, interrupted the attorneys general after a few minutes. "You keep asking for things back. I don't see how we're going to make progress," he said.

Mike Moore suggested it was time to end the meeting.

"We have to go back and talk among ourselves, gentlemen," Moore said. "Then we'll get back to you."

Scruggs, Mike Moore's closest adviser, was disappointed at the turn the talks had taken. Over a dinner of tacos, chicken fajitas, and chimichangas at La Paloma, a Mexican restaurant in the nearby suburb of Plano, Texas, Scruggs told Moore, Butterworth, Gregoire, Coale, and Rodham that he'd had enough.

"Maybe Mississippi should just settle its own case; the other states be damned. This all seemed so promising a few weeks ago, but maybe it's impossible to do a national settlement that includes everybody."

"What about Florida?" Bob Butterworth said.

Christine Gregoire added nervously: "We're just going to protect kids in Mississippi? What about the rest of the kids?"

"I don't know," Scruggs said, shaking his head. Moore sat silently. He couldn't soothe Scruggs's frustration, and besides Moore knew that Scruggs was right. If he didn't limit the number of negotiators, Moore thought to himself, the talks were going to break down, perhaps forever.

On Tuesday, May 6, Moore and Scruggs met with the attorneys general again in the Patio Room. By now, even more attorneys general were uncomfortable with Big Tobacco's demands for immunity.

"This is too complex. You can't explain it in a speech to a Rotary Club," Butterworth said. "And if you could, they wouldn't like it anyway." He suggested the attorneys general up their demands and refuse to cap any payouts to individual smokers.

Moore and Scruggs were sure Big Tobacco wouldn't stand for this. They both knew they had no choice but to try and negotiate on their own and then convince the other attorneys general it was the best they could do. Several times, Scruggs ducked out to the patio by the pool to use his cell phone to call Phil Carlton, who was waiting at the Dallas offices of Jones Day with the rest of the tobacco attorneys.

Finally, Moore and Scruggs looked at each other and decided to break from their colleagues.

"The tobacco companies don't want to meet with you guys," Moore said. "We're going over there to talk and we'll come back and report." Moore and Scruggs stormed out.

Shortly after they had left, Ron Motley and Woody Wilner, fresh from losing the Connor case in Florida, walked into the conference room. The two were briefed on the talks, prompting Wilner to launch into a rousing defense of punitive damages.

"The punitive damages phase is where we get to show how egregious their conduct is," Wilner said. "These cases are winnable. The evidence is strong that the industry is culpable and irresponsible. We should not let them off the hook. We're getting more and more documents all the time—that's why the industry wants to settle. Why do you want to take that tool away from us?"

Wilner's speech struck a nerve with Gregoire and with several of the newcomers to the talks. They quickly decided to take up his cause.

Moore and Scruggs returned shortly thereafter. Moore gave the report.

"This is where we are," Moore said. "The tobacco companies want plaintiffs to jump through certain hoops before they can sue. Smokers have to try to quit first before they could file a claim."

As Moore spoke, the conference room full of once boisterous attorneys general fell quiet. Grant Woods, sitting at a corner of the table, stared straight at Moore and felt his anger rise.

"Mike, we can't do this. We can't negotiate a new form of tort law. We can't give up punitive damages. We have to go back to the tobacco companies and tell them they're out of their minds," Woods said.

Moore turned to face Woods. He needed agreement, not a debate.

"That's easy for you to say. Your trial is far away. Mine is coming up. I don't have much more time to negotiate."

"Look, we went through this with Liggett," Wood said. "Every time LeBow or Kasowitz refused to go along with our demands, we told them to get lost. And every time, we got what we wanted. We're going to go back over there with you guys."

What Woods said was true. And Moore saw that he wasn't going to convince his colleagues to go along with the tobacco company plan for punitives.

A short time later, all the attorneys general left the Fairmont and walked the three blocks to the Jones Day offices, taking what seats were available in the now crowded conference room.

Scruggs stood to speak.

"Some of my people want to talk about the punitive damages issue."

Woods and Blumenthal seized the opportunity and spoke for several minutes on how punitive damages couldn't be limited.

At one point, Arthur Golden, RJR's attorney, tried to soften the argument by suggesting that the companies weren't asking for that much.

"It's not a big deal to change the tort system because the tort system is already broken," Golden said.

Woods swiveled in his chair. "It's got to be up to the jury to decide what dollar amount should be awarded," Woods said. "This is the heart of the jury system. I won't go along with any cap."

Blumenthal added: "If ever there was an industry that deserved to get hit with punitive damages, it's the tobacco industry."

The tobacco company attorneys were aghast.

Herb Wachtell, who had been quiet during most of the session, reddened and spluttered with rage. "Why is it you people think everyone has some God-given right to punitive damages?" he yelled.

Golden was more controlled, but he too glared at Moore. "We're not going to take this kind of abuse every time we get together," he said. "This isn't acceptable."

The negotiations were all but ended. With the two sides unwilling to bend, the attorneys general left the session.

The tobacco company attorneys picked up their briefcases and headed for the elevator. Tired and frustrated, they felt that all their hard work during the past four weeks had dissipated.

In the elevator, Philip Morris Senior Vice President Steve Parrish sighed and slumped against the wall. He didn't say anything. He didn't have to. The lawyers in the elevator knew how Parrish felt. Marc Firestone, a Philip Morris attorney, patted Parrish's shoulders and offered to buy him a bourbon back at the Adolphus. Parrish smiled grimly.

Back at the Fairmont hotel, Scruggs was just as dismayed as Parrish. In the lobby, Scruggs cornered Steve Berman, the Seattle private attorney who had supported Grant Woods's stand for no limits on punitive damages.

Scruggs, who is taller than Berman, stared down at him and erupted. "Fuck you guys," Scruggs said. "You guys are asking too much. You guys are smoking dope."

Scruggs was concerned that the fruitless negotiations were causing his team to fall behind on the preparation for their trial in Mississippi, which was now just over two months away.

The next morning, Scruggs announced to Moore and Rice that he had thought about what to do overnight. "I'm getting out of here," he announced.

He looked at Moore, his longtime friend and close ally. "Some of our guys are basically prohibitionists, and you're being too deferential to them," Scruggs said.

"Dickie, c'mon," Rice said. "There's a light at the end of the tunnel. We can negotiate this."

Scruggs had made up his mind, though. He said he had told some people he had to get back to in Mississippi because it was his wedding anniversary. After lunch, he called Phil Carlton and gave him a different story: that his mother was sick so he was returning to Mississippi. Carlton said he understood, and that he, too, was frustrated by the recent failures at the negotiations.

Scruggs got on his jet and flew home in such haste that he left his luggage at the Fairmont.

By the afternoon of Wednesday, May 7, the talks officially came to a halt. Too many attorneys, too many positions, the lack of structure, no agreement on how to manage the negotiations—all had led to a breakdown.

Mike Moore, looking haggard and defeated, still held out hope that the negotiations would resume. He couldn't publicly admit failure. So, he lied to reporters.

"This is one of the best days we've had," he said. In reality, he was seriously upset that Dick Scruggs had dropped out.

Most of the antitobacco attorneys left Dallas that day. Of the attorneys general and their supporters, only Mike Moore, Joe Rice, and Tom Green, a 37-year-old Massachusetts assistant attorney general, stayed behind, hoping to patch up some of their differences with Big Tobacco's lawyers and leave the door open to resume negotiations. They, along with several Castano attorneys, set up a meeting with the full tobacco negotiating team—Koplow, Parrish, Carlton, Golden and Wachtell, and others—at Jones Day on Thursday afternoon.

Golden spoke first.

"We have to get something, or there's no reason to keep on going," he said. "What about a limit on how much the industry would have to pay in all suits in any one year?"

The few remaining antitobacco attorneys looked at each other and shrugged. Moore thought to himself that at least the cigarette makers were still talking. It showed Moore that Big Tobacco was serious about settling.

Golden then said Big Tobacco would agree to pay up to a combined $4 billion a year to individual smokers who won lawsuits against the industry. (Eventually, in the final settlement, that number would rise to $5 billion annually.) Golden suggested that the most a smoker could collect in any one year be set at $1 million, with any larger awards to be paid out over multiple years.

"We don't want to make one smoker into a lottery winner, and not give others help to quit if they want," Golden said.

This reasoning was in line with that of the Castano attorneys. Under their arrangement with the attorneys general, annual payments by the industry would be split down the middle between the public and private sectors. The public half would go to the states for their Medicaid expenses. The private half would be split again, with one half to compensate individuals who had sued and the other half to pay for cessation programs.

Moore thought this would be fairly easy to sell to the public health advocates, who were chronically underfunded. But he knew there would be resistance from the attorneys general, especially the hard-

Outgoing Food and Drug Administration chief David Kessler made regulating tobacco a top priority, committing himself to the political and legal battle of his career. In February 1997, he went to Greensboro, North Carolina, to explain the FDA's position at a one-day hearing where Big Tobacco was challenging his agency's authority to control cigarettes.

Matt Myers (left), executive vice president of the National Center for Tobacco-Free Kids and one of the industry's most outspoken critics, shocked his fellow public health advocates by joining Mississippi's Mike Moore to negotiate with the cigarette companies. Here the two confer while deflecting criticism at a May 1997 meeting in Chicago.

President Bill Clinton made reducing teen smoking a key initiative of his second term, hoping to make that public health gain a part of his presidential legacy. He lent crucial support to (left to right) Mike Moore, Florida Attorney General Bob Butterworth, and others fighting the politically potent tobacco industry, such as cancer-stricken former industry lobbyist Victor Crawford.

In December 1996, Clinton tapped his confidant Bruce Lindsey, deputy White House counsel (on cellular phone), to shepherd the landmark settlement talks. In the final week of the negotiations, Lindsey provided the crucial solution to overcoming the last stumbling blocks in the talks.

Ron Motley, the fiery Charleston, South Carolina, lawyer, demonstrated to jurors how the scales of justice should tip in favor of deceased smoker Jean Connor in a trial against RJR Nabisco. The Jacksonville, Florida, jury narrowly sided with the cigarette company.

Hugh Rodham (standing), the First Lady's brother, joined the Castano coalition of trial lawyers in 1995 and provided critical entree to the White House for such coalition members as Bob Redfearn and Will Kemp (shown seated).

John Coale of Washington, D.C. (left), and Russ Herman of New Orleans (right), two of the lead negotiators for the Castano lawyers, worked the phones in Washington to move the settlement talks ahead.

Negotiators for the states, including attorneys general Grant Woods of Arizona, Christine Gregoire of Washington, and Dick Blumenthal of Connecticut, huddled in a corner of the ANA Hotel in Washington to hash out their demands for FDA control of nicotine.

(Left to right): Former Maine Attorney General Jim Tierney, Blumenthal, Woods, and Mike Moore poll the 39 states that sued the tobacco industry on their support for the settlement proposal.

Phil Carlton (left), former North Carolina Supreme Court justice, managed to hold the talks together at several key junctures when they threatened to fall apart, helped by a down-home negotiating style. Arizona's Grant Woods, in contrast, took a hard line on liability issues that remained unsolved until the last days. Below, Washington Attorney General Christine Gregoire meets in an ANA Hotel corridor in early June with (left to right) Woods, New York Attorney General Dennis Vacco, Jim Tierney, and Florida Attorney General Bob Butterworth to discuss breaking off the talks over nicotine.

By mid-June, more than 100 print, radio, and television reporters had surrounded the negotiators, creating a zoolike atmosphere as attorneys general including Grant Woods and Indiana's Jeff Modisett worked to resolve the last issues.

Bennett LeBow came to Washington, D.C., to keep the national settlement from bankrupting his small Liggett Tobacco Company. He learned minutes before the deal was announced that he had failed.

The lead attorneys general strike a stern pose for a Time *magazine photographer. From left to right: Dennis Vacco, Dick Blumenthal, Christine Gregoire, Mike Moore, Grant Woods, Bob Butterworth.*

On June 20, the entire settlement came down to the fate of one man: former Brown & Williamson research and development chief Jeffrey Wigand (left). After the company finally agreed to drop its lawsuit against Wigand, he celebrated with attorney Ron Motley.

Toasting brings out the hidden flavor of the world's finest tobaccos. A combination millions can't resist.

LUCKY STRIKE
"IT'S TOASTED"

Gone forever under the proposed settlement would be the billboards and neon signs that have dotted the American landscape for generations. Joe Camel, the Marlboro Man, and alluring models would be banned, ending—after a century—nearly every form of cigarette advertising.

liners who didn't want to reduce a smoker's right to sue one bit. Moore decided that he had to show that he could deliver support of the attorneys general. He needed to look in control, especially after the debacle of the previous two days.

"I think we can sell that to the others," Moore said confidently.

Just at that point, Russ Herman, a rotund, 55-year-old Castano lawyer from Louisiana, cleared his throat. "I haven't said too much so far, so I'd appreciate your giving me 10 or 15 minutes uninterrupted," said Herman, his eyes bulging behind gold, wire-rim glasses.

Herman, author of a book on courtroom persuasion, delivered an impromptu, funny, and profane speech, complete with slaps on the table for emphasis, during which he laid out the Castano positions to date.

The Castano attorneys were in a sort of middle ground between their official allies, the attorneys general, and their official enemies, the tobacco industry. Used to being reviled for actual or assumed greed, the private lawyers had fewer qualms about settling with Big Tobacco than did the state attorneys. Some had already been accused of an unseemly willingness to give in in exchange for attorney fees to be awarded later. But they were also more experienced in these sorts of negotiations than the attorneys general, and wouldn't take a position one day only to reverse it the next.

Herman's goal was a settlement, no matter what the public thought about it. To get there, both sides were going to have to get serious: "Let's cut to the chase and either agree that we'll let go of the deal killers, or end the negotiations. We all have a lot of things that we could be doing," Herman said.

For the companies, "There isn't going to be any immunity," he said, because for decades the companies had lied to and addicted a quarter of the American public. "This isn't about how much you're willing to give in order to settle this," he bellowed, "it's about how much we will accept for not destroying you in court!"

Then Herman turned and told the attorneys general that they were going down the wrong path by insisting on giving people the right to sue for punitive damages. They were already going to get sweeping public health changes and billions of dollars annually for the states and for smokers.

"You're not going to sit at Jones Day, eat the industry's food, negotiate a deal, and at the same time say, 'We're going to go back out there and sue your ass,'" he said. "That's not how it works."

Herman's voice grew grave, and he stopped clowning. "We are at a historic moment in this country," he said. "There has never been a public health crisis that could be resolved at a negotiating table. There's been a lot of talk about asbestos, breast implants, and other big cases. If those cases were M&Ms, they'd fill a fishbowl. Tobacco litigation would fill a swimming pool.

"We can't afford to be children," Herman concluded, looking each lawyer around the table in the eye. "If we let this opportunity pass by without acting in good faith, then shame on us. And shame on the legal profession."

There was a pause after Herman's tour de force had ended.

Then Moore nodded slowly in agreement.

Reflexively, the negotiators looked to the pit bull, Wachtell, half expecting an explosion in response to Herman's broadside against the tobacco companies.

Instead, Wachtell spoke quietly. "There's a lot of food for thought there," he said.

"I wish the other AGs had been here to hear that," Golden said. "But maybe we can get this moving again anyway."

Both sides agreed to break for the day, with some of them meeting again on Friday.

On Friday morning, as Mike Moore walked over to Jones Day, he knew that despite Russ Herman's eloquent speech, the attorneys general just weren't giving in on the punitive awards issue. Regrettably, he was going to have to send a stern message to Big Tobacco to ease off their demands to be shielded from punitive damages.

Moore spoke for 30 minutes. He used the first 20 minutes to repair the damage wrought by his colleagues, trying to explain that there were just going to be some issues the attorneys general weren't going to be able to stomach.

"Punitive damages continue to be a problem for my group," Moore said, looking dejected and disappointed. "They're not going to bend on this issue."

Then, with 10 minutes left to speak, Moore, gambling that the tobacco companies wouldn't walk out of the talks, began to explain that there would be no more negotiations over limits of a lawsuit.

"There can be no more bells and whistles," Moore said. "There will be no caps on jury awards. And we can't ban secondhand-smoke cases. That's just the way it is going to be."

Big Tobacco's attorneys stared at Moore in silence. They sat in the Jones Day conference room, red-faced and disgusted as they listened to Moore, now backing off another agreement to cap jury awards.

Moore then left, taking with him the antitobacco lawyers who attended the meeting—Rice, Tom Green, Russ Herman, and others. When they were gone, Carlton spoke, telling the tobacco attorneys that they were going to have to give Mike Moore breathing room to reach a consensus within his own ranks.

On Friday night, May 9, Moore flew home to Mississippi on a jet with Joe Rice. They were worn out. They barely talked, and when they did it wasn't about the negotiations. At one point, though, Moore looked out the window, then turned back to Rice. "I got to call my man Scro and get him back on the reservation," he said.

AFTER A ONE-WEEK layoff, the talks resumed on Monday, May 19, in New York City at the East 45th Street offices of Davis Polk & Wardwell, where RJR attorney Arthur Golden was a partner. The meeting was set up in large part by Moore, who had held a series of ad hoc conference calls with various negotiators.

Mississippi's lawsuit against the cigarette makers was scheduled to start in about six weeks—the first of the state lawsuits against Big Tobacco. Time was running out. Soon Mike Moore would have to face his adversaries in court.

Moore convinced Dick Scruggs to return to the talks after he promised his Mississippi partner that he'd reduce the number of attorneys at the table and would designate a separate group of attorneys on both sides to work on the issue of FDA authority. The tobacco attorneys agreed that this made sense.

Moore was less successful at deciding which attorneys he didn't want at the talks and making his choices stick. He was planning to negotiate without consulting with attorneys like Arizona Attorney General Grant Woods and Seattle private attorney Steve Berman, who represented a handful of states. Both lawyers had been at the negotiations since the first session, but Moore felt that his group simply had grown too big, and that had hurt the talks in Dallas.

It didn't take long for word to spread.

Berman called Woods, concerned with reports that Moore and Scruggs were negotiating FDA and money issues in New York.

"Grant, what the fuck is going on?" Berman asked. "I'm getting calls from my clients. They want to know what's going on in New York. They want me to go to New York."

"I'm hearing the same stuff," Woods said.

They decided that Woods would fax a warning to Moore. The memo said that if Moore didn't allow Woods, Berman, and others, such as Connecticut Attorney General Richard Blumenthal, to join the talks, Woods was going to send letters to all the attorneys general, telling them that Moore was conducting talks without consultation. "We are considering taking this matter to the media if a change is not made," he concluded.

Moore got the fax and called Woods.

"Come to New York," Moore told Woods, who quickly flew to the city, as did Berman. Woods and Berman would prove to be crucial players as the negotiations progressed. But Moore had succeeded in keeping the huge crowd of attorneys that had appeared in Dallas from taking part in the talks. For most of the rest of the sessions, the only attorneys general who would participate would be Moore, Woods, Butterworth, Blumenthal, and Gregoire.

Gregoire's plan of breaking up into four negotiating committees—to handle money, immunity, FDA, and enforcement—had pretty much fallen apart. Too much had been happening each day at the table to keep everyone separated. Nevertheless, the most complex part of the negotiations, the part dealing with FDA regulations, had stayed with Gregoire.

During the sessions that began May 19, this group made a lot of progress. On the antitobacco side were Gregoire, Tom Green, an assistant attorney general from Massachusetts, and Matt Myers, the executive vice president of the National Center for Tobacco-Free Kids.

Myers, a short, slight, dark-haired man with glasses and a visceral hatred of even the faintest whiff of smoke, had been an ACLU lawyer, working for prisoners' rights before joining the staff of the Federal Trade Commission. At the FTC, he argued for tougher cigarette warning labels and enlisted then House member Al Gore to help him. Ultimately, they were successful.

In 1982 Myers started a small law firm and was leading a new group called the Coalition on Smoking or Health—a joint venture of the American Cancer Society, the American Heart Association, and the American Lung Association. He lobbied Congress to double the cigarette tax to 16 cents a pack, its first increase in three decades. He had a shoestring budget but was making some inroads against Big Tobacco.

In 1996, the Robert Wood Johnson Foundation and the American Cancer Society chipped in a combined $30 million to create the National Center for Tobacco-Free Kids. Myers was named executive vice president and began waging the most aggressive antismoking advertising blitz in history.

Bruce Lindsey had demanded that Myers, who had ties to the White House through his relationship with Gore, be actively involved in the negotiations to ensure that the talks included the views of a leading public health advocate. That didn't endear Myers to other health advocates—typically tobacco's most virulent foes—who were so mistrustful of the cigarette makers that they felt it was unsavory to even negotiate with them.

The cigarette makers delegated Steve Parrish, the Philip Morris senior vice president for corporate affairs, and Marc Firestone, Philip Morris's senior vice president for regulatory affairs, to negotiate with Gregoire's team on the issue of FDA regulation.

This new setup worked. With fewer attorneys talking to each other, areas of agreement were found quickly. When they disagreed, it was easier to arrive at a compromise.

Missteps occurred, but they were sorted out more rapidly than before. For instance, both sides on the FDA panel were concerned that if the agency used its power to reduce or ban nicotine, a huge black market in nicotine-rich cigarettes would develop, making it virtually impossible to regulate cancer-causing ingredients.

The attorneys came up with the idea to include in the settlement a provision that gave the FDA the option to reduce or ban nicotine after 10 years, but not before then. The agency could only use this option after demonstrating that reduction was technologically feasible, would have public health benefits, and wouldn't create a significant black market, Gregoire, Myers, and Firestone agreed.

At that moment, Mike Moore and Bob Butterworth, their work done for the moment in their own sessions, entered the room. Picking up the thread of the discussion—hearing Firestone talk about somewhat vague

FDA options—Butterworth misunderstood and butted in: "No, nicotine has to be banned in 10 years. Period. There is no option."

Firestone, 38 and a 10-year veteran at Philip Morris, had just taken a sip of water and was so stunned by Butterworth's statement—by his attempt to undo what had just been agreed upon—that he gagged and sprayed water over the lawyers. (The attorneys general nicknamed Firestone "Egghead" because he frequently carried a phonebook-sized folder of FDA regulations with key segments underlined in red ink.)

Gregoire quickly called a break and pulled Moore and Butterworth outside the room. "It's just the option to ban nicotine we want," she said. "Next time I need a pit bull, though, I'll be sure to call on you two."

Back in the room, Gregoire told Firestone that her colleagues had got it wrong. The FDA option was back; there was no change in the position of the attorneys general on this, she said. That issue was close to resolution.

Aside from the matter of overall FDA regulation, Gregoire also made headway on the provision to penalize tobacco companies if teen smoking rates didn't fall below a certain amount after the accord was passed by Congress.

This first came up in early April, during the initial meetings between Big Tobacco and the attorneys general in Crystal City, Virginia, near Washington, D.C. At that time—the day after tobacco CEOs Geoff Bible and Steve Goldstone sat down with Moore and the other attorneys general—health advocate Matt Myers told the industry's attorneys that President Clinton's goal of cutting teenage smoking in half must be met by the settlement. If not, the cigarette makers would be penalized. Big Tobacco assented.

Since then, teen-smoking penalties were put aside while the more thorny question of FDA regulation was sorted out. With that matter almost resolved, at the May 20 meeting Gregoire once again made a pitch to deal with teen smoking. Her proposal: If teen smoking didn't fall by 60 percent within 10 years of the agreement, the cigarette companies would have to pay back all profits they would receive from those kids over their lifetimes. This became known as the look-back provision.

The tobacco attorneys again said they could go along with it.

Now the two sides just had to work out what the annual maximum penalty would be if teen-smoking-reduction targets weren't met. Meyer Koplow, who was handling this part of the negotiations for the tobacco companies, said by the industry's calculations—looking at what it could pay and what its profits might be—a cap of $1.4 billion a year would be acceptable.

Gregoire was thinking of asking for $1.7 billion. But with Koplow so close to that number already, she decided to stretch a bit and see how much more money she could squeeze from the cigarette makers.

"I'll agree to a cap of $2 billion, and not a penny less," she said.

Koplow grumbled, but he didn't say no.

Gregoire pounced: "I take that as an affirmation."

After lunch, when both sides had reconvened in full, Carlton told the tobacco foes that "the look back is done"—Big Tobacco could agree to what had been worked out by Koplow and Gregoire. That provision was the first significant piece of the settlement to be fully resolved.

The lawyers applauded. Finally, some good news. Scruggs and Moore gave Gregoire high fives.

ON WEDNESDAY, MAY 28, Mike Moore and Matt Myers, executive vice president of the National Center for Tobacco-Free Kids, met at the Sofitel Hotel near O'Hare International Airport in Chicago with 100 health advocates—people from groups such as the American Cancer Society and the American Lung Association as well as outspoken public health supporters such as Clifford Douglas, a Chicago attorney who specialized in federal tobacco legislation and regulations. Also there were Dr. Lonnie Bristow, the past president of the American Medical Association who had been pulled into the settlement talks during the Dallas round, and Mike Ciresi, the lead outside lawyer for Minnesota Attorney General Hubert Humphrey III.

Gaining the support of these groups, who had fought for decades to reduce smoking, was crucial. The White House had made it clear that the public health community had to back the national pact before the president would approve it.

This would be a tough crowd to convince, though. As a group, the health advocates hated the settlement talks. They didn't know exactly what was being agreed to in the negotiations—Moore and Myers weren't about to divulge that in this open session—and they felt that if Big Tobacco was supporting an accord, it must be because its foes were caving in.

As the meeting started, Moore and Myers sat at a long table on the stage. The tone of the meeting was quickly set when the crowd was asked for a moment of silence for people who had died from smoking-related illnesses.

This proved to be a difficult moment for Mike Moore. A steadfast and unswerving opponent of Big Tobacco, he had taken on the industry before any other state attorney. Yet he felt somehow that this moment of silence was directed at him; it seemed to carry a message—cigarette makers are killers, and there's no negotiating with killers.

Finally, it ended. Then the moderator, Tom Houston, director of preventative medicine and public health for the American Medical Association, introduced the speakers.

As the crowd murmured and got comfortable in their seats, Moore began with a joke about stickers being passed out at the meeting. They read: "No Moore Sellout."

"I've seen some of the nice signs people have on today," he said, stopping to put one of the stickers on. "I'm very much used to these. As a young politician, you see, people in my state had stickers that said, 'No More Moore.'"

Few laughed.

Moore then summoned all the political skills and down-home Mississippi charm he had in an attempt to rally the health advocates to his side. He came from a part of the country that produced evangelical showmen like Jimmy Swaggart and powerful political demagogues such as Huey Long—men who thundered like freight trains when they spoke to people and were hypnotically seductive. Moore, a student of that preaching style, decided now was the time to use it.

With a cordless microphone, he stepped down off the stage and roamed the room. Taking a far different tone from the one he offered at the negotiations, he chastised the cigarette makers: "These are sorry, rotten, no-good scoundrels who have killed thousands of people. Am I right?" he shouted, a preacher's hoarseness slipping into his usually silky voice.

"Amen," came a voice from the room.

The hecklers quieted.

Moore continued by ticking off the years that had passed since he filed his lawsuit in May 1994, trying to show that nothing had been accomplished, nothing had happened to change the thinking of tobacco executives: "1994. 1995. 1996. 1997. Has anybody been indicted yet? If I win my lawsuit, you know what I get? I don't get to expand health care."

Moore looked across the crowd, trying to get them to buy into his sense of frustration. He explained why the settlement was worthwhile.

"Our plan is to stop the allure of Joe Camel and the Marlboro Man. If we're successful, there'll be no marketing in concerts. No movies. No more sponsorships. No more race cars.

"We're going to get $500 million a year—maybe more—to do countermarketing and advertising campaigns.

"Nicotine in cigarettes will be regulated."

Moore continued in that vein for a half an hour, desperately trying to stir the audience. But when he was done, the room was quiet. He had failed to move the crowd. Moore walked back to the table in front of the room and sat down next to Myers.

People in the crowd began to ask pointed questions. "Mike, what's wrong with relying on the court system?"

"The tort system is not effective," Moore said. "Fifty years has been pretty much a failure. We've had some victories in court. We've had some losses. It's a mixed bag in court."

The next person asked why Moore had conducted the talks in secret.

"In settlement negotiations, what you *don't* do is walk outside and tell everyone what is going on," Moore responded.

The crowd grew more strident in their questioning.

"All we've gotten from you is soundbites. This was supposed to be a briefing."

Moore wasn't going to apologize. "I didn't set up the meeting. The talks are confidential. I can only do what I came here to do."

One person asked Moore what guarantees he had that a settlement wouldn't be changed in Congress after the tobacco lobbyists get at the legislators.

"There are no guarantees," he said, adding that he'd "count on a veto from President Clinton if lawmakers radically changed the proposal."

Then it was Mike Ciresi's turn. Ciresi, a private lawyer, spoke from his seat at the front of the room. The Minnesota attorney and his boss, Hubert Humphrey III, not only opposed the settlement, but had gathered 30 million internal tobacco industry documents to use in their Medicaid suit, expected to go to trial in 1998.

Humphrey was the most passionate antitobacco attorney general. The death of his father, vice president under Lyndon Johnson and the Democratic presidential candidate in 1968, played a role in this. The elder Humphrey, a heavy smoker for much of his life, died of pelvic cancer in 1978. Humphrey soured on the settlement talks early on, mostly because he and Ciresi felt they had a winnable case—the documents were solid evidence, and Minnesota had tough state and consumer fraud statutes.

"Mike Moore wants to suggest you get more by settling," Ciresi said, raising his voice. "I disagree with that."

"On April 13, nicotine regulation was off the table and I know it," he added, accusing Moore incorrectly of caving in quickly on the issue of FDA control. In fact, that hadn't been resolved yet.

Still, Ciresi was touching the crowd, which was skeptical of Moore's motives.

"No one knows how you should ratchet down nicotine," he said. "That should be left to the FDA," not the attorneys at the negotiating table.

The attorneys general wanted to change Big Tobacco's corporate culture, he went on. That was no good. "What changes their culture is unfettered civil liability. The negotiators should not presume they speak on behalf of us."

Myers spoke next. This was a tough session for him, too. As one of the nation's top public health advocates, Myers should have had this crowd on his side, but most of the people in the audience considered him a traitor—someone who had been co-opted by Moore and the tobacco companies.

"We initially said we would not participate," Myers told the audience. "But I decided to be in on the talks to ensure public health issues remain front and center."

Myers explained that a settlement would provide the public health advocates with what they wanted—sharp limitations on Big Tobacco's ability to promote and sell its products, more money for antismoking campaigns and an increase in smoking-cessation programs. And they would get all of this much more quickly than if they waited for the courts.

The session ended at 5:00 P.M. When it was over, the audience hadn't been swayed. Moore slumped against a wall, fatigue spreading throughout his body.

Later, he boarded Dick Scruggs's Learjet for New York, where the negotiations would resume the next day. From the plane, he called Scruggs. At a litigation conference earlier in the year, Scruggs endured a critical grilling from University of Chicago law professor Richard Epstein, who wouldn't let up as Scruggs wilted.

"Man, I've just had an Epstein on steroids," Moore told his friend.

10

WALKOUT

This was not kids trading baseball cards or the creation of a prenuptial agreement between loving parties trying to accommodate each other. This was hardball negotiating every step of the way.

—DR. LONNIE BRISTOW

past president of the American Medical Association
who was involved in the later stages of the talks

Mike Moore returned to New York City from Chicago after dark and took a cab to the Sheraton New York Hotel & Towers on 53rd Street, 10 blocks from Times Square. He was exhausted from the grueling session with public health advocates. The flashing lights and laser-streaked billboards on Broadway made him squint. Though it was nighttime, it felt like the sun was in his eyes.

The hotel was no relief. The lobby was all noise and activity. Still dazed from the drubbing he took from the public health community only hours before, Moore checked in, then walked across the street to eat a quick dinner. He was relieved when he finally got to his room, silent except for the soothing hum of the air conditioner. He kicked his shoes off and lay down on the bed. Closing his eyes, he thought about how much he missed Mississippi.

On Thursday, May 29, the talks resumed in the offices of Philip Morris's counsel Wachtell, Lipton, Rosen & Katz on the 33rd floor of the CBS building, the charcoal, granite skyscraper on Sixth Avenue known as Black Rock. At 11:00 A.M., about two dozen attorneys and assistants had wedged themselves into the law firm's largest conference room, 33F, decorated with prints of Greek urns. They sat in soft, black leather chairs around the pale, wooden table—jackets off, sleeves rolled up—surrounded by huge windows that offered sweeping views of Manhattan's midtown skyline and the Hudson River.

The two sides were still at loggerheads over what to do about punitive damages and civil liability. Big Tobacco hadn't shifted its stance that the settlement ban all punitive damage for past actions and that punitive awards in future litigation by smokers be limited. Mike Moore wasn't able to convince the tobacco foes that some sort of compromise had to be reached on this issue.

Scruggs, sitting next to Mike Moore, began the session by tackling this subject head-on.

"Look, I know we said we could come to some agreement on punitive damages, but we just can't, we're not even near your position," Scruggs said, eyes darting from Arthur Golden to Meyer Koplow, Steve Parrish, and Phil Carlton. They just stared back. "We can't sell limiting or eliminating civil liability to our group."

Moore and Scruggs had hit hard resistance from all sides on this issue, including the Chicago health groups and such hard-line attorneys general as Maryland's Joe Curran and Iowa's Tom Miller. None of them were willing to free the cigarette makers from punitive damages.

Miller in particular was suspicious of Moore's shifting positions and desire to compromise on punitive damages, and he made sure other attorneys general backed his efforts to block any attempt to yield on this issue.

"The tobacco companies have more to lose than we do by not settling," Miller told Connecticut Attorney General Richard Blumenthal on a call before the negotiations resumed. "They can win most of the Medicaid cases and still wind up in bankruptcy. And even if we try all our cases and lose them all, we have achieved some good in terms of public opinion and getting documents released. We could hold our heads high."

Scruggs knew he had to make sure the tobacco companies understood the depth of opposition to limiting punitive damages that existed in his group.

"We can live with an annual cap on how much the cigarette companies would pay for future lawsuits," Scruggs said, essentially echoing the last offer of Big Tobacco. "But we can't accept a ban on punitive damages for past misconduct."

In effect, the cigarette companies were being asked to pay a huge fee to settle lawsuits and at the same time being told they would still have to go to court to fight potentially massive cases brought by individual smokers. Thirty seconds passed, then Golden banged his hands on the table.

"What the hell have we been doing here?" Golden asked, his face reddening as he stared at Moore. "You knew immunity from punitives for past misconduct was an absolute condition of these talks. We said that from the beginning, and it's the only reason why we're here."

He stopped short. Then he looked around at his colleagues on his side of the table.

Golden got up. "That's it. There's not going to be a deal." He stormed out of the room. The other Big Tobacco attorneys watched Golden leave and were unsure what to do next. Then they walked out without saying a word.

"This is just posturing," thought Stan Chesley, the Castano group attorney from Cincinnati, Ohio.

Others weren't so sure. "They've never done this before," Christine Gregoire said to herself. "We're in trouble."

Then the door to the conference room opened and the tobacco attorneys walked back in, single file. They had forgotten their suit coats and briefcases. They grabbed their belongings and strode out again.

Joe Rice ran out to the hallway and saw Golden by the elevator.

"When are we meeting again?" Rice asked.

"I don't know."

"And it looks like you don't care."

"That's right," Golden said, and got on the elevator.

The tobacco lawyers left the CBS building and climbed into their fleet of cars for the short trip to Philip Morris headquarters at 120 Park Avenue. In his limousine, seated next to Phil Carlton, Golden couldn't contain his anger.

"They have to understand we're serious," Golden said.

When they arrived at Philip Morris, the attorneys marched into a conference room. Golden stepped off to the side and called RJR CEO Stephen Goldstone. He wasn't in.

"Find him!" Golden yelled at Goldstone's secretary. "This is an emergency."

Five minutes later, Goldstone, who was at a nearby airport taking flying lessons, called Golden back. After telling Goldstone what had happened in the talks, Golden said the cigarette makers had to draw the line on this issue—even though the industry had previously never been ordered by a jury to pay punitive damages.

"Moore told us this would work, and now they're going back on it," Golden said. "We're already paying for our sins in this settlement, to the tune of at least $300 billion. Isn't that enough? We have to get something back for giving up more than a quarter of a trillion dollars."

"You're right," Goldstone said. "If they won't be reasonable, we can't deal with them."

With Goldstone's go-ahead to stonewall, Golden went to the conference room and told the other attorneys that RJR's position was to end the talks, at least until the attorneys general changed their stance.

"This is ridiculous," Golden said. "Some of these people don't want a deal, and Moore can't keep them in line. They're dealing in bad faith. We should go back and tell them we're through talking. When they wake up, they can come see us."

Murray Bring, Philip Morris's general counsel, didn't want to give up. "We can't throw out everything we've done over one bad day," he said. "If we tell them we're not going to move on this—and we're not—we can keep talking about the other issues. When they realize we're serious, they'll come around."

The men hashed out their options for hours, with Philip Morris playing the dove and RJR the hawk. Golden argued that even with an annual cap on payouts for lawsuits, a ban on punitive damages was crucial. The possibility of large awards would give plaintiff attorneys more incentive to sue, and if many multibillion-dollar awards ensued, Congress would be tempted to raise the annual cap. Finally, they came to a compromise: They would tell the attorneys general that the talks were over until they got their positions unified and made a serious proposal on liability. Phil Carlton and Meyer Koplow drafted a memo for the tobacco foes that said: "Today's developments threaten what we have accomplished.

There is only one way to save the process. Within four days, we need a firm list of demands."

Golden took a car crosstown to his office to meet with two of the Castano lawyers, Stan Chesley and Russ Herman, who wanted to know if the talks would survive the day's events.

"It's pretty bad," Golden said. "They aren't shooting straight with us."

Golden had expected Chesley and Herman to argue to resume the talks. After all, the Castano attorneys had a lot to gain financially from settling. Instead, though, they agreed with Big Tobacco, declaring themselves equally frustrated with the attorneys general's lack of unity.

"Walking out was the best thing you could have done," Chesley told Golden. "If you don't draw the line, they'll keep backing away forever."

Herman agreed. "You have to be tough," he said. "The AGs are like kids in a candy store."

The attorneys general, meantime, were in disarray.

Christine Gregoire, deflated by the sudden negative turn, left the CBS building and went out into the heat of midtown, across 52nd Street. She needed to walk off some of her frustration.

Once a hesitant participant in the tobacco talks, Gregoire had become one of the biggest backers. Her subgroup, hashing out the scope of the FDA's regulatory power over nicotine, had accomplished a lot in a few short weeks.

The Gregoire group had hammered out the so-called look-back provision, a creative way to punish the cigarette companies with billions of dollars in fines if teen smoking rates didn't fall. They had reached agreement with the tobacco companies on broad changes in the role of smoking in public society, from banning cigarettes in hotel lobbies and almost all office buildings to getting rid of the pervasive billboards that dotted America's landscape.

And they were making steady progress on how the FDA could regulate ingredients, including nicotine, in cigarettes, and how to allow tobacco companies, for the first time, to advertise any innovative, safer products as less-dangerous cigarettes, if they could prove it.

Now, walking through the New York streets—oblivious to the hundreds of people passing by—Gregoire wondered: Was all her work worthless? Were all those red-eye flights between Seattle and New York, and Dallas and Chicago, a waste of time?

Connecticut's Richard Blumenthal soon followed Gregoire out of the CBS building. Living up to his nickname, the Hawk stopped for the TV cameras at the corner of 52nd Street and Avenue of the Americas.

"The elimination of punitive damages and limiting future damages, in our view, are off the table," Blumenthal told TV viewers. "Giving these things up might be too high a price for the industry to pay. But we're willing to walk away from the table if the industry continues to insist on unreasonable protection from liability."

Those attorneys general who were still at Wachtell Lipton were stunned by what had transpired that morning.

At one point, Castano attorney Charles Zimmerman tapped Dick Scruggs and asked what he thought was going on at Philip Morris headquarters.

Without pausing, Scruggs replied: "Tobacco is debating whether to say 'Kiss my ass' or 'Please kiss my ass.'"

MARC KASOWITZ, LIGGETT'S attorney, wasn't aware that the negotiations had taken such a bad turn when he rendezvoused with Scruggs, Moore, Joe Rice, and Grant Woods for lunch that day at Palio's, an upscale Italian restaurant in the Equitable Building on Seventh Avenue.

Kasowitz called the meeting to ensure that the states held to their settlement with Liggett—and plead his case to exempt the tiny cigarette maker from an industrywide accord. There was no way that Liggett could afford its share of the multibillion-dollar payments that would be part of the settlement with Big Tobacco.

Entering the dark bar, encircled by a two-story-high mural of the centuries-old annual Il Palio horse race in Siena, Italy, Kasowitz was told that his party was one floor up in a private dining room.

As he sat down, Kasowitz thought Moore looked tense. He wondered if the talks were spiraling out of Moore's control. Kasowitz, of course, didn't care if Big Tobacco and its foes worked out a deal or not. In fact, it would be better for him and LeBow if they didn't. It would render moot the question of whether Liggett's settlements with the states could be superseded by a new accord.

"Well, if you do work out a deal with the other companies, is Liggett still separate, as you promised?" Kasowitz asked.

"It's getting tougher to stick to that," Moore said. "The other companies' position is that if Liggett is exempted from the settlement, you'd be able to keep prices low while they'd have to raise prices to pay for the deal. That would give you an unfair advantage."

Kasowitz tried to bargain.

Try this, he said: Liggett is exempted from the deal, as long as its market share doesn't rise above its current 3 percent. If Liggett's market share exceeds that, the company would have to join the proposed national settlement, Kasowitz added.

"That might work," Moore said. "It's good to know you have that flexibility."

But Moore also knew—and he wasn't telling Kasowitz—that he wasn't about to push Big Tobacco on the Liggett issue because of the precarious nature of the talks. Moore's main goal was to work out a settlement with all of the cigarette makers, not to protect Liggett. If Liggett had to be sacrificed, Moore would do it.

After lunch, Kasowitz called Bennett LeBow: "It went well," he said. "They're keeping their promise."

THE NEXT MORNING, Friday, May 30, the antitobacco attorneys returned to Wachtell Lipton in the hope that the other side would show. No one did, except for Meyer Koplow, who had been designated to tell the attorneys general that they couldn't continue to shift their stance on punitive damages.

But then Phil Carlton, who had a noon flight to North Carolina, decided on a whim to stop by the law firm. He stepped off the elevator and saw Dick Scruggs and Koplow walking toward a conference room.

Carlton hailed Koplow, and the Wachtell Lipton attorney pulled Carlton aside.

"This is a perfect time to read them the riot act," Koplow said. "I'm going to talk with Dickie. Come on."

Koplow, Carlton, and Scruggs sat down in the small conference room. They met for an hour. Koplow had rehearsed his points and he ticked them off for Scruggs, at times flailing his arms in frustration.

"Dickie, the companies are at a point now where we're not getting anything back," Koplow said. "There's no reason for the companies to settle, especially because you all keep moving the goalposts. You come up with a plan of what you want and are willing to give by next Wednesday, or forget it."

Scruggs listened quietly. Near the end of the talk, Scruggs nodded his head.

"I understand," Scruggs told the two tobacco company attorneys. "Let me go work on it."

Before heading home, the attorneys general held a conference call with the antitobacco forces nationwide. Moore told the attorneys that they weren't bending on punitive damages. The other attorneys general quickly supported Moore, telling him he was doing the right thing.

"You guys are doing a great job," said Indiana attorney general Jeff Modisett.

Despite the mostly conciliatory tone of the call, it turned ugly at one point.

Peter Angelos, the private attorney who represented Maryland (and the owner of the Baltimore Orioles baseball team) broke in. Under his breath, thinking he couldn't be heard, he cursed Moore.

"That lying S.O.B. has probably worked out all the money," Angelos said.

The comment by the feisty attorney was heard by everybody on the call. It surprised some people because Angelos up to this point had been outwardly friendly to Moore and supportive of him.

Now, Angelos, who had made millions of dollars winning asbestos lawsuits in the 1980s, was showing his hand. His success was driven by fees, and he feared that the attorneys at the talks—led by Moore—had negotiated how much money the lawyers would get from the settlement and that they were keeping that a secret from the group on this call.

"What was that you said?" Moore asked. "You said Mike Moore is a lying S.O.B.? Well, I'm not. We haven't talked about money."

Moore explained that they had been trying to take a hard stand on punitive damages, and that some of the others, such as Christine Gregoire, had been working out the FDA provisions.

After Moore was done speaking, Betty Montgomery, the Ohio attorney general who had just sued Big Tobacco, came to Moore's defense.

"That is totally unprofessional," she said, upbraiding Angelos. "We trust each other. We're not going to stand for it."

Maryland Attorney General Joe Curran later apologized to Moore for Angelos's rude outburst.

THAT WEEKEND, MOORE was on the telephone virtually nonstop, trying to get everyone in his camp to agree on a punitive damages plan that would be acceptable to the cigarette makers. Otherwise, it was almost pointless to show up for a scheduled meeting on Thursday, June 5, in Washington, D.C.

Moore also was working against time. His Medicaid lawsuit against the tobacco companies was slated to begin on July 7, and he needed either to focus on the settlement talks or walk away and prepare for the opening of the trial.

The weekend before the Washington meeting, Joe Rice returned to his home in Charleston, South Carolina, and reviewed what the attorneys general had accomplished in the talks and what was left to be done. He went through his notes, making a list of issues, preparing for an upcoming meeting with Moore, Scruggs, and Florida Attorney General Bob Butterworth.

On the morning of June 2, Moore, Scruggs, and Butterworth met with Rice at the Charleston office of Ness, Motley, Loadholt, Richardson & Poole, a modern, brick building across the street from a 1696 Charleston graveyard, the oldest in the southern port city. The attorneys took their seats in a conference room decorated with framed Civil War stamps.

Rice passed out a five-page memo outlining issues for the attorneys to read. "We need to keep the ball moving," Rice said. "Here's where we are. We've made tremendous progress on the public health and FDA issues."

Reading the draft, it was clear where the two sides were divided. On the FDA, how would the agency be allowed to regulate nicotine? On money, the two sides still had to agree on a final amount, though they knew it would be more than $300 billion. And finally, there was the issue of civil liability; how would punitive damages be settled?

The antitobacco attorneys knew they had to refuse to shield the companies from punitive damages, for both past and future wrongdoing. Moore suggested that they stand firm on this issue, but offer Big Tobacco some form of relief from postsettlement lawsuits.

"What if we banned new class-action lawsuits?" Moore said.

The attorneys were silent. Without class-action lawsuits—in which hundreds, thousands, or millions of plaintiffs band together to sue a company, spreading the high costs of litigation—there would be less incentive for individual smokers to sue. It was just too expensive, and plaintiffs' attorneys were generally unwilling to take on these cases, considering Big Tobacco's mostly winning record in the courts. However, the Castano attorneys, who already had more than 20 lawsuits seeking billions of dollars, were willing to cede their right to file additional class-action cases against Big Tobacco. They decided to propose the ban on new class-action lawsuits.

In addition, the attorneys decided to pitch other proposals to Big Tobacco, such as capping punitive damage awards at three times compensatory damage awards.

Moore hoped this would be enough to convince Big Tobacco to resume talks.

ON THURSDAY, JUNE 5, Mike Moore, Dick Scruggs, and Joe Rice arrived at the ANA Hotel, five blocks from Georgetown, to prepare for what they hoped would be a resumption of negotiations. The 10-story-tall ANA had become a familiar place to Moore and Scruggs. Since late 1996, they had stayed there every time the negotiations took them to the nation's capital. By now, they knew the staff by name.

After the grime and bustle of New York—especially the noisy, overlit, crowded hotels—the airy ANA seemed like a quiet oasis, complete with soothing piano music and a dark, backlit bar in the lobby.

Directly across 24th Street, the tobacco companies took three floors of the Park Hyatt. The hotel is even more posh than the ANA: At the Hyatt, uniformed staff escort guests through the revolving doors into the rose-colored lobby, and a cup of coffee costs $2.75.

The two sides weren't scheduled to meet until the evening, so both used the day to prepare their positions. This was shaping up to be a showdown, and neither set of attorneys wanted to be ambushed.

At 6:30 P.M. that evening, Moore and Scruggs met with Meyer Koplow and Arthur Golden in an ANA conference room, the first face-to-face meeting since the industry attorneys stormed away from the negotiating table in New York.

Scruggs and Moore read the latest terms to Golden and Koplow.

"To reach an agreement on punitive damages, the tobacco companies are going to have to include in the settlement money for past misconduct; we can't eliminate that," Moore said. "It's going to have to be a lot of money."

Koplow and Golden listened.

"We might be able to move on class-action lawsuits," Moore added. "We're willing to ban future class actions."

Moore said he had spoken by telephone with Christine Gregoire, Richard Blumenthal, and Grant Woods about his proposal. They had agreed to the ban on future class-action lawsuits. It would make filing a lawsuit much more expensive for individuals, even though it would still hold the industry open to such suits.

Moore then brought up the other points that had been discussed in Charleston. Punitive damages for past misconduct could be limited, for example, by restricting them to triple the amount of compensatory damages in each case. Otherwise, he reiterated, the companies would have to pay punitive damages now, an amount that would be included in the settlement.

At least it was a place to start, Golden thought.

"That's a lot better," he said. "I'll see what we can do." Soon, Golden relayed word to Moore that the full negotiating teams could resume work the following Monday.

SUNDAY, JUNE 8, brought a new problem for the negotiators. B.A.T Industries' CEO Martin Broughton, a fiery, cigar-smoking, 50-year-old Englishman, told the other tobacco company chiefs privately that he couldn't back the proposed provisions on FDA control of nicotine.

Broughton specifically was bothered by wording in the latest settlement proposal which could let the FDA ratchet down nicotine levels within a short time frame and ban nicotine entirely under some circumstances. In effect, Broughton thought, this provision gave the agency far too sweeping regulatory authority over nicotine.

Broughton wanted more safeguards to protect his company—the maker of Kool, Lucky Strike, Carlton, and Misty cigarettes—from potentially overzealous regulators. In particular, Broughton asked for a mechanism written into the settlement that would force the FDA to go to court and prove that reducing nicotine levels would directly lead to fewer people smoking. That, Broughton figured, would be hard to prove and would thwart the FDA's regulatory abilities.

Broughton's tactic was a surprise. B.A.T's U.S. tobacco unit, Brown & Williamson, had endured the most damaging legal and public-relations blows of all the companies—the cache of confidential documents leaked by Merrell Williams; the subsequent emergence of its former research chief, Jeffrey Wigand, as the industry's highest-ranking defector; and the 1996 courtroom loss in Jacksonville, Florida, when a jury awarded $750,000 to Grady Carter.

Even so, B.A.T wouldn't go away quietly. The company was becoming more strident.

Broughton's hard-line stance roiled the talks on June 9 in Washington. The FDA subgroup was back at the negotiating table. Gregoire, Matt Myers, and Tom Green represented the antitobacco groups, while Marc Firestone, Robert Fiske, and Steve Parrish represented Big Tobacco.

Almost immediately, it was apparent that Big Tobacco—coaxed by Broughton—was backing off from some of its initial positions. For instance, the tobacco attorneys now said that each time the FDA wanted to order a cancer-causing chemical ingredient banned or reduced, it should have to prove in court that there would be a health benefit and that there would be no significant black market. Previously, the sides had agreed only to require a formal hearing at which the FDA simply presented its position but didn't have to prove it. The industry could then challenge the agency's findings and actions in court.

Gregoire and her team were stunned by this change. They gradually realized, though, that something had shifted behind the scenes. There was no other explanation for the tobacco attorneys' backing off their earlier agreement.

At 2:00 A.M., after a long arduous day, Gregoire left the room where the FDA subgroup was meeting and walked downstairs to find tobacco attorneys Phil Carlton and Arthur Golden in the Park Hyatt Hotel's ballroom area.

"We're not going to keep trying to fix this until we know what's going on," she told them. "Just be straight with us, and we'll deal with the problem."

Carlton and Golden looked at each other in silence.

"One of the clients has cold feet," Golden said finally.

Gregoire went to her room and called Mike Moore.

"We've got a big problem with FDA," she said. "I think it's B.A.T. I don't think they're trying to solve it. They're just saying no. I don't think we can get there from here."

Moore slumped. "We've hit a brick wall," he said, wondering whether B.A.T was bluffing. Maybe they're just playing bad cop, Moore thought.

Tuesday morning, June 10, Gregoire tried another approach. "Based on this conduct, I would just as soon not settle with B.A.T," she told Carlton and the other tobacco lawyers. "How about we split them out of it?"

"No way," Golden said. "We have to stay together."

Later that day, Meyer Koplow gave the bad news to Moore, Scruggs, and some of the Castano attorneys: B.A.T couldn't go along with the FDA regulation proposal.

"We got a big problem with B.A.T," Koplow said.

This latest roadblock put particular pressure on Mike Moore, with Mississippi's trial date approaching. Moore said that unless talks concluded within a week, he'd have to walk away from the table and turn his attention to his lawsuit.

At 11:00 A.M. on June 11, Moore, Butterworth, and Woods, at the ANA Hotel, held a conference call with the attorneys general from the 31 states that had sued.

Moore was in a delicate position. He knew he needed to build consensus on the call, and that meant telling the attorneys general the suggestions he and Scruggs had proposed but hadn't actually been agreed to yet—especially about punitive damages and banning future class-action lawsuits. If the other attorneys general voiced little disagreement, he knew he could push forward with the tobacco companies. He had to sound confident. He wasn't, though, so he had to bluff.

"We worked Monday and Tuesday with these guys in Washington," Moore told the other state attorneys. "I think we've hammered just about everything we can hammer out. We're as close to getting some kind of resolution as we can get. Obviously, there's always some final details to be worked out."

Moore paused, then went on.

"They're down to two [demands] that they want, which is limitation of class actions against the industry in the future, and limitation of punitive damages in the future.

"On the public health stuff, I think we're there. The children's look-back provisions, FDA language, we are there and worked out something that will both maintain the jurisdiction of the FDA over nicotine as a drug, and allow them to regulate it sometime in the future, if it's the feasible thing to do or the safe thing to do for this country."

Moore knew he was on shaky ground here. Indeed, these provisions had been agreed upon, but now B.A.T had forced Big Tobacco to backtrack.

A few minutes later, Moore turned to money.

"I feel comfortable that at the end of the day, our money is going to be way in excess of $300 billion in the 25 [-year] period."

Then Moore switched subjects to the problem at hand in the talks. He brought up B.A.T's latest objections.

"The hitch right now is that on the nicotine piece, Brown & Williamson got very, very worried that what we had negotiated with the industry and what the public health folks had been talking about would put them out of business. Of course, we've taken the position, so be it."

Moore changed the subject again, back to money.

"I think they're going to pay us at least $10 million in cash up front."

Two callers quickly corrected Moore.

"Uh, $10 billion. I think they will meet the numbers—and we have not discussed the annual payments again since this Brown & Williamson balk yesterday. But as soon as that's done, we'll get down to the final numbers."

Moore then told the attorneys that they had consulted with the White House and the Office of Management and Budget about the payments.

Moore asked the attorneys general for a response.

"Do y'all like what you hear? Are we doing okay?" he asked.

Nobody demurred. Good, Moore thought to himself. Now if only Big Tobacco would sort out the disagreements among their group and get back to the negotiating table.

B.A.T, THOUGH, REMAINED the spoiler. The tobacco companies and their attorneys decided that they needed to meet with Broughton for a summit. Broughton would fly to New York from London on the Concorde.

The meeting was set for Friday morning at Philip Morris's headquarters.

One by one, the heads of the five biggest tobacco companies entered the building. They walked to the bank of elevators in the middle of an enclosed, four-floor-high, pedestrian mall containing shops, greenery, and modern sculpture. The Whitney Museum had designated the area as its downtown branch and filled it with works of art.

Philip Morris's Geoff Bible, B.A.T's Martin Broughton, RJR's Steven Goldstone, Loews's cochairmen Laurence and Preston Tisch, and UST Chief Executive Vincent Gierer Jr. were joined by their general counsels and the negotiating team in a windowless fifth-floor conference room adorned with lithographs of plants. The executives settled into black leather armchairs.

Koplow, Golden, Carlton, and Parrish briefed the group on the talks, including how much money would be required and what else was needed to forge a settlement.

When FDA regulation was brought up, the executives expected disagreements. Murray Bring, Philip Morris's vice chairman and general counsel, tried to defuse the situation.

"If the FDA acts rationally, it will never ban nicotine," Bring said.

Bible, who chaired the meeting as always, was again the most committed to getting a deal made.

"We ought to accept FDA control," he said, backing up Bring.

Broughton was still reluctant to give the FDA the "death penalty," the right to ban nicotine. "We'd be allowing future generations of bureaucrats to decide whether our product is legal," he said.

Two separate times, the chief executives and top in-house lawyers went to another room for private sessions.

"Why is nicotine so important to you?" Bible asked Broughton. "The FDA is never going to ban it. Even if they wanted to, they couldn't without proving the ban would help public health."

Bible offered a compromise. There would be no deal unless the industry received a provision that would allow the FDA to control or eliminate nicotine only after a dozen years. Plus, the agency could do so only if it could prove there wouldn't be a black market for cigarettes. The industry also would demand the right to appeal the provision in court.

The FDA would never be able to prove their case in court, the executives said. Big Tobacco's attorneys could tie them up in lawsuits for years.

"All right," Broughton said. "I'll go along with you on the FDA, if these conditions are met."

After seven hours, the tough-talking Broughton was convinced the talks should continue.

11

SETTLEMENT DAY

Never in my wildest dreams would I have ever envisioned that we could produce anything like what we have today for consideration by the president, the Congress, the American people.

—CHRISTINE GREGOIRE
Washington attorney general

O n the evening of Friday, June 13, as the tobacco companies were ending their meeting at Philip Morris's headquarters, Moore and Scruggs slumped down into two plush chairs in the ANA lobby. Moore, the sleeves of his white shirt rolled up and his tie loosened, was worn out after a year of settlement talks—and recent late-night negotiations that had stretched into the early hours of the next day.

The two men ordered drinks, then discussed how far they had come in the past few months.

Many of the public health provisions had been completed. The sides had agreed to the dramatic wording of the black-and-white warnings on cigarette packs: "Cigarettes are addictive"; "Cigarettes cause fatal lung disease"; "Cigarettes cause cancer'; and "Smoking can kill you." Cigarette ads on billboards would be banned. So would cigarette sales from vending machines.

Yet, three hurdles remained. The negotiators hadn't reached a final agreement to allow the FDA to reduce the nicotine levels in cigarettes. An earlier accord would have let the agency regulate nicotine, if the FDA could show that it was technically feasible, that it wouldn't create a black market, and that there would be a proven benefit to public health. But B.A.T. had balked at this provision.

The issue of punitive damages persisted; the industry wanted some protection from lawsuits that could result in potentially crippling punitive judgments. The attorneys general were slowly coming up with some alternative plans, such as banning future class-action litigation. Both sides had yet to agree on the issue of punitive damages in lawsuits over the industry's past actions.

And, finally, there was money. The industry originally wanted to pay $230 billion, though it knew it would have had to come up with at least $300 billion to satisfy the demands of the public health advocates, the attorneys general, and the Castano lawyers.

Still, Moore and Scruggs were pleased with how much had been achieved in the talks. And as they spoke they realized two men deserved a lot of the credit for where they were that day: Jeff Wigand, the scientist who had led the FDA through Brown & Williamson's documents related to alleged nicotine manipulation, and Merrell Williams, the legal assistant who had stolen thousands of the company's documents.

The Mississippi attorneys decided that while they had to remain focused on the big unresolved issues, they'd make sure that tobacco whistle-blowers would be shielded in any settlement. After all, they thought, without the documents and information these men provided, Moore and Scruggs might never be so close to extracting a $300 billion-plus settlement from Big Tobacco.

"We're going to protect people like Jeff Wigand and Merrell Williams," Moore said. "They don't have to worry about that."

The next morning, Moore and Scruggs flew home to Mississippi, to squeeze in time at home for the weekend before what would turn out to be the final week of the tobacco settlement negotiations.

During this hiatus, Scruggs competed in a sailing race in the Gulf of Mexico, where his crew finished second. Meanwhile, Moore worked the phone, speaking with Phil Carlton, the White House, other tobacco attorneys, and the industry's foes.

On Saturday, Moore, Scruggs, and Joe Rice had a conference call with Meyer Koplow and Arthur Golden. The two tobacco attorneys had to update Moore's team about the Friday meeting at Philip Morris's headquarters with the tobacco CEOs.

Golden proposed a trade-off.

"The cigarette makers are willing to agree to give the FDA the authority to regulate tobacco if your side would forgive punitive damages for past misdeeds," Golden said, repeating the position that the CEOs had agreed upon in New York the day before.

Moore and Scruggs liked this proposal, because it focused on past punitive damages, not future ones. In other words, they figured, their proposal to ban new class-action lawsuits but not new cases by individual smokers seeking punitive damages might be acceptable to Big Tobacco. Still, getting backing for the elimination of punitive damages for past conduct was going to be tough to sell to the hard-liners among the attorneys general.

Moore told Golden that the proposal sounded interesting and he would bring it up with the tobacco foes. Actually, Moore wanted to discuss the issue of punitive damages with Bruce Lindsey at the White House, to see if he could help break the stalemate.

Lindsey had pushed both sides to come up with a draft agreement the week before, but B.A.T's sudden rejection of the proposed FDA provision made that impossible. Moore called Lindsey from his home in Jackson, Mississippi.

"Bruce, the talks are looking good," Moore told the deputy White House counsel. "But we'll need to meet with you this week. It looks close. We're down to the final details."

He told Lindsey that it was likely the negotiators would need his help to resolve the persistent snag over punitives.

They decided to meet on Monday. Lindsey reminded Moore that he wanted an agreement early in the week to give to the president, who was flying to Denver, Colorado, on Thursday morning to discuss global economic matters with the so-called Group of Seven, or G-7—the leaders of the United States, Germany, the United Kingdom, France, Canada, Japan, and Italy—plus Russia's Boris Yeltsin.

On Sunday, June 15, most of Washington's attention was on the U.S. Open at the Congressional Golf Club in nearby Bethesda, Maryland. Perhaps the most disappointed golfer that day was Tiger Woods, the 21-

year-old phenomenon who could eke out only a 19th-place finish in this showcase event. Fatigued and frustrated by his performance, Woods arrived at a private Washington airport that night, heading home, in no mood to be disturbed. Still, Woods stopped briefly to scrawl his autograph for a couple of lawyers who just arrived by plane. Mike Moore and Dick Scruggs thanked Woods for being so gracious.

ON MONDAY, JUNE 16, the *Wall Street Journal* reported on the stalemate over punitive damages. In a story by Alix Freedman and Hilary Stout, the newspaper quoted people close to the talks as saying that the negotiations were at a standstill over whether all punitive damages would be wiped out by the settlement, something that the tobacco companies had absolutely demanded since nearly the first day of talks. It appeared, the article continued, that unless the two sides could come up with a solution to this intractable issue, the final pact could be incomplete or the talks could be completely derailed.

Scruggs and Moore awoke early that morning and darted down to the ANA's fitness center without picking up a copy of the *Wall Street Journal.* At 7:30 A.M., a reporter found Scruggs in the fitness center and asked if the story was correct. Scruggs grimaced and turned toward Moore, who was on a Nautilus machine.

"The *Journal*'s reporting that we're having problems with punitive damages," Scruggs said to Moore. Turning back toward the reporter, Scruggs said the story was true, and he wasn't pleased that it was out.

After breakfast, Moore and Gregoire met with Arthur Golden and Phil Carlton.

"Let's get this done," Golden said. "We'll give you FDA control over nicotine, and you give us protection from punitive damages."

Gregoire shook her head.

"Look, if the game is quid pro quo, we don't do that," she said. "I will never trade FDA jurisdiction for punitive damages. We are going to agree on each of these things individually, or we are not going to agree."

To try to break the deadlock, both sides sent their lead representatives to the White House for the meeting with Bruce Lindsey.

Around noon, the negotiators began to assemble in the office of Bruce Reed, President Clinton's chief domestic policy adviser. Present were Moore and Scruggs, representing the attorneys general; Chesley and Coale on behalf of the Castano lawyers; and Carlton and Golden, speaking for Big Tobacco.

They told Lindsey that they had reached agreement on many FDA issues, including the one that was designed to appease President Clinton: setting up penalties for the industry if it failed to reduce teen smoking by at least 50 percent over seven years.

But the *Wall Street Journal* was right, they said. The issue of how to handle punitive damages for presettlement actions had, indeed, become intractable. The attorneys told Lindsey they had agreed that a set amount of money in the overall settlement would be earmarked for damages, so that the industry didn't have to worry about huge jury awards with no cap. But Big Tobacco didn't want to pay punitive damages for past sins. The industry wanted to swap giving the FDA power to regulate nicotine, which had been agreed to previously, for a ban on punitives for prior acts.

Lindsey thought this wasn't fair. He looked at Carlton and Golden.

"If you are going to ask them to give up punitive damages, you're going to have to give them something," he said. Lindsey wasn't more specific.

"Come up with some bright, shining thing," Lindsey told them.

The negotiators headed back to 24th Street, where the Park Hyatt and the ANA Hotels faced each other. A conference room at the Park Hyatt served as the main negotiating room.

As it stood now, two issues remained: the extent of FDA authority and past punitive damages. The latter, of course, was linked to how much money the industry would pay. Both sides interpreted Lindsey's directive to construct a "bright, shining thing" as an order to come up with a staggering multibillion payment to cover presettlement punitives.

Golden and Koplow made the first offer: $15 billion to get rid of punitive damages for presettlement conduct. In effect, the tobacco companies would be paying that amount to wipe out all past suits by smokers in the states.

The attorneys general rejected this offer. Too little, they thought. It's not big enough to win over the White House, or them. But at least there was an amount on the table; Big Tobacco was willing to write a check and admit to past misdeeds—such as covering up health-related research and destroying documents.

In the meantime, Gregoire and her FDA team—which included Matt Myers and Tom Green—were meeting with their industry counterparts—Bob Fiske, Steve Parrish, and Marc Firestone—to finish the regulatory section of the agreement. Now that Lindsey had essentially vetoed the industry's plan of using FDA regulation as a bargaining tool, Big Tobacco began negotiating for the amount of time before the FDA authority would be enforced.

ON TUESDAY AFTERNOON, June 17, Moore and his attorneys general walked through a maze of TV cameras and wiring to give an impromptu press conference in a back corner of the patio of the ANA Hotel. As a spring breeze swept through the courtyard, Moore stepped to the phalanx of microphones. He wanted to send a message that his attorneys general were ready to walk away from the negotiations—even though they weren't—if they didn't get their way on key issues. Moore hoped to bluff Big Tobacco into believing that the attorneys general weren't going to budge either on FDA regulation or on getting at least a staggering payment to make up for the industry's past deeds.

"I'm still very optimistic that the industry will either give us what we want, or we'll go to trial," Moore said.

Time magazine correctly sensed that Moore was fibbing and sent a photographer to shoot pictures for the issue when the settlement was announced. The photographer first took a portrait of Moore and then a group photo of all the attorneys general.

Next, the photographer wanted to take pictures of the Castano attorneys. As they posed, the trial lawyers joked about their reputations for being greedy. The electronic flash went off and instead of saying "cheeeeese," a half-dozen Castano attorneys—including Hugh Rodham, Stan Chesley, John Coale, and Charles Zimmerman—yelled out "feeeeees."

As this was going on, Christine Gregoire, Matt Myers, and Indiana Attorney General Jeff Modisett went with tobacco lobbyist and former Texas Governor Ann Richards to meet with U.S. Senator Ted Kennedy. They wanted to convince the Massachusetts Democrat to support the settlement by promising that some of the amount paid by the tobacco companies would be set aside for providing health insurance for the 10 million uninsured American children, a Kennedy pet project.

Just the night before, the Senate Finance Committee had rejected a bill cosponsored by Kennedy and Utah Republican U.S. Senator Orrin Hatch to hike the federal cigarette tax by 43 cents a pack. The idea was to use the revenue from the tax increase for childrens' insurance.

The antitobacco attorneys walked into the waiting room of Kennedy's office, past photos and paintings of America's Camelot, a period frozen in time on the wall, memorializing the early 1960s administration of President John F. Kennedy, Ted's brother.

They had barely sat down in front of the red-faced Massachusetts senator before his face grew even more crimson. Christine Gregoire began discussing the idea to give money from the settlement to a medical insurance pool for children when Kennedy cut her off.

"What are you doing here?" Kennedy snarled.

Gregoire and Modisett glanced at each other nervously as the same horrible thought ran through their minds: Kennedy thought Gregoire, like Richards, represented the tobacco industry that had lobbied against his legislative proposal.

Gregoire never had a chance to clear up Kennedy's mistake. The senator railed against the industry he blamed for scuttling his bill.

Matt Myers, trying to get back on track, made things worse when he praised Scott Harshbarger, the attorney general of Massachusetts, for lending his assistant Tom Green, to work on the FDA part of the settlement. That angered the Senator because Harshbarger was the main Democratic opponent for an upcoming Massachusetts gubernatorial race against Ted Kennedy's nephew, U.S. Representative Joe Kennedy. (Joe Kennedy later dropped out of the campaign, citing a family scandal; his brother allegedly had an affair with his baby-sitter.)

Kennedy dismissed the attorneys, and once they'd left, he emerged from his office, still angry. The fact that the tobacco companies were fighting a bill to provide children's medical care "is not winning them any friends up here," Kennedy said to a reporter as he stepped into an elevator.

The plan by the attorneys general to garner the support of the Massachusetts senator had failed. But at least, they thought, the tobacco companies and the attorneys general were in lockstep in that the cigarette makers were going to have to pay a lot of money to settle punitive damages for prior actions—even though they had yet to work out the sum.

The Castano attorneys were also on board. They had been promised cessation programs for all smokers and were likely to be rewarded with sizeable attorney fees after the settlement passed.

Of course, there was still one big question. Would the attorneys general from around the country be willing to accept money from Big Tobacco in exchange for a ban on punitive awards for past misdeeds? Moore needed to find out where they stood on this issue. So he held a conference call at 4:00 P.M. on Wednesday afternoon, June 18.

Moore started by filling in the attorneys general on the status of the negotiations. Once again, he said, he didn't have the details neatly wrapped up. Money had not been decided. FDA regulation was close, but not done. And Moore was far from certain what Big Tobacco would pay for presettlement punitive damages. But he couldn't let the people on the call know about these potential stumbling blocks.

"We think we have negotiated this thing about as far as we are going to go," Moore said.

One of the first topics was money. Moore did the math: $308 billion over 25 years, with a $10 billion up-front payment. This hadn't been decided, of course, by the negotiators, but Moore wanted to see what the attorneys general felt about this amount. Moore assured the people on the call that the states, not the federal agencies that administered Medicaid programs, would keep all of the money. This was a provision, Moore said, that the White House promised to support.

On punitive damages for past misconduct, Moore went even farther out on a limb. To settle that, he said, the cigarette makers would pay a staggering $50 billion, the bulk of it to the states. Actually, this was more than triple what the industry so far had offered to pay.

"That's a pretty good extraction of pain," Moore said.

The sum would be tax deductible, Moore said.

Then, Moore called for a vote. Did the attorneys general like what they heard? Could they support it?

Alabama? "Yes."

Alaska? "Yes."

Arizona? "Yes."

Moore continued down the list of states alphabetically. Maryland's Joe Curran was the first to voice a major concern, saying he still didn't like the fact that Moore had agreed to ban class-action lawsuits—a part of the pact that had been agreed to a week earlier. Curran abstained. So did a few others, including the attorneys general from New Mexico, Montana, and Oregon.

The call was typical of Moore, who somehow had cajoled his attorneys to vote on something that didn't exist as a formal document; it was, so far, only Moore's wish list.

Mike Fisher of Pennsylvania wasn't even sure what he was voting for. And Moore wasn't quick to provide an answer when Fisher asked. He earnestly wanted to avoid a lot of no votes.

Fisher: "You know, I thought when we started this roll call we were just voting on the punitive damage piece, is how I thought we started it out."

Moore: "There you go."

Fisher: "Is that a yes or a no?"

Moore: "That's right."

"If we're just talking about the punitive damage piece as described, I vote yes."

"Alright," Moore said. "Thanks."

While not unanimous, the attorneys general had voted in support of a settlement. The tally was 30 in favor; seven abstained.

Then Moore asked if anyone had any questions.

One attorney general wanted to know how the hundreds of billions of dollars would be divided among the states. Moore replied that that would be discussed in Jackson Hole, Wyoming, at the annual get-together of the attorneys general. The calculations, he said, would be based on a combination of a state's Medicaid population and the costs of running the health care plan for the poor.

Then California Attorney General Dan Lungren asked Moore if the settlement included making good the payment agreements between the private attorneys and the states, struck when they signed on these lawyers to help in the Medicaid suits.

It was the first mention of fees for such men as Dick Scruggs, Ron Motley, and Steve Berman. The press had reported that the private attorneys would receive hundreds of millions of dollars from the settlement. That kind of news, which was generally received unfavorably by the public, worried some attorneys general.

"Can you give us a little bit of an idea of what's being discussed, because frankly I've heard some things that I can accept and some things that are alarming," Lungren said. "I don't know what's true. And I also have to be in a position to be able to go to [California's] 54 members of Congress and tell them that this is a fair deal for all the states, including my own."

Moore expected the question to arise, and he had an answer ready.

"We would like to handle this attorneys'-fees issue above and beyond any money that we have contemplated in the deal. And what I mean by that is that just like any other case, when a side loses, the other side ought to pay the costs and ought to pay the attorneys' fees. So what we're working on right now is the concept that the tobacco companies would pay the attorneys' fees above and beyond this agreement."

Moore elaborated, addressing the bad publicity about the fees—and the criticism by House Speaker Newt Gingrich, who said that he wouldn't support a settlement that provided hundreds of millions of dollars to trial lawyers. That money has to come from the industry, Moore told the attorneys.

"Frankly, my estimation, if I was attacking the deal, I'd say you've got $350 billion, and the lawyers are going to get 25 percent of it," Moore said. "I can add that up. Everybody is going to get 85, you know, the lawyers are going to get $85 billion. We'd get killed if that money came from the settlement. That money has to come from the industry."

That mollified Lungren.

"I appreciate what you're trying to do, but I think you've got to realize that's a question you're going to be asked by members of Congress," Lungren said.

"No question about it," said Moore, who further explained that an idea likely to get into the settlement was to have a three-judge panel that would assess the lawyers' fees, and Big Tobacco would pay them as well.

At the end of the call, Moore said that an agreement might come as soon as that night or the next day—meeting Bruce Lindsey's deadline of getting the proposed settlement to the president by Thursday, before he left for the G-7 meeting in Denver.

"Our mission here in the next few hours is to punch it across," Moore said. "We're there. We're in the shadows."

Bloomberg News was the first to report that it would take tens of billions of dollars to settle the punitive damages issue. The news story that revealed the payment came after the stock market closed on Wednesday. But Wall Street analysts were shocked by the $50 billion payment, which, after all, represented the industry's entire annual sales.

"That's a stunning number," said David Adelman, a tobacco analyst at Morgan Stanley. "But it shows how committed the companies are to the settlement."

Of course, Big Tobacco hadn't agreed to that yet.

ON WEDNESDAY AFTERNOON, June 18, after Moore's conference call with the attorneys general, he, Dick Scruggs, and Grant Woods went back to the White House. It was another critical meeting, because both sides hoped Lindsey would once again help steer the negotiators to the amount Big Tobacco would have to pay.

As awed as Moore was each time he came to the White House, it was the M&M candy with the presidential seal that intrigued him the most. Each time Moore went there, he'd take some packages for his 10-year-old son, Kyle.

Phil Carlton was representing Big Tobacco at this meeting. The Castano lawyers present were John Coale, Stan Chesley, and Hugh Rodham.

When Woods was asked for his identification to enter the White House, he opened his wallet and pulled out a phony Elvis Presley driver's license that he had picked up as a souvenir at Graceland when the negotiations took him to Memphis.

The White House guard didn't smile, and Woods was detained for 15 minutes before the Secret Service felt comfortable enough to let him go in.

Over coffee in the Roosevelt Room, just off the Oval Office, Lindsey asked how much the industry was willing to pay year by year for the settlement.

The tobacco negotiators, who didn't want to pay much more than $300 billion, said they could afford $308.5 billion over the first 25 years, starting at $6.5 billion a year and increasing payments each year until they hit $15 billion annually. The money would reimburse the states for Medicaid expenses and pay for smoking-cessation programs, which had been sought by the Castano class actions. It also would be used for anti-smoking educational campaigns.

Lindsey said he understood the industry needed to ramp up the payments, but said it was taking Big Tobacco too long to get to the $15-billion-a-year figure. What's more, the $308 billion wasn't enough to cover punitive damages for lawsuits alleging past misconduct by the cigarette companies, he thought.

How about if the industry gets to $15 billion in four or five years? Lindsey asked. He took out a pen and started writing on a napkin. He thought it would make more sense if the numbers started with $10 billion up front, then went to $7.5 billion in the first year, then $9.5 billion in year two, $11.5 billion in year three, and $15 billion annually thereafter.

He added those numbers together and came up with $368.5 billion through the first 25 years. He circled the number and slid the napkin over to Carlton.

"It's going to be $368.5 billion," Lindsey said. "You're going to have to come up with an extra $60 billion. That amount will cover all punitive damages for past misconduct."

Carlton wasn't surprised by this. Privately, Big Tobacco was already resigned to paying billions more than at first hoped to satisfy the attorneys general, the public health advocates, and the White House. When Carlton saw the figure he said to himself: "That's the 'bright, shining thing' Lindsey was talking about."

Moore sighed with relief. If this number stuck, he could now go back to the attorneys general with $10 billion more than the $50 billion that he promised them for past punitive damages.

"Fine," Carlton said; it was in the price range that his clients were prepared to accept.

"We'll recommend that when the president speaks about the settlement, that he say the punitive damage fund is a reasonable way to settle the issue," Lindsey said.

The biggest sticking point of the negotiations was solved. Big Tobacco would pay $60 billion as punishment for past misconduct. And the industry would get at least some relief from future punitive damage awards, in that class-action lawsuits would be banned and there would be an annual combined $5 billion cap on judgments or settlements in future lawsuits by individual smokers.

After dinner, Coale and Chesley met Meyer Koplow and Arthur Golden at the Park Hyatt to discuss the details of the $368.5 billion settlement. When they mentioned the price tag, Koplow looked puzzled.

"Carlton and the others said it was *$386* billion, not $368 billion," Koplow said.

Coale and Chesley looked at each other.

"I'm positive it's $368 billion," Coale said. "Phil must have misheard."

Chesley called Hugh Rodham and told him to double-check.

Rodham phoned Lindsey at home. They did the math again. "It's $368.5 billion," Lindsey said.

Rodham relayed this to Chesley inside the negotiating room, and

Chesley told Golden the lower sum was correct.

"We just saved you $20 billion," Chesley said, rounding up a little. "Don't forget it."

THE OTHER NEGOTIATORS were down to the final details, including how to handle the disclosure of the industry's secret documents—the memos detailing research that smoking was unhealthy and the maneuvering to hide these data from the public.

Ever since Merrell Williams's stolen Brown & Williamson papers were released to the newspapers and over the Internet, few other tobacco industry documents had seen the light of day. Even the papers that Liggett turned over to the attorneys general were still locked in Florida and Mississippi state courts. The tobacco companies were so far able to argue successfully in court that the files should remain sealed because they were the private communications between the industry and its lawyers.

The document-disclosure debate carried into Thursday morning, June 19. That's when the issue of Jeffrey Wigand emerged.

Wigand, the 54-year-old former head of tobacco research at Brown & Williamson, had been instrumental in FDA chief David Kessler's crusade against Big Tobacco. When he led Kessler through a series of internal documents from Brown & Williamson showing that the tobacco companies manipulated the level of nicotine in cigarettes, the FDA used this evidence to assert that cigarettes were drug-delivery devices. This backed up the agency's claim that it should be allowed to regulate tobacco products.

Wigand had paid a hefty price for blowing the whistle. He lost his $300,000-a-year job at Brown & Williamson and couldn't get another high-level research job in Louisville, Kentucky. By June 1997, Wigand was living on $30,000 a year, teaching high school science in the city. His marriage fell apart largely due to the stress of the industry's repeated attacks against him, worries about legal bills, and constant media attention. He was being followed by industry-paid detectives. And he faced a lawsuit from Brown & Williamson for breaking a confidentiality agreement.

Moore and Scruggs had made protection for whistle-blowers one of their initial demands in the talks, stemming from the first meetings they had with Big Tobacco in April. The cigarette companies initially had said it wouldn't be a problem. The issue had been pushed to the side as more critical areas took the attention of the lawyers on both sides of the table.

Now, Arthur Golden told the tobacco foes that the companies could accept some level of protection for whistle-blowers, but that it had to be reasonable. "There are federal laws protecting whistle-blowers at government contractors, things like that," Golden said. "Show me a statute you like, and we can adapt it."

But Moore and Scruggs, who had a close relationship with Merrell Williams—Scruggs found him a job in Mississippi, bought him a house, and loaned him money to buy a boat and car—wanted to make sure that Williams and Jeff Wigand were happy with whatever was worked out. Scruggs had already told Wigand's lawyer, Laura Wertheimer, that before long he would ask her to be present at the talks. On Thursday morning he invited her to attend.

After breakfast, shortly before Clinton flew to the G-7 meeting in Denver without the settlement proposal he had wanted, Scruggs called Wertheimer at her office, Shea & Gardner. She hopped in a cab, which took her to the Park Hyatt. Scruggs met her at the entrance.

"We're almost there," Scruggs said. "I think B.A.T will drop its suit against Jeff [Wigand]."

In order to obtain medical benefits for a daughter who needed expensive treatments, Wigand had settled, early on, a Brown & Williamson complaint accusing him of discussing the terms of his severance package. In return, Wigand had signed a strict confidentiality agreement, which said he couldn't discuss anything he learned while working at the company. Wigand had breached this, according to the cigarette maker, by speaking to Scruggs, the FDA, and the media, including *60 Minutes*. Wertheimer went upstairs to meet Golden and Brown & Williamson's No. 2 in-house lawyer, Neil Mellen.

"Are you ready to drop your suit right now and release Dr. Wigand from his agreement?" she asked.

Golden said the company might eventually drop its suit, but couldn't allow Wigand to go around saying whatever he wanted about his former employer.

"What if the settlement doesn't get through Congress?" he asked. "Is Brown & Williamson supposed to let a man who stole company secrets and broke the law go around bad-mouthing the company?"

Wertheimer was stunned. She had thought Big Tobacco was going to leave her client alone.

"Don't overplay your hand," Golden told her. "You've got no leverage. The attorneys general will not walk away from this deal because of Jeff Wigand."

Wertheimer left the meeting and decided that since Brown & Williamson wasn't going to shelve its case against Wigand easily, she'd try to rewrite the confidentiality agreement to something both sides could live with.

The original contract was so broad that Wigand couldn't even speak about public records if he had learned about them while working at Brown & Williamson. It was all but a lifetime gag order. Wertheimer changed it so that Wigand would immediately have the right to talk about public documents and general health issues, just not about Brown & Williamson trade secrets. And Wigand would be allowed to criticize the industry as a whole, just not Brown & Williamson alone. Then, in six months, this document would be ripped up, and Wigand could talk freely without any restraints.

Wertheimer worked late that night in a Park Hyatt hallway, pounding out a more limited version of the confidentiality agreement on a laptop computer borrowed from Florida attorney Kim Tucker. She wanted to stay close to the talks so she could ask the negotiators for feedback. That evening, Wertheimer gave Dick Scruggs a copy of her proposal to present to Big Tobacco.

WHILE WERTHEIMER WAS working to revise the confidentiality agreement between Wigand and Brown & Williamson, Arthur Golden, Meyer Koplow, Phil Carlton, and Mike Moore went back to the White House to meet with Lindsey. The four negotiators slipped through a back entrance to avoid the press and went straight to Lindsey's office.

"We're just about there," Moore said. For most of the next two and a half hours, the men went over a draft of the agreement.

Golden said the companies could handle paying the extra money instead of punitive damages.

As Carlton took notes on Park Hyatt stationery, Lindsey mapped out how much should be paid each year for a "public health trust fund," for medical research. He wrote: $2.5 billion the first two years. Then $3.5 billion, $4 billion, $5 billion, and $2.5 billion in the final three years.

ON THURSDAY EVENING, after the attorneys had returned from the White House, Bennett LeBow and Marc Kasowitz were making a last-ditch effort to keep Liggett out of the settlement. They knew the talks were almost over; they were running out of time to get themselves excluded from any industrywide agreement. Liggett couldn't afford to pay its share of the settlement, and the company had pleaded to the attorneys general to grant it an exemption.

In the ANA's restaurant, Kasowitz and LeBow met with Moore and Scruggs along with Arizona attorney general Grant Woods and Steve Berman, who had helped negotiate the March settlement between Liggett and the then 22 states suing the tobacco industry.

The antitobacco lawyers were noncommittal, knowing that they weren't going to buck Big Tobacco on this issue; if the other cigarette companies wanted Liggett included in the deal, then that's the way it would be. Liggett didn't matter enough to Moore and Scruggs to stand in the way of the settlement.

Still, the attorneys offered LeBow and Kasowitz one small hope. "What if we get the tobacco companies to agree to letting the White House decide whether Liggett should be included or not?" Moore asked.

Berman suggested that the attorneys general write a strongly worded letter to the White House, urging the President to exempt Liggett from the deal.

"Let's see what the letter is going to say," LeBow answered. "If the letter is really strong, okay."

Later, walking across 24th Street to the Park Hyatt, Berman had another idea about Liggett. He approached Arthur Golden about it.

"Arthur, look, I've got a solution to Liggett," Berman said. "Your worry is that Liggett is going to be a low-cost competitor. What if we allow the company to be exempted from the national settlement until their market share exceeds 3 percent?"

Golden's nostrils flared, shocking Berman, who thought Golden looked as if Berman had jabbed a hot poker in his eye.

"We're walking on this issue," Golden said. "We're stopping all the computers. It's over."

Berman had misunderstood how much RJR hated Bennett LeBow, who, along with Carl Icahn in 1995, had launched a failed hostile takeover attempt of the company. When the Seattle attorney, backpedaling, broached the idea of the letter to the White House supporting Liggett's exemption from the accord, Golden shook his head again.

"If you send a letter to the White House, we're out of the agreement," Golden said.

With that, Berman knew Liggett would have to be included in the settlement.

THE LIGGETT ISSUE was just one of several still to be completed as the clock ticked toward Friday, June 20, and the haggard negotiators shuttled in and out of a handful of Park Hyatt conference rooms, occasionally stopping for a cup of coffee or a sandwich.

Attorneys on both sides felt they had to have a settlement in the next 12 hours. With most of the issues agreed upon, allowing the tobacco companies to continue the talks into the weekend would open the door for them to reconsider.

The attorneys general, meanwhile, were planning to attend one of their national conferences the following week among the soaring mountains in Jackson Hole. If the talks carried into the conference, many felt it would be a repeat of Dallas, Texas, when too many attorneys general at the table had only caused havoc.

Outside the rooms where the negotiations were continuing through the night into the predawn hours of Friday, the small group of reporters that had followed the talks most closely—Doug Levy of *USA Today*, Mark Curriden of the *Dallas Morning News*, Keith Summa of ABC News, author Dan Zegart, and Joe Menn and Carrick Mollenkamp of Bloomberg News—sat in chairs, waiting for word that it was over.

Some slept, others read anything they could get their hands on, but as time dragged on they got restless. So they brought cocktails up from the bar and were laughing so loudly after the liquor hit that one junior attorney came out and asked for some quiet.

Inside the conference room Moore was reading line-by-line drafts of the parts of the settlement that had been completed. By now, Moore, Koplow, and the other exhausted attorneys felt as if they were back in law school, trying to finish exams.

Meanwhile, the FDA subgroup was finalizing the mind-numbing public health portion of the settlement, including an agreement to disclose the ingredients in cigarettes. Massachusetts Assistant Attorney General Tom Green pecked out the wording on his Compaq computer, then downloaded the files into a computer that held the main draft.

Earlier, in a smaller Park Hyatt conference room, Gregoire and Myers had been able to reach an accord with the tobacco attorneys that the agency would be able to ban nicotine, but only after a formal rule-making process. The negotiators had agreed that the FDA could regulate nicotine as a drug but couldn't ban it until 2009. After that, the FDA would have to prove that outlawing nicotine would result in a "significant" reduction of health risks, was technologically feasible, and wouldn't create a black market for cigarettes high in nicotine.

Gregoire realized it was the best deal she could get from Big Tobacco. She told Moore the news, and Moore relayed it to the Castano attorneys.

AT 5:00 A.M., the first draft of the proposed agreement rolled out, page by page, from a laser printer in the conference room.

By 6:00 A.M., attorneys from both sides were back at the Park Hyatt, poring over the settlement, proofreading the drafts carefully to make sure not even a word got into the document that they couldn't live with.

There was still one problem to resolve, though: Would Brown & Williamson drop the suit against Jeffrey Wigand? And if the cigarette maker refused to, would the tobacco foes be willing to approve the deal? After years of taking on Big Tobacco, after months of tumultuous settlement talks, it had all come down to one man: Jeffrey Wigand, the highest-ranking defector in the industry's history.

At 10:00 A.M., June 20, Washington, D.C., was sweltering. All week long, a cool, spring breeze had blown through the nation's capital, but Friday was blazing hot, and it wasn't even noon.

Wigand's attorney, Laura Wertheimer, met with Bob Fiske of Davis Polk & Wardwell and David Murphy of Wachtell, Lipton, Rosen & Katz to get their answer on her proposal, which called for Brown & Williamson to drop its suit immediately and allow Wigand to speak at least generally about the cigarette industry. In six months this new con-fidentiality agreement would be voided, and Wigand would be freed of all restraints.

Fiske said it was close to acceptable, but not quite. The original nondisclosure agreement said Wigand couldn't "disparage" the company. That was so vague that any criticism of the industry as a whole could have landed Wigand in court again. Wertheimer had proposed changing the clause to a ban on "directly disparaging" the company or its products.

Fiske suggested changing the phrase to "defaming," and Wertheimer agreed. Fiske and Murphy left to take the new agreement to Brown & Williamson.

Moore and Scruggs, meanwhile, had left the Park Hyatt to return to the ANA. Moore was wearing a blue-checkered shirt and his aides had recommended that he change to a white shirt for the TV cameras. Though far from certain that there would be a press conference to announce the agreement, Moore wanted to look his best if there was one. Dodging cameras, Moore and Scruggs crossed 24th Street. Inside the ANA, they rode the elevator to their rooms. Moore, who had run out of clean white shirts, had to borrow one from Scruggs. It was a half size too big, but Moore didn't have a choice. He tried it on with a blue tie in front of a mirror. Then they returned to the Park Hyatt.

At 12:29 P.M. a press release written by the assistant attorneys general of Mississippi and Arizona crossed the news wires: "The attorneys general who have sued the tobacco industry will make a major announcement regarding their ongoing negotiations in pursuit of a global settlement protecting children and the public health, changing the way the tobacco companies do business, and providing relief to those injured by smoking."

The press release said the announcement was scheduled for 1:30 P.M. in Ballroom I of the ANA.

Around 1:00 P.M., CNN went live, reporting that a settlement would be announced within an hour.

But it wasn't to be—yet.

Brown & Williamson's general counsel Mick McGraw and his deputy Neil Mellen wouldn't accept the new Wigand agreement.

As Wertheimer waited in an adjoining room, Fiske arranged a conference call for 1:00 P.M. that would include Philip Morris's chief executive Geoff Bible, RJR's CEO Steve Goldstone, and Martin Broughton, head of B.A.T, in London.

As he set up the call, Fiske was told by the B.A.T attorneys that the unbending Broughton likely wouldn't approve the latest Wigand proposal. So Fiske hoped that Bible and Goldstone could help convince Broughton to come around, just as they had in New York a week earlier, when Broughton opposed the provision in the settlement to grant the

FDA authority over nicotine.

"They want the Wigand suit dropped now, and the agreement modi-fied," Fiske said on the call. "I think the new agreement is reasonable." He outlined the terms of Wertheimer's proposal.

Bible jumped in first. "That makes sense," he said.

"No," Broughton interjected. "That's not acceptable. Tell them that after the settlement passes Congress, we'll keep the existing agreement in place for one more year, *then* rip it up."

"All right," Fiske said, "I'll try that."

At 1:30 P.M., Fiske relayed Broughton's counterproposal to Wertheimer: Wigand's current stringent confidentiality agreement would remain in force until one year after the settlement passed in Congress, he said. Then, Wigand could speak freely, without any restraints.

Wertheimer called Wigand, who was waiting in her office at Shea & Gardner, and recommended against the proposal.

"Jeff, your life shouldn't hang in the hands of Congress passing this agreement," she said. "I recommend you turn it down."

Wigand agreed.

Wertheimer then went in to tell the attorneys general about her con-versations with Fiske and Wigand.

"I've talked to Dr. Wigand," she told the lawyers. "He's extremely appreciative that you're standing behind him. He's risked everything to tell the truth."

Bob Butterworth, the Florida attorney general, stood up quickly. "We're not going to leave a wounded soldier on the battlefield. It's over."

New York Attorney General Dennis Vacco called for a quick vote. Everyone raised their hands in support of Wigand.

Grant Woods stepped into the hallway and borrowed Butterworth's line; "We're not going to leave any wounded behind," he told the crush of reporters that quickly gathered. "Past and future whistle-blowers will be protected, and one company doesn't understand that."

The attorneys general went into the room where Fiske and the other tobacco lawyers waited.

"We've taken a vote," Scruggs said. "We can't go forward."

Butterworth pulled Carlton aside.

"Phil, I don't want to tell you how to do your business, but if you guys can't make a decision right now, it's over," Butterworth said.

Carlton looked ashen. "How do you think I feel?"

"I don't give a damn," Butterworth said, walking away.

Then Butterworth went over to Fiske and issued a warning: "You've got an hour to fix this."

Fiske complained he didn't know if that was even possible. "I've been told Broughton's on a train for two hours, under the channel," Fiske said. It wasn't true, but the B.A.T lawyers were trying to buy time and asked Fiske to say that.

"Somebody knows how to reach him," Butterworth shot back. "Try his wife."

With that, Fiske went up to Murray Bring's suite to call Broughton and arrange a second call among the CEOs. Seated in the room were Wachtell, Golden, Bring, Carlton, and Rob Sharpe, RJR's general counsel. The attorneys general waited in the conference room below.

At 1:45 P.M., Bible and Goldstone dialed in from their New York offices; Broughton called from London.

"We have to solve this," Fiske said. "What if we leave some of the confidentiality agreement in place until the settlement passes, but drop the suit now?"

"That's not possible," Broughton said.

"Martin, they're going to make a martyr out of this man," Bible said. "Let's get this done."

Goldstone backed him up. "This is stupid," he said.

Wertheimer was pacing back and forth in a hot, cramped kitchen off the main conference room, awaiting the outcome of this conference call. The entire tobacco settlement had come down to the fate of her client, and hundreds of reporters were massed shoulder-to-shoulder in the hall 15 feet away, anxious for answers.

"This isn't a negotiation," Wertheimer thought. "This is a jihad."

Under pressure from everyone else on the call, Broughton finally gave in. "They want six months from now to void the confidentiality, and we wanted a year [after Congress passes it]," Broughton said. "Let's call it nine months from today, and we'll drop the suit now."

Broughton also agreed to immediately free Wigand to talk about the industry in general and about public documents.

Fiske felt his spirits lift. He hung up and raced downstairs with Carlton to find Wertheimer.

"They'll drop the suit," he said and laid out the other terms that Broughton had offered.

Wertheimer let out a deep breath. Finally, this worked. She called Wigand and advised him to accept. He did.

Then, she walked back into the conference room to tell the antitobacco attorneys.

"Wigand's fine, and he thanks all of you," Wertheimer said.

The lawyers, relieved, applauded.

The settlement was finished. It was 3:15 P.M. on June 20, 1997, a full 79 days since both sides first met in Crystal City, Virginia.

Golden called RJR CEO Steve Goldstone.

"The deal's done," Golden said.

"I hope we're doing the right thing," Goldstone said.

Murray Bring, Philip Morris's chief counsel, called Geoff Bible to tell him the news.

"It's done," Bring said.

Bible barely responded. Bring told him that the other side would hold a press conference soon and that the defense attorneys would fly back to New York. "Good work," Bible said, and hung up. He lit a cigarette.

ABC News broke into *The Oprah Winfrey Show;* Peter Jennings reported that the settlement was complete. Wire-service headlines saying that an agreement had been reached scrolled across computer screens.

Arthur Golden walked into the conference room where the five main attorneys general who had crafted the agreement—Moore, Gregoire, Woods, Butterworth, and Blumenthal—plus Attorney General Dennis Vacco of New York, were reading copies of the so-called Memorandum of Understanding, the preface to the 68-page settlement.

"We might as well start signing these," Golden said.

The attorneys shook hands all around. Philip Morris's Marc Firestone hugged Christine Gregoire. The two had spent dozens of hours working out the FDA provisions in the settlement. Gregoire was stunned by such spontaneous emotion from Firestone. The awkwardly formal regulatory expert—the "Egghead"—hadn't shown anything but a passion for numbers. Firestone had never even called Gregoire anything other than "General."

When the signing was completed, the tobacco foes began to leave the Park Hyatt to cross the street to the ANA Hotel, where the press conference announcing the settlement would be held. None of the Big Tobacco attorneys would attend it.

Mike Moore asked Dick Scruggs to walk with him as they descended the steps of the Park Hyatt to the street. They started this crusade together four years ago when Mike Lewis came up with the idea of suing cigarette makers for the costs of treating the sick and dying. And Moore wanted to end it side by side with Scruggs.

INSIDE THE ANA, Moore, Scruggs, and the other attorneys turned left and headed down two flights of stairs to Ballroom I.

The room they walked into was crammed with dozens of journalists and numerous still and television cameras on tripods. Flashguns went off in rapid fire and TV reporters improvised into their microphones, telling their audiences for the umpteenth time how this agreement had come about and what they were about to see. All the attorneys could hear, though, was the sound of their own hearts and footsteps.

Mike Moore, Christine Gregoire, Bob Butterworth, Grant Woods, Richard Blumenthal, Dennis Vacco, and Jeff Modisett ascended the podium.

Moore stepped forward.

"We are here today to announce what we think is—we know, we believe is—the most historic public health agreement in history," Moore said, staring into the cameras, imbued by a moment in the spotlight that had been so difficult to reach, yet never entirely out of his grasp. "We wanted this industry to have to change the way it did business, and we have done that.

"The attorneys general of America, the trial lawyers of America, the public health community has fought a war. A very long war," he continued. "We had to punish this industry in such a way that everybody in this country, and everybody in this world, would recognize that they had paid a higher price than any other corporation in history. Because, frankly, this corporation has done more harm than any other corporation in history."

For an hour, all the attorneys general gave statements about the settlement, and none of them, not even those who had grown close to some of their opposing counsel during the arduous talks, had anything good to say about Big Tobacco.

Blumenthal was especially harsh, declaring that the attorneys general knew they were "dealing with the devil," with an industry responsible for millions of deaths.

Then Florida's Bob Butterworth started to speak.

"The Marlboro Man is riding off into the sunset on Joe Camel," said Butterworth, and he began paying tribute to those who had fought Big Tobacco, people like Yul Brynner, the actor who died of lung cancer and was an outspoken critic of cigarette smoking late in his life; and Victor Crawford, the ex-lobbyist who had died of throat cancer. Then another man on Butterworth's list walked into the conference room.

The hundreds of reporters and guests recognized Jeffrey Wigand from his appearance on *60 Minutes* and began applauding. Butterworth and the other tobacco foes clapped as well.

BIG TOBACCO ATTORNEYS watched the press conference from the Park Hyatt conference room.

With them was one renegade from the other side: Hugh Rodham, the president's brother-in-law and one of the Castano attorneys. Rodham's colleagues had asked him to skip the press conference to avoid politicizing the event and having questions raised about Clinton's role in the settlement. Angry at this rebuff, Rodham lit up a so-called safer cigarette, an Eclipse—the low-smoke cigarette made by RJR—that he found in the room. The tobacco attorneys watched as Rodham, an ex-smoker, puffed deeply. It tasted horrible to him, too clean and purified, like smoking through a porcelain tube.

Rodham made a face and put out the cigarette firmly in the ashtray. "Fuck it," he said and left the room, heading over to the press conference.

Philip Morris's counsel Steven Parrish waited until the attorneys general were finished, then walked to the press briefing to read a dry, six-paragraph statement from the industry: "Our companies have made concessions that were extremely difficult. But on balance this plan is preferable to the continuation of a decades-long controversy that has failed to produce a constructive outcome for anyone."

Parrish left abruptly, refusing to answer questions. Later, when he called his wife to tell her that the deal had been struck, and he was coming home, his wife was still overcome from watching the attorneys general speak on TV. She was in tears.

At Washington National Airport, Bennett LeBow was waiting to catch a flight home to Miami, Florida. LeBow watched the press conference on a public TV without sound. He listened to it by calling his office on his cell phone and asking his assistant to put the phone next to a television. This was tough for LeBow to see. Liggett was included in the settlement. There would be no special rules for his tobacco company, and no letter to the White House recommending that his company be exempted. Geoff Bible, after all, had got his revenge.

After the press conference, Moore and Scruggs took a car to the White House to drop off a copy of the agreement with Bruce Reed, Clinton's top domestic policy chief. Bruce Lindsey had left for Denver to be with the president at the G-7 conference.

LATER, MOORE AND Scruggs went with their staffers and Jeffrey Wigand to the Japan Inn in Washington for a sushi dinner.

In Ocean Springs, Mississippi, in the dark of his living room, Merrell Williams clicked on the TV and sat back to watch the press conference.

It had been nearly a decade since Williams strode into a Louisville law firm, a research assistant on his first day, ready to read secret Brown & Williamson documents. He ended up walking out with thousands of photocopies that, on an airstrip in Orlando, Florida, were turned over to Dick Scruggs to be locked away in the lawyer's bank vault.

The papers had haunted Williams, making an already difficult life of low-paying jobs and a trail of divorces even tougher. Once Williams turned over the memos to Scruggs, it didn't take long for them to end up in books, newspapers, and on the Internet—making it useless for Brown & Williamson to try to reclaim them.

The walls of his home featured photos of his two young daughters. They didn't seem to understand what he had done. He had felt sorry for them when they had to climb on a school bus and hear their father was a thief.

In his living room is a Mexican-made table that swings open on both sides. A few sailing magazines rest on the wings, but the former drama teacher doesn't read. Instead, he waits. He waits for his life to get better. He waits for his daughters to visit.

The tobacco settlement did have a provision to protect whistle-blowers to the fullest extent against any recriminations. And it called for previously confidential industry memos to be made public before long. But all of this is too late for Merrell Williams.

Upstairs, in a closet in one of his daughter's rooms, are the boxes with the Brown & Williamson documents. The company, he says, doesn't want them anymore. Neither do the tobacco foes. In fact, nobody does.

He could scatter them into the wind and no one would care.

12

THE LEGACY OF JACKIE THOMPSON

Joe Camel is dead. He had it coming.

—BRUCE REED
White House domestic policy adviser

A t the Democratic National Convention in Chicago in August 1996, Vice President Al Gore lamented his lone sibling's premature death 12 years earlier from lung disease. Nancy Gore Hunger had been 45—and started smoking cigarettes at age 13. Gore choked back tears as he recalled her voice, her eyes, and how much he missed her.

"Until I draw my last breath I will pour my heart and soul into the cause of protecting our children from the dangers of smoking," Gore said. That pure sentiment moved the 20,000-strong Democratic faithful at United Center. Several delegates wept openly, caught up in a brother's deathbed compact with his sister.

But, like everything else in the storied and complicated history of tobacco in the United States, not much is black and white.

There's a little-known fact that the vice president neglected to mention at the convention—one that would have raised a skeleton that he preferred to keep buried: Until 1988, the Gore family farmed tobacco, growing acres and acres of the golden leaf in Carthage, Tennessee. It was the family's most lucrative crop.

Money from softly rolling, dark-brown fields of tobacco helped build a political base for the vice president's father, Al Gore Sr., who was elected U.S. senator from Tennessee in 1953. And though the sincerity of the vice president's now passionate hatred for the cigarette industry is unquestioned, his family bears at least a tangential responsibility for Big Tobacco's growth. Some people smoking today undoubtedly took their first puff on leaf harvested and cured by a Gore farmhand.

The fact that even one of Big Tobacco's most powerful opponents has a link to the industry underscores just how entwined tobacco is in the fabric of American life. It is the No. 1 nonfood crop in the United States, putting, the industry says, more than three million Americans to work; 50 million people smoke in the United States and tobacco kills 425,000 people a year, making it America's most dangerous legal consumer product.

Because Big Tobacco is so fundamental, so close to the core of U.S. day-to-day existence, it's no surprise that the $368.5 billion settlement of lawsuits against cigarette makers encompasses scores of staggering changes for society. Several of these were huge shifts all by themselves:

➤ Banning all outdoor advertising, including billboards for tobacco products, and limiting magazine ads to black-and-white text in periodicals with more than 15 percent youth readership.

➤ Prohibiting distribution of tobacco through vending machines, free samples, and containers of fewer than 20 cigarettes.

➤ Forbidding brand-name sponsorship of cultural and sports events like the Winston Cup auto racing series and the use of cigarette-brand logos on nontobacco merchandise like "Marlboro Gear" outdoor clothing.

➤ Prohibiting the industry from paying to get its cigarette brands used in movies or named in pop songs.

➤ Requiring the industry to pay as much as $15 billion yearly forever, about one-third of its U.S. revenue, to state and federal governments, private litigants, and antismoking groups.

➤ Empowering the Food and Drug Administration to regulate the manufacture and sale of tobacco products, including the right to ban or reduce the amount of ingredients (like nicotine) by 2009.

➤ Penalizing the industry if teen smoking rates do not decline to meet set targets.

➤ Eliminating class-action lawsuits and banning the award of punitive damages based on past acts by the companies, in addition to limiting to $5 billion annually the total amount of damages that the industry would have to pay smokers who win lawsuits.

Those wanting to gauge the settlement's importance could find some perspective in the decades-long battle to control handguns. Despite impetus from a rash of assassinations—two Kennedy brothers, King, Malcolm X, and Lennon, among others; the woundings of Reagan, Brady, and Wallace; and shoot-outs in playgrounds, housing projects, and fast-food restaurants, staunchly opposed gun manufacturers and the National Rifle Association have cited the law—the Second Amendment of the Constitution—to stay out of regulation's reach.

Proponents of handgun control had nobody to go to but Congress to get serious reform done. And Congress, carrying dozens of lobbyists on its back anytime it tries to move, was never able to pass a law that stuck and was really effective. After 30 years, a dangerous product is still less regulated than milk or ground beef.

What Mike Moore's initiative did in the spring and summer of 1997 went beyond controlling cigarettes; it may have changed the way vital public policy issues are resolved. The past 50 years have seen an interventionist government stepping in when private, corporate, or states' interests collided. But in the tobacco case, an ad hoc coalition of groups who wouldn't speak to each other in public found their way to an agreement and then intervened on government, offering a precedent for making crucial national decisions.

THE MASSIVE AGREEMENT—far bigger than any legal settlement in the history of the United States—immediately drew enthusiastic praise and virulent criticism. Ironically, the most vehement attacks came from interests who benefited from its gains but had never been able to come this close to getting them.

David Kessler, the former head of the FDA who began his quixotic campaign against Big Tobacco some three years earlier, blasted the agreement for being far too lenient—specifically for taking away from the FDA some of the regulatory control over cigarettes that the agency had won in Judge William Osteen's Greensboro, North Carolina, court-room in the spring of 1997.

The settlement claimed to maintain what Judge Osteen's decision gave the FDA—authority to reduce and even eliminate all levels of nicotine in cigarettes. But troubling to Kessler and other health advocates was a series of hurdles written into the settlement that the agency would have to clear before it could tinker with nicotine. Chief among them: The FDA would have to prove that reducing nicotine in U.S. cigarettes would not create "significant demand for contraband"—in other words, a thriving black market.

What's more, Judge Osteen had ruled that FDA tobacco decisions couldn't be overturned unless a judge deemed them "arbitrary and capricious." That was also changed under the settlement. Now, the agency would have to provide "substantial evidence" to back up its attempts to regulate nicotine, making it far easier for the industry to tie up and block the FDA in court.

"These provisions have been very well lawyered by the tobacco industry to thwart gains already made," Kessler told reporters after the settlement was announced. "It's giving away the farm."

Minnesota Attorney General Hubert Humphrey III also criticized the negotiated plan. The second attorney general to sue the industry, Humphrey was considered by many tobacco defenders to be a greater threat in court than Mississippi's Mike Moore. He had strong state antitrust and consumer fraud laws on his side, had amassed more than 30 million potentially damaging tobacco documents, and had won a series of rulings that the documents could be admitted in court because they showed evidence of criminal activity. Humphrey urged Congress to hold off approving the settlement at least until the documents were unsealed.

"It's outrageous," Humphrey said, the day the agreement was announced. "What about getting to the real truth? This deal allows the lies and cover-up to live on. Is this the kind of justice we want?"

But even those who spoke out against the settlement were not opposed to an agreement; their chief criticism was that it should have gone further, not that it shouldn't exist. And the champions of the freedom to sue had to contend with the fact that millions of dollars had begun flowing to the states under the settlement's provisions, while Big Tobacco still had the only pending monetary award against it tied up in court and had not yet paid a dime.

The settlement's $368.5 billion price tag over 25 years, as staggering as it is, almost immediately appeared unlikely to survive intact to final passage of the agreement. As soon as President Clinton and legislators began examining the pact in the summer of 1997, there was strong sentiment that at least another $75 billion or so should be added to the amount that the cigarette makers will have to pay.

"When the dust clears and the settlement is signed, the industry will pay between $420 billion and $450 billion," predicted Gary Black, the analyst at Sanford C. Bernstein & Co.

That would be galling for Big Tobacco. When Philip Morris CEO Geoff Bible and RJR CEO Steven Goldstone entered the negotiations in April 1997, they intended to pay about $200 billion, maybe even $250 billion, in exchange for full protection from lawsuits. Instead, they may have to pay twice that amount for limited protection. (Big Tobacco would still be vulnerable to punitive damage awards for future lawsuits, though the industry's total annual punitive damage payments would be capped at $5 billion a year.)

Still, there were mitigating aspects that made these provisions a bit more palatable to Big Tobacco. Part of the massive settlement would be paid for by raising the retail price of the 24 billion packs of cigarettes sold each year in the United States by as much as $1.

Indeed, in September 1997, tobacco companies raised cigarette prices 7 percent, its biggest price hike in four years, in an effort to amass cash to pay for the settlement. What's more, because of the advertising and promotion restrictions in the settlement, cigarette makers would save billions of dollars per year on marketing costs, which also would go towards paying for the settlement.

Higher prices and less advertising could cut the number of smokers by 15 percent over the next few years, but the agreement has a provision that protects the cigarette makers against too drastic a drop-off. If unit sales of cigarettes purchased by adults fall below 1996 levels, Big Tobacco would get a decrease in their annual settlement payments in proportion to the drop in sales. In turn, the industry could lower prices and entice more customers.

"In order to get the $368 billion, we need to keep people smoking," says Attorney General Joseph Curran of Maryland. "This is a real paradox that's very troubling."

WHEN MIKE MOORE and the other attorneys general announced the settlement in Washington, D.C., on June 20, they did it with passion, like well-trained stump speakers who had just fought the people's war and won. As if to stamp their patriotism, draped behind them was an American flag—not subtle, but ideal for the moment. It was a reminder, though, that the state prosecutors hadn't wrestled for smokers' rights anywhere else but in the United States.

There are an estimated 1.5 billion smokers globally, almost 30 percent of the world's population. Subtracting the 50 million U.S. smokers leaves plenty of customers for the cigarette makers to target. And they've done so with lethal gusto, concentrating less on the West than on the emerging markets in eastern Europe and Asia.

In eastern Europe, for example, smokers consumed 660 billion cigarettes in 1996. Philip Morris's market share in that region was forecast to rise to 32 percent in 1997, from 28 percent in 1996, and 22 percent the year before, according to Smith Barney analyst Martin Feldman.

No wonder, then, that Geoff Bible, Philip Morris's CEO, advocated a U.S. settlement. He knew the future for the Marlboro Man was in emerging markets. In 1995 he stood before stock analysts and said it succinctly: "International tobacco is our star business."

The antitobacco attorneys did consider trying to insert stipulations into the pact that might have reduced global smoking. In the early weeks of the settlement talks, the attorneys thought about pumping millions of dollars into groups like the World Health Organization for an antitobacco campaign. But the proposals never made it into the 68-page accord.

Of course, reducing global cigarette consumption would have been a difficult trick for the attorneys general. In China, for example, the biggest cigarette maker is the Chinese government—symbolized by leader Deng Xioaping who puffed his beloved Panda cigarettes until his death in early 1997. Cigarette sales in China topped $5 billion in 1996.

Cigarette makers have been crafty in building market share overseas. In Japan, for example, an RJR executive moved quickly to introduce a "better-smelling" cigarette after noticing a growing demand for products in that country that erased cigarette smoke. RJR's "sweet-smelling" brand, Salem Preferred, had failed in the United States—but reintroduced as Salem Pianissimo in Japan, the cigarette became a hit.

Put plainly, when Big Tobacco makes one of its annual payments to the states, the money won't likely be coming from U.S. cigarette sales. As Greg Connolly, director of the Massachusetts public health department, puts it: Mississippi's Medicaid bills will be paid with the money that children in Manila use to buy cigarettes.

THOUGH THE SETTLEMENT was nothing more than a three-week-old proposal on July 15, 1997, the state of Mississippi received a $170 million wire transfer from a coalition of the United States' biggest tobacco companies to its account in Pascagoula's SouthTrust bank.

To avoid going to court against Big Tobacco while the accord worked its way through Congress, Mississippi had agreed to a separate $3.4 billion settlement with the cigarette makers. In effect, that would be Mississippi's portion of the overall agreement if it becomes law. The $170 million represented the tobacco industry's initial installment on its debt to Mississippi. It also marked the first time Big Tobacco ever paid any money to settle health-related lawsuits.

Mike Moore had done what no one before him had ever accomplished. He had gotten Big Tobacco to pay for the sins of its product. In less than a year, Moore had transformed his image from a little-known attorney general in one of the poorest states in America into a household name with a viable shot at filling Moore's ultimate dream: becoming a politician on the national level.

All in all, the 50 states likely will divide the lion's share of the $368.5 billion settlement—if the total amount doesn't go up.

Others, also, stand to benefit in a big way from the settlement. Matt Myers's National Center for Tobacco-Free Kids and scores of other public health organizations—the American Heart Association and the American Cancer Society among them—will get $500 million a year for antismoking ad campaigns and other tobacco-control programs, especially those targeted on curbing teen smoking. That's more than double what these groups spend on those activities currently.

Even the FDA and the Department of Health and Human Services, among the settlement's most implacable foes, will get more than $425 million a year for enforcing tobacco regulatory activities and other antismoking initiatives.

As for the high-profile private attorneys hired by the states to argue their Medicaid lawsuits in court, it didn't take long after the settlement for rifts over fees to turn ugly. Very ugly.

Florida followed Mississippi's lead in settling independently, agreeing to an $11.3 billion pact with Big Tobacco. Not long after the Florida settlement was reached, trial attorney Bob Montgomery demanded $1.4 billion in fees—an amount that angered Florida Attorney General Bob Butterworth. The fees, he said, were enough to "choke a horse." Montgomery filed a lien against the state to secure the money he felt was owed him for months of trial preparation.

The tobacco companies have yet to work out how much they will pay in fees to the 65-member Castano coalition. Estimates start at $500 million, which, if split equally among the group, would give each attorney more than $7 million.

Those hurt the most from the settlement are magazine publishers and billboard companies. With the ban on cigarette advertising, they lose millions in revenue and get nothing in return. Cigarette makers spent one-third of a billion dollars in 1996 on ads in magazines, especially those that cater to young readers, like *Rolling Stone*, *Vogue*, and *Sports Illustrated*. Additionally, tobacco companies earmark about $150 million a year for billboard advertising.

Also, under the agreement, thousands of stores and supermarkets face tough enforcement of laws that could result in $50,000 fines if retailers are caught selling to minors. For convenience stores, any cut in tobacco sales will hurt, because cigarettes represent about 25 percent of their $17 billion in annual sales.

The human pain from the settlement is being felt in tobacco country —cities like Owensboro, Kentucky; Moultrie, Georgia; and Edgefield, South Carolina. Tobacco farmers received nothing in the settlement. And they're concerned that the agreement will cut smoking in the United States so severely that tobacco growing will become an unprofitable way of life.

In Smithfield, North Carolina, a 40-minute drive southeast of Raleigh, the talk around the batting cage at the ball field off Bright Leaf Boulevard, even among the 11- and 12-year-olds, was about how the tobacco settlement would change their lives.

"We've been told that there could be some cutbacks around town and that has us wondering who's going to pay for our uniforms and bats," said Brad Stephenson, a dusty-haired 12-year-old who pitches for a team sponsored by the K. R. Edwards's tobacco-leaf-processing plant.

And in South Richmond, Virginia, a dad, Marv Stanley, worried about his job and his ability to support his family. Stanley operates a packing machine at Philip Morris's manufacturing plant there.

"I'm afraid the cost of the settlement might force the companies to cut jobs or benefits," he said, clutching a lunch box with a sticker that says 'I Smoke and I Vote.' "I feel I'm at risk and it's all about extortion."

THE CLINTON ADMINISTRATION took three months to scrutinize the settlement (longer than it took to negotiate), even though the White House had played a key role in crafting the compromise. It was White House deputy counsel Bruce Lindsey who informed both sides during the negotiations of the White House's stance on key issues and it was Lindsey who got the deal over its biggest hurdle with a creative suggestion: having the cigarette makers pay $60 billion to smokers as punishment for past misdeeds.

Lindsey slipped out of the spotlight in late June after the agreement was struck. In his place Donna Shalala, head of the Department of Health and Human Services, and Bruce Reed, senior White House domestic policy adviser, moved to the forefront to study the proposal.

The shuffling of top aides was designed to assure President Clinton that he would gain consensus within his administration before he went to Congress and the public to back any version of the settlement. That would enable the president to skirt around the divisiveness which thwarted his doomed plan to overhaul the nation's health care system in 1993.

The process of forging agreement on the tobacco settlement in the White House, however, proved tumultuous. Shalala and Reed shellacked the deal as being too soft on the industry and urged the president to step up the power of the FDA and raise the penalties Big Tobacco would have to pay if teen smoking failed to decline.

That infuriated the negotiators, who charged that administration officials were simply trying to take credit for the historic compromise.

"I am amazed at Donna Shalala," Dick Scruggs, Mike Moore's associate, said late in the summer of 1997. "They can't even get $34 million out of Congress in funding for tobacco enforcement. Here's a settlement where the industry's gotta put $300 million into it every year"—he laughs—"and now they say, 'That's horrible! It weakens the FDA!'

"The whole thing is ego," Scruggs continued. "The game is, your idea is horrible. Go back and change a comma, change a word, call it their idea, and now, they've saved it, they've fixed it and it's their plan."

By mid-September, things were looking so bleak that the *New York Times* led its Sunday, September 14, edition with a story that pronounced the settlement in dire straits. "Tobacco Accord, Once Applauded, Is All but Dead," read the headline.

That turned out to be premature. Clinton never gave up on the tobacco settlement which he had always considered an integral part of his legacy—especially in light of his failed overhaul of health care four years earlier.

On September 17, on a stage flanked by Mike Moore, C. Everett Koop, David Kessler, and Matt Myers, Clinton delivered his much-anticipated verdict on the agreement. While he stopped short of a full endorsement, Clinton urged Congress to put the tobacco settlement into law. He put his own stamp on the deal, proposing that cigarette prices be boosted $1.50 a pack over 10 years if the strict marketing and advertising measures fail to curb teenage smoking rates. And he said he wanted nondeductible, uncapped penalties on tobacco companies if targets for reducing teenage smoking aren't met.

"I want to challenge Congress to build on [the settlement]," Clinton said. "We're building on the agreement. We're not tearing it down and I think we can get legislation to reflect it. We have moved from confrontation and denial to the brink of action."

Public health advocates, Big Tobacco representatives, and state attorneys general all said the president's fine-tuning of the accord improved the chances of reaching a national settlement.

"It'll work," said C. Everett Koop, the former U.S. surgeon general. "I wouldn't have been as optimistic as this two months ago."

After Clinton's statements it was up to Congress to draft the final settlement and approve the accord. Awaiting the president's position on the pact, Senate Majority Leader Trent Lott said little about it since it was crafted. Publicly, Lott surfaced only briefly in the summer of 1997 when he and Speaker of the House Newt Gingrich quietly backed in Congress a short-lived controversial provision that would have provided a $50 billion tax credit to Big Tobacco to ease the impact of its settlement costs.

But, in little more than four years since Lott began guiding his brother-in-law Dick Scruggs and Mike Moore to piece together a legislative solution to the tobacco industry's mounting litigation, the saga had come full circle: The landmark tobacco settlement was back in the hands of Trent Lott.

IN THE END, it's difficult to connect the death of Mike Lewis's friend Jackie Thompson to the $368.5 billion settlement.

Thompson, dying of cancer, was the inspiration for Mike Moore's lawsuit in May 1994—the Medicaid suit that eventually led to the agreement with Big Tobacco. But people like Jackie Thompson—the individual, sick smoker—are the forgotten ones in this settlement. For one thing, the agreement freed the tobacco companies from liability for virtually all prior lawsuits. That means that while the states will be reimbursed for their Medicaid cases and the Castano lawyers will get paid for withdrawing their class-action suits, no smoker will directly see any money out of the settlement. All they'll get is the right to attend a smoking-cessation program for free.

If individual smokers want to get any money from the cigarette makers, they'll have to sue just like before the settlement—well, not quite like before. The agreement bans class-action suits against Big Tobacco. And it limits the amount of damages an individual can collect from the cigarette makers.

On August 25, two months after the settlement was announced, a dialogue on CNN summed up the plight of the sick smoker. Castano attorney John Coale was a guest on CNN's *Talk Back Live* hosted by Susan Rook.

Rook: "Let's go to the phone. George is joining us from Mississippi. George, welcome. We're glad you're here. Tell us your story."

George: "I've smoked for over 50 years. I had to stop about five years ago because of emphysema. As I watch your show, I'm hooked up to a breathing machine. I have two oxygen tanks: one a large one that I take with me if I go any distance, a short one I put over my shoulder when I go a short distance.

"I have eight or nine pills I have to take a day. Breathing instruments I have to use. Now I understand that the government wants to cut off— withhold some of my oxygen therapy. They want to start charging me for home health care.

"I don't want billions of money. I don't want hundreds of thousands of dollars. But when we're talking about all this money, what does a little individual like me [do to] be able to get a little bit of the pie? How would I go about it?"

Rook then passed the question to John Coale, who told George that he might be able to apply for programs to help him pay for the medical costs if the settlement was passed.

But if the caller wanted more than that, if George wanted to extract a little pain for his own suffering, then he was out of luck. He would have to sue.

Coale: "Now what he can do is he can go down to Mike Moore's lawyer, Dickie Scruggs. And Scruggs's firm can sue for you individually, where you can have an individual case against the companies and get compensated for what was done to you."

George: "Well, I'm kind of homebound, and Scruggs's office is in Pascagoula. That's about 50 miles from my home."

Coale: "Dickie will take a collect call."

George: "Pardon?"

Coale: "Dickie Scruggs will take a collect call from you."

That afternoon, the offices of Scruggs and Moore were deluged with telephone calls. A lot of them had to be put on hold.

For smokers, not much had changed.

Chronology

1492—Within a week of landfall Christopher Columbus and his crews encounter Indians chewing aromatic leaves and smoking them through a Y-shaped pipe called a tobaga. A century later, tobacco has spread throughout the globe and, along with coffee, chocolate, and cane sugar, is one of the unexpected gifts of the New World to the Old.

1560—Jean Nicot, France's ambassador to Portugal, learns that court physicians prized tobacco for its curative powers; when tobacco was credited with curing a relative's ulcer he writes to Paris rhapsodizing about the leaf's healing powers. Within two generations, tobacco is widely accepted as an antitoxin and disinfectant. Nicot's name would later be used to name nicotine, the addictive element in tobacco.

1604—King James I issues "A Counterblaste to Tobacco," calling smoking "a custom loathsome to the eye, hateful to the nose, harmful to the brain, dangerous to the lungs." He increases the import tax on tobacco by 4,000 percent.

1612—John Rolfe, an English colonist, raises Virginia's first commercial tobacco crop in Jamestown, providing the fledgling colony with its main resource.

1640—What is today known as Greenwich Village in New York City is known to Native Americans as Sapponckanican—"tobacco fields" or the "land where tobacco grows."

1665—The plague sweeps through Europe; smoking is thought to have a protective effect.

1760—Pierre Lorillard establishes a plant in New York City for processing tobacco.

1776—During the American Revolution, tobacco helps finance revolutionaries by serving as collateral for loans from France.

247

1794—The U.S. Congress passes its first tobacco tax. The tax applies only to snuff.

1828—Scientists in Germany conclude that nicotine is a "dangerous poison."

1839—Tobacco manufacturers in North Carolina use charcoal for the first time in the process of flue curing tobacco leaves, turning them into a "bright leaf" and making the tobacco more mild in taste when smoked.

1847—Philip Morris opens a shop in England to sell Turkish cigarettes.

1849—J. E. Liggett and Brother is established in St. Louis, Missouri. Fifty years later, the company teams up with George Myers to form Liggett & Myers.

1852—Washington Duke builds a home in Durham, North Carolina; later he uses it as a tobacco factory.

1854—Philip Morris begins making his own cigarettes in London.

1857—James Buchanan "Buck" Duke is born to Washington Duke and his wife.

1860—Bull Durham is established as a popular "roll-your-own" cigarette.

1861–65—Union armies fighting in the Civil War are introduced to tobacco as a spoil of battle. They raid Confederate warehouses, including Washington Duke's, for tobacco they can take home to the North.

1873—Philip Morris dies. His cousin Leopold takes control of the company and sells stock to investors. It prospers for 20 years before well-heeled rivals begin offering free samples and drive the smaller company into bankruptcy.

1874—Washington Duke and his sons build their first tobacco factory.

1875—Richard Joshua Reynolds founds R. J. Reynolds Tobacco Co. to make chewing tobacco, including Dixie's Delight and Yellow Rose brands, in Winston, North Carolina.

1884—James Buchanan "Buck" Duke heads north to New York City to build his family's company into a national concern that will eventually be called American Tobacco Co. and dominate the market.

1889—Duke spends $800,000 to market cigarettes in a single year.

1894—Creditors in control of Philip Morris hand the company over to British industrialist William Thomson, who plans to nurse the company back to health by exporting cigarettes to the United States.

1899—Liggett & Myers is folded into Duke's tobacco empire.

1900—R. J. Reynolds is sold to Duke's tobacco trust for $3 million.

1901—Buck Duke enters the British market, merging American Tobacco Co. with Continental Tobacco, into Consolidated Tobacco.

1902—British tobacco companies, uniting to fight Duke, form the Imperial Tobacco Group.

1902—Philip Morris incorporates in New York to sell British brands, including a brand that will prove popular—named for the London street where the home company's factory was located: Marlborough.

1906—Brown & Williamson Tobacco Corp. is formed by a group of farmers as a Winston-Salem, North Carolina, maker of plug, snuff, and pipe tobacco.

1907—President Theodore Roosevelt's Administration files antitrust charges against Buck Duke's American Tobacco, which controls 90 percent of the world's tobacco market. In 1911, Duke's empire is dissolved, breaking into American Tobacco Co., R. J. Reynolds, Liggett & Myers Tobacco Co., Lorillard, and B.A.T.

1912—Liggett introduces Chesterfield brand.

1913—The American Society for the Control of Cancer (later, the American Cancer Society) is created to inform the public about the disease.

1919—R. J. Reynolds dies.

1921—The "I'd Walk a Mile for a Camel" slogan is introduced by R. J. Reynolds; by 1923, Camel has 23 percent of the U.S. market.

1925—Buck Duke dies. A year before his death, he establishes Duke University in Durham.

1927—British-American Tobacco Co. buys Brown & Williamson.

1929—Philip Morris buys a factory in Richmond, Virginia, and begins making its own cigarettes.

1930—Large cigarette companies such as R. J. Reynolds hike cigarette prices, opening the door for small firms like Philip Morris and Brown & Williamson to counter with low-priced brands.

1933—Brown & Williamson introduces Kool menthol brand.

1939—*Fortune* finds that 53 percent of adult American men smoke.

1941—Dr. Michael DeBakey publishes a report citing a correlation between increased sales of tobacco and increasing lung cancer.

1950—American scientists Ernst L. Wynder and Evarts A. Graham publish a report that 96.5 percent of lung-cancer patients are moderate-to-heavy smokers.

1951—The TV series *I Love Lucy* begins, sponsored by Philip Morris.

1952—Liggett publicizes a study by Arthur D. Little showing that smoking Chesterfields has no adverse effect on the throat.

1953—A landmark study by Ernst Wyndner shows that painting cigarette tar on the backs of mice creates tumors.

1953—Tobacco executives meet at New York City's Plaza Hotel to discuss ways to deal with scientific studies that report the health hazards of smoking.

1954—Eva Cooper sues R. J. Reynolds Tobacco Co. for the death of her husband from lung cancer. Cooper loses the case.

1954—Philip Morris hires attorney David Hardy to defend the company in litigation, beginning the company's association with Shook, Hardy & Bacon. Philip Morris wins the first case handled by Hardy.

1954—The Tobacco Industry Research Committee issues a "Frank Statement" to the public, a nationwide two-page ad that states that cigarette makers don't believe their products are injurious to a person's health. The same year, advertising agency Leo Burnett creates the "Marlboro Man" for a brand that has only 1 percent of the U.S. market.

1963—Brown & Williamson general counsel Addison Yeaman notes in a memo, "Nicotine is addictive. We are, then, in the business of selling nicotine, an addictive drug."

1964—U.S. Surgeon General Luther Terry issues the first surgeon general report citing health risks associated with smoking.

1965—The U.S. Congress passes the Federal Cigarette Labeling and Advertising Act, requiring a surgeon general's warning on cigarette packs.

1968—Philip Morris introduces its Virginia Slims brand, aimed at women.

1971—R. J. Reynolds begins its sponsorship of NASCAR auto racing.

1972—Philip Morris's Marlboro becomes the best-selling brand in the world.

1975—Philip Morris's Marlboro overtakes R. J. Reynolds's Winston brand for a U.S. market share lead.

1982—U.S. Surgeon General C. Everett Koop finds that secondhand smoke may cause lung cancer.

1983—Rose Cipollone, a smoker, sues the tobacco industry. She dies in 1984 and her family takes up the lawsuit.

1985—Philip Morris buys General Foods; R. J. Reynolds purchases Nabisco Brands, Inc. and, in 1986, renames itself RJR Nabisco, Inc. Ross Johnson assumes control of RJR, Inc.

1988—Michael Moore is elected attorney general of Mississippi.

1988—Merrell Williams begins working for the Louisville, Kentucky, law firm Wyatt, Tarrant & Combs, which represents Brown & Williamson.

1988—Judge Lee Sarokin rules that he has found evidence of tobacco industry conspiracy in the Cipollone case; Liggett is ordered to pay Cipollone $400,000 in compensatory damages.

1988—Ross Johnson informs RJR's board that he plans the management buyout of the company. The investment firm Kohlberg, Kravis, Roberts & Co. ends up winning control of the company for $29.6 billion.

1990—Don Barrett, the Mississippi attorney representing smoker Nathan Horton, wins a case against the industry, but his client is awarded no money.

1990—Smoking is banned on U.S. passenger flights of less than six hours' duration.

1992—The U.S. Supreme Court rules that the 1965 warning label on cigarette packs does not shield companies from lawsuits.

1992—Wayne McLaren, who modeled as the "Marlboro Man," dies of lung cancer.

1993—Philip Morris announces it will slash prices on Friday, April 2, cutting the price of Marlboros by 40 cents a pack. Philip Morris stock tumbles 23 percent—$13 billion—on what is soon known as "Marlboro Friday."

1993—Wyatt Tarrant sues Merrell Williams for stealing top secret Brown & Williamson documents.

February 1994—FDA Commissioner David Kessler announces plans to consider the regulation of tobacco as a drug.

March 1994—ABC airs a *Day One* segment about the tobacco industry's alleged manipulation of nicotine.

March 1994—A national class-action lawsuit is filed on behalf of smokers. It is known as the Castano suit, after Peter Castano, a former Louisiana attorney who died of lung cancer.

April 1994—B.A.T Industries buys American Tobacco from American Brands.

April 1994—Seven tobacco company executives testify before the U.S. Congress, saying in a widely televised broadcast that they believe nicotine is not addictive.

May 1994—The *New York Times* reports that Brown & Williamson documents showed that tobacco company executives knew of the risks tied to smoking.

May 1994—Stanton Glantz, a professor at the University of California at San Francisco, receives a box of Brown & Williamson documents from "Mr. Butts." He later disseminates the documents on the Internet.

May 1994—Mississippi Attorney General Mike Moore sues the tobacco industry on behalf of his state, seeking to recoup $940 million the state spent treating sick smokers. Other states soon follow.

June 1994—Geoffrey Bible is named Philip Morris's president and chief executive, replacing Michael Miles.

October 1995—Steven Goldstone is named chief executive of RJR Nabisco Holdings Corp., after having served as president and general counsel.

November 1995—Dr. Jeffrey Wigand, a former top scientist at Brown & Williamson, becomes a whistle-blower, providing tobacco industry secrets to Mississippi lawyers and to CBS's *60 Minutes*.

March 1996—Brooke Group, Ltd. and its tobacco division, Liggett, settle with five states and 67 law firms suing the industry—the first such agreement in 40 years of litigation.

March 1996—RJR Nabisco Holdings Corp.'s chief executive Steven Goldstone says the industry would consider settlement if the terms are right.

May 1996—A federal appeals court dismisses the Castano national class-action lawsuit. Lawyers in the Castano group begin filing class-action lawsuits in individual states.

August 1996—A Jacksonville, Florida, jury awards $750,000 to Grady Carter, who had sued Brown & Williamson. Philip Morris's stock loses $12 billion in value within an hour.

October 1996—B.A.T Industries Plc's chief executive Martin Broughton says a settlement of tobacco lawsuits would be "common sense."

December 1996—RJR hires North Carolina lawyer Phil Carlton to lobby the White House and try to meet with Mississippi Attorney General Mike Moore.

February 1997—Phil Carlton meets with White House deputy counsel Bruce Lindsey.

February 1997—The tobacco industry argues in U.S. district court in Greensboro, North Carolina, that the FDA does not have power to regulate tobacco.

March 1997—The Mississippi Supreme Court rules that the state's lawsuit can proceed to trial.

March 1997—Brooke Group settles with more than 20 states, agreeing to release tobacco industry documents.

March 18, 1997—Joe Rice, an attorney working with Mike Moore, meets in Charlotte, North Carolina, with tobacco company attorneys to discuss a settlement of all lawsuits facing the industry, the first time a major tobacco company representative sits across a table from an antitobacco attorney, apart from litigation.

March 31, 1997—Mike Moore, Dick Scruggs, Matt Myers, and John Coale meet with Phil Carlton.

April 3, 1997—Philip Morris's CEO Geoff Bible, RJR's CEO Steven Goldstone, and their attorneys meet in Crystal City, Virginia, with state attorneys general to discuss a national settlement.

April 25, 1997—A U.S. district judge in Greensboro rules that the FDA has the authority to regulate nicotine as a drug.

May 5, 1997—RJR wins a lawsuit in Jacksonville filed by a smoker who died and blamed the cigarette maker for not adequately warning her of the dangers of smoking.

June 20, 1997—The tobacco companies and state attorneys general announce the landmark $368.5 billion settlement agreement in Washington, D.C.

Notes

In the preparation of *The People vs. Big Tobacco,* more than 100 people were interviewed at length, including negotiators in the settlement talks, state attorneys general, tobacco company executives and attorneys, senior officials in the White House and federal agencies, key congressmen, public health advocates, whistle-blowers, private trial lawyers, and lobbyists. Some of the interviews were taped and extensive word-for-word notes were taken during them all.

In addition, the writers combed through thousands of documents, including Securities and Exchange Commission and court filings, books and articles on tobacco, and internal memos from the tobacco industry and state attorneys.

Special mention—sincere gratitude and appreciation—is owed to several of the key negotiators and players in this story. They spent numerous hours being interviewed, sharing their notes, insights, late nights, and weekends with the authors; among them: Phil Carlton, Mike Moore, Dick Scruggs, Don Barrett, Steve Berman, Christine Gregoire, Grant Woods, Bob Butterworth, Mike Lewis, Tom Green, Merrell Williams, Charles Zimmerman, John Coale, Dick Blumenthal, Stan Chesley, and Russ Herman. Will Kemp kindly provided several photos.

Each person named in the book was interviewed or was provided with ample opportunity to comment. Most of the tobacco industry executives and attorneys would only agree to speak on a not-for-attribution basis.

People's thoughts and feelings at particular moments came directly from the person identified or from others close to the person. Quoted statements came directly from the speaker, someone who heard the remark, or from transcripts. In three cases, the authors reconstructed conversations, and in all instances at least three people who knew the details of these conversations provided specifics as to what was said. The reconstructed conversations are listed under the appropriate chapter heading in the notes that follow.

PROLOGUE

Information on Thomas Sandefur came from:
—Andrew Wolfson, "B&W Chairman Little Known, and Likes It That Way," *Louisville Courier-Journal,* June 19, 1994

—Glenn Collins, "Thomas Sandefur, Tobacco Leader, Dies at 56," *New York Times,* July 16, 1996

—Philip Hilts, *Smokescreen*, Reading, Massachusetts: Addison-Wesley Press, 1996

Jeffrey Wigand's deposition can be found at: (www.gate.net/~jcannon/documents. wigand.html)

The section on James Morgan and Andrew Schindler relied on depositions reprinted on the *Miami Herald's* Internet site (www.herald.com); and Victoria Cherrie, "Island VFD Failed," *Wilmington (North Carolina) Star-News,* April 20, 1997

Information for the history of Big Tobacco came from:

—Richard Kluger, *Ashes to Ashes,* New York: Alfred A. Knopf, 1996

—Benjamin Weiser, "Tobacco's Trials," *Washington Post* magazine, December 8, 1996

CHAPTER 1
THE PEOPLE vs. BIG TOBACCO

Mike Lewis, Pauline Lewis, Alice Craven, Mike Moore, Dick Scruggs, Don Barrett, Joe Rice, Hugh Rodham, Bennett LeBow, one unnamed tobacco company executive, and two other unnamed tobacco negotiators were interviewed for this chapter. Mike Espy has pleaded not guilty to charges of illegally taking gifts.

Sources for the section on the Mississippi attorneys include:

—Weiser, "Tobacco's Trials"

—Jim Yardley, "The Small-Town Lawyer Who Finally Caught Big Tobacco," *Atlanta Journal-Constitution,* July 27, 1997

—Tom Donnelly, "Mike Moore's Persona Softer Away from Work," *Mississippi Press,* February 1991

—Henry Weinstein and Jack Nelson, "Untested Theory Becoming Tobacco Firm's Top Threat," *Los Angeles Times,* August 4, 1996

Sources for the settlement section include:

—Alix Freedman and Suein Hwang, "Burning Questions: Tobacco Pact's Limits— and Its Loopholes—Presage Fierce Debate," *Wall Street Journal,* June 23, 1997

CHAPTER 2
THE THIEF

Merrell Williams, Dick Scruggs, Don Barrett, Norwood Wilner, Grady Carter, Mike Moore, Grant Woods, two tobacco industry executives, and two tobacco industry negotiators were interviewed for this chapter.

Sources for the section on Merrell Williams include:

—David Barstow, "The Thief and the Third Wave," *St. Petersburg (Florida) Times*, April 6 and 7, 1997

—Michael Orey, "Fanning the Flames," *American Lawyer*, April 1996

—Mark Curriden, "The Paralegal Who Smoked the Tobacco Industry," *National Law Journal*, May/June 1997

—Stanton Glantz, *The Cigarette Papers*, Berkley, California: University of California Press, 1996

—University of California Web site: (http://www.library.ucsf.edu/tobacco/bwsearch. html)

Sources for the section on Dick Scruggs include:

—Marie Brenner, "The Man Who Knew Too Much," *Vanity Fair*, May 1996

—Mollie Gore, "Mississippi Lawyer Targets Cause," *Richmond Times–Dispatch*, September 1, 1996

—Frank Fisher, "State Receives $11 Million in Asbestos Suit Settlement," Mississippi Press, July 7, 1992

The section on the depositions from the seven tobacco executives relied on Hilts, *Smokescreen*

Sources for the section on Wilner and Carter include:

—Suein Hwang, Milo Geyelin, and Alix Freedman, "Jury's Tobacco Verdict Suggests Tough Times Ahead for the Industry," *Wall Street Journal*, August 12, 1996

—Weiser, "Tobacco Trials"

Sources for the section on Moore and Scruggs's recruiting efforts include:

—Pat Kossan, "Anti-Tobacco Groups Slam Junket," *Arizona Republic*, February 18, 1997

Sources for the section on the tobacco CEOs include:

—Patricia Sellers, "Geoff Bible Won't Quit," *Fortune*, July 21, 1997

Portions of the conversation between CEOs in this section were reconstructed from interviews with tobacco company executives.

CHAPTER 3
BREAKING RANKS

Bennett LeBow, Marc Kasowitz, Marc Bell, Steve Goldstone, and Geoffrey Bible were interviewed for this chapter.

Sources for the section on Bennett LeBow include:

—John Schwartz, "A Maverick's Complaint," *Washington Post*, July 24, 1997

—Suzanne Woolley, "Western Union Banks on the Unbanked," *Business Week,* April 5, 1993

—Riva Atlas, "Now You See It, Now You Don't," *Forbes,* April 24, 1995

—Glenn Collins, "Breaking Ranks: Profile," *New York Times,* March 21, 1997

—David Rovella, "Fear at an October Meeting Spurs Liggett Settlement," *National Law Journal,* April 7, 1997

Sources for the section on Geoff Bible include:

—Sellers, "Geoff Bible Won't Quit"

—Kluger, *Ashes to Ashes*

—Alix Freedman and Elizabeth Jensen, "Capital Cities, Philip Morris Settle Lawsuit," *Wall Street Journal,* August 22, 1995

—Alix Freedman and Elizabeth Jensen, "Why ABC Settled with the Tobacco Industry," *Wall Street Journal,*. August 24, 1995

CHAPTER 4
THE BROKERS

Dick Scruggs, Mike Moore, Grant Woods, Wendell Gauthier, Russ Herman, John Coale, Hugh Rodham, Hubert Humphrey III, Richard Blumenthal, Jim Hunt, Phil Carlton, and two tobacco industry representatives were interviewed for this chapter.

Sources for the section on Trent Lott include:

—James Barnes, "Lott: The Senate Broker," *National Journal,* December 21, 1996

—Milo Geyelin and Suein Hwang, "Plan to Settle Tobacco Cases Draws Fire," *Wall Street Journal,* August 27, 1996

—Milo Geyelin, "States Greet Plan to Settle Tobacco Suits with Skepticism, but Leave Door Open," *Wall Street Journal,* August 29, 1996

—Bruce Ingersoll and Michael Frisby, "Smoke Signals: Omens of Tobacco Truce Are in the Air," *Wall Street Journal,* December 19, 1996

—Richard Tonkins, "The Ifs and Butts of Litigation," *Financial Times* (London), March 22, 1996

Sources for the section on the Castano coalition include:

—David Greising, "The Big Four Who Battle Big Tobacco," *Business Week,* April 16, 1997

—Joel Obermayer, "Tobacco Lawsuit Not So Easy for Judge," *Raleigh (North Carolina) News & Observer,* February 9, 1997

—Weiser, "Tobacco Trials"

—Claudia MacLachlan, "Warning: Hot Coale," *National Law Journal,* June 7, 1993

—Stephanie Mansfield, "The Lawyer and the Thrill of Disaster," *Washington Post,* March 12, 1987

—David Morgolick, "Trouble in the Trial Bar," *New York Times,* May 25, 1990

Sources for the section on North Carolina officials in the talks include:

—Rob Christensen, "Voice for Big Tobacco Speaks with N.C. Accent," *Raleigh, (North Carolina) News & Observer,* April 23, 1997

—Danny Lineberry, "Scannergate Was No Trifling Matter," *Durham (North Carolina) Herald-Sun,* April 17, 1994

—Suein Hwang, "Tobacco: Carolina Lawyer Helps Smooth Tobacco Talks, *Wall Street Journal,* April 21, 1997

—Rob Christensen, "Today's Power Holders Stood Out 40 Years Ago at NCSU," *Raleigh, North Carolina, News & Observer,* April 28, 1997

—"Under the Dome: Carlton Talking Tobacco," *Raleigh (North Carolina) News & Observer,* April 19, 1997

—Barry Meier, "Tangled Web of Factors Led to Tobacco Talks," *New York Times,* April 21, 1997

CHAPTER 5
PAGE ONE NEWS

Phil Carlton, Mike Moore, Wendell Gauthier, John Coale, Richard Blumenthal, Christine Gregoire, Gary Black, Steven Goldstone, Joe Rice, Ron Motley, Dick Scruggs, and two tobacco attorneys were interviewed for this chapter.

For the section on settlement news reports sources include:

—Dave Greising and Catherine Yang, "Peace Talks in the Tobacco Wars," *Business Week,* February 10, 1997

—Peter Hardin, "Possibility of Deal Seen in Smoking Fight," *Richmond Times-Dispatch,* February 2, 1997

For the section on Bruce Lindsey sources include:

—David Von Drehle, "Little-Known Arkansas Lawyer Plays Big Role in Clinton's Decisions," *Washington Post,* January 17, 1997

—Peter Baker and Frank Swoboda, "Pilots Say Showdown Only Delayed," *Washington Post,* February 16, 1997

—Richard Dunham, "Collision Course for Bruce Lindsey," *Business Week,* June 9, 1997

For the section on the Charlotte meeting sources include:

—Steve Weinberg, "Hardball Discovery," *ABA Journal,* November 1995

CHAPTER 6
THE FDA AND THE WHISTLE-BLOWER

Bruce Lindsey, Bennett LeBow, Grant Woods, Don Barrett, Steve Berman, Marc Kasowitz, Russ Herman, Tom Miller, Hubert Humphrey, Richard Blumenthal, and Christine Gregoire were interviewed for this chapter.

Sources for the section on FDA, Wigand, and Greensboro include:

—Hilts, *Smokescreen'*

—Kluger, *Ashes to Ashes*

—Alix Freedman and Suein Hwang, "How Seven Individuals with Diverse Motives Halted Tobacco's Wars," *Wall Street Journal,* July 11, 1997

—Obermayer, "Tobacco Lawsuit Not So Easy for Judge"

—John Schwartz, "With Leadership in Transition FDA to Face Many Challenges in New Congress," *Washington Post,* December 1, 1996

—John Schwartz, "FDA's Kessler Will Resign Early in 1997," *Washington Post,* November 26, 1996

—John Schwartz, "FDA Chief Discloses High-Nicotine Leaf," *Washington Post,* June 22, 1994

—Tim Friend, "Kessler's FDA Makes Headway," *USA Today,* February 4, 1992

—Malcolm Gladwell, "FDA Chief Relishes Label of Lawman," *Washington Post,* October 24, 1991

—Malcolm Gladwell and Paul Valentine, "FDA Battles for Authority amid Generic-Drug Scandal," *Washington Post,* August 16, 1989

—Brenner, "The Man Who Knew Too Much"

—Transcript of *United States Tobacco Co. vs. U.S. Food and Drug Administration,* U.S. District Court, Greensboro, North Carolina, February 10, 1996

CHAPTER 7
MEET THE CHAIRMEN

Mike Moore, Don Barrett, Dick Scruggs, Phil Carlton, Mike Easley, Steve Berman, Grant Woods, Christine Gregoire, Bob Butterworth, Richard Blumenthal, Steve Parrish, John Coale, Hugh Rodham, Stan Chesley, Wendell Gauthier, and three tobacco negotiators were interviewed for this chapter. Herb Wachtell's firm and Philip Morris say that Wachtell was kept away from the talks by commitments to the Walt Disney Company.

Sources for this chapter include:

—Alix Freedman and Suein Hwang, "Peace Pipe: Philip Morris, RJR, and Tobacco Plaintiffs Discuss a Settlement," *Wall Street Journal,* April 16, 1997

—Sellers, "Geoff Bible Won't Quit"

—Rob Christensen, "Carlton Talking Tobacco," *Raleigh (North Carolina) News & Observer,* April 19, 1997

CHAPTER 8
OSTEEN'S RULING

Mike Moore, Gary Black, Phil Carlton, Joe Rice, Dick Scruggs, Grant Woods, Christine Gregoire, Steve Berman, John Coale, Wendell Gauthier, Bob Butterworth, Richard Blumenthal, Hubert Humphrey, Woody Wilner, and five tobacco industry lawyers were interviewed for this chapter.

Sources for the section on Philip Morris and Richmond include:
—Chip Jones, "Philip Morris USA Payroll Undergirds Area Economy," *Richmond Times-Dispatch,* July 13, 1997
—Chip Jones, "Bible Hints He'll Take Compromise," *Richmond Times-Dispatch,* April 25, 1997
—Sellers, "Geoff Bible Won't Quit"
—Obermayer, "Tobacco Lawsuit Not So Easy for Judge"
—Scott Solmo, "Judge's Past Poses No Conflict, Observers Say," *Greensboro (North Carolina) News & Record,* April 19, 1995

For the section on Ron Motley sources include:
—Greising, "The Big Four Who Battle Big Tobacco"
—Catherine Yang, "Look Who's Talking Settlement," *Business Week,* July 18, 1994

CHAPTER 9
TOO MANY LAWYERS

Mike Moore, Grant Woods, Christine Gregoire, Bob Butterworth, Joe Rice, Dick Scruggs, John Coale, Charles Zimmerman, Marc Kasowitz, Russ Herman, Bennett LeBow, Steve Berman, Phil Carlton, Tom Green, Richard Blumenthal, Hugh Rodham, Wendell Gauthier, and four other tobacco attorneys were interviewed for this chapter. One source asserts that Herb Wachtell was not at the meeting described on page 182.

Sources for this section include:
—Laura Barrow, "Why My Jury Let R. J. Reynolds Off," *Washington Post,* May 25, 1997
—Sheryl Gay Stolberg, "Beleaguered Tobacco Foe Holds Key to Talks," *New York Times,* June 4, 1997

CHAPTER 10
WALKOUT

Mike Moore, Grant Woods, Christine Gregoire, Bob Butterworth, Joe Rice, Dick Scruggs, John Coale, Charles Zimmerman, Marc Kasowitz, Russ Herman, Bennett LeBow, Steve Berman, Phil Carlton, Richard Blumenthal, Stan Chesley, Tom Miller, and three other tobacco attorneys were interviewed for this chapter.

Sources for this chapter include:
—Alix Freedman and Hilary Stout, "Tobacco Talks Hit Impasse on Immunity for Companies from Punitive Damages," *Wall Street Journal,* June 16, 1997
—Suein Hwang, "B.A.T Chief Tells Colleagues to Toughen Up," *Wall Street Journal,* June 17, 1997

Portions of the conversations between tobacco CEOs in this chapter were reconstructed from interviews with several company executives.

CHAPTER 11
SETTLEMENT DAY

Mike Moore, Grant Woods, Christine Gregoire, Bob Butterworth, Joe Rice, Dick Scruggs, John Coale, Marc Kasowitz, Russ Herman, Bennett LeBow, Steve Berman, Phil Carlton, Richard Blumenthal, Tom Green, Stan Chesley, Laura Wertheimer, Jeffrey Wigand, Bruce Lindsey, Hugh Rodham, Merrell Williams, and three other tobacco attorneys were interviewed for this chapter. Matt Myers denies mentioning Scott Harshbarger in the meeting with Senator Ted Kennedy. Other attendees dispute his account.

Sources for this chapter include:
—David Barstow and Lucy Morgan, "Tobacco Deal Now a Matter of Time," *St. Petersburg (Florida) Times,* June 17, 1997
—Saundra Torry and John Schwartz, "Tobacco Agreement Needed Nudge from White House," *Washington Post,* June 23, 1997
—Adrianne Flynn and Tim Koors, "Anatomy of the Deal," *Arizona Republic,* June 29, 1997
—Freedman and Hwang, "Burning Questions: Tobacco Pact's Limits—And Its Loopholes—Presage Fierce Debate"
—Matthew Cooper, "Ifs, Ands, and Butts," *Newsweek,* June 30, 1997
—Gregg Otolski, "The Tobacco Wars: Wigand's Credibility," *Louisville Courier-Journal,* March 29, 1996

Portions of the conversations between tobacco CEOs in this chapter were reconstructed from interviews with several company executives.

CHAPTER 12
THE LEGACY OF JACKIE THOMPSON

Hubert Humphrey, Mike Moore, Dick Scruggs, Gary Black, and Allan Kaplan were interviewed for this chapter.

Sources for this chapter include:
—Kluger, *Ashes to Ashes'*
—Freedman and Hwang, "Burning Questions: Tobacco Pact's Limits—And Its Loopholes—Presage Fierce Debate"
—Anne Platt McGinn, "Cigarette Traffickers Go Global," *World Watch,* July/August 1997
—Jill Smolowe, "Big Tobacco Fesses Up and Pays Up—$368.5 Billion, but Congress Must Approve the Deal," *Time* magazine, June 30, 1997
—Michael Frisby, "Opponents of Tobacco Pact Face Big Hurdle: Clinton," *Wall Street Journal,* August 8, 1997
—"The World to Play For," *Economist,* April 19, 1997

—Transcript for CNN, *Talk Back Live,* August 25, 1997

—"Fee Dispute in Florida Tobacco Case Gets Testy," CNN Interactive (Web site office), September 10, 1997

—Milo Geyelin, "Florida's Anti-Tobacco Lawyers Try to Stall Pact for More Fees," *Wall Street Journal,* September 10, 1997

—Bob Williams, "Looking East for Salvation," *Raleigh (North Carolina) News & Observer,* April 10, 1995

—"European Tobacco Industry Sees Little Effect from U.S. Settlement," *Extel Examiner* (London), June 23, 1997

—Norihiko Shirouzo, "Low-Smoke Cigarette Catches Fire in Japan," *Wall Street Journal,* September 8, 1997

—Tim Carvell, "Counsel for the Plaintiff," *Fortune,* September 29, 1997

Appendix

The Settlement

Contents

(continued)

Appendix

The Settlement

June 20, 1997

PREAMBLE

This legislation would mandate a total reformation and restructuring of how tobacco products are manufactured, marketed and distributed in this country. The nation can thereby see real and swift progress in preventing underage use of tobacco, addressing the adverse health effects of tobacco use and changing the corporate culture of the tobacco industry.

The Food and Drug Administration ("FDA") and other public health authorities view the use of tobacco products by our nation's children as a "pediatric disease" of epic and worsening proportions that results in new generations of tobacco-dependent children and adults. There is also a consensus within the scientific and medical communities that tobacco products are inherently dangerous and cause cancer, heart disease and other serious adverse health effects.

The FDA and other health authorities have concluded that virtually all new users of tobacco products are under legal age. President Clinton, the FDA, the Federal Trade Commission ("FTC"), state attorneys general and public health authorities all believe that tobacco advertising and marketing contribute significantly to the use of nicotine-containing tobacco products by adolescents. These officials have concluded that because past efforts to restrict advertising and marketing have failed to curb adolescent tobacco use, sweeping new restrictions on the sale, promotion and distribution of such products are needed.

Until now, federal and state governments have lacked many of the legal means and resources they need to address the societal problems caused by the use of tobacco products. These officials have been armed only with crude regulatory tools which they view as inadequate to achieve the public health objectives with which they are charged.

This legislation greatly strengthens both the federal and state governments' regulatory arsenal and furnishes them with additional resources needed to address a public health problem that affects millions of Americans, including most importantly underage tobacco use. Further, it is contemplated that certain of the obligations of the tobacco companies will be implemented by a binding, enforceable contractual protocol.

The legislation reaffirms individuals' right of access to the courts, to civil trial by jury and to full compensatory damages. Resolution through the Act of potential punitive-damages liability of the tobacco industry for past conduct is only made in the context of the comprehensive settlement proposed by the legislation. It is not intended to have precedential effect, nor does it express any position adverse to the imposition of punitive damages in general or as applied to any other specific industry, case, controversy or product and does not provide any authority whatsoever regarding the propriety of punitive damages.

Among other things, the new regime would:

Confirm FDA's authority to regulate tobacco products under the Food, Drug and Cosmetic Act, making FDA not only the preeminent regulatory agency with respect to the manufacture, marketing and distribution of tobacco products but also requiring the tobacco industry to fund FDA's oversight out of ongoing payments by the manufacturers pursuant to the new regime ("Industry Payments").

Go beyond FDA's current regulations to ban all outdoor tobacco advertising and to eliminate cartoon characters and human figures, such as Joe Camel and the Marlboro Man, two tobacco icons which the public health community has long assailed as advertising appealing to our nation's youth.

Impose and provide funding out of the Industry Payments for an aggressive federal enforcement program, including a state-administered retail licensing system, to stop minors from obtaining tobacco products, while in no way preventing the States from enacting additional measures.

Ensure that the FDA and the states have the regulatory flexibility to address issues of particular concern to public health officials, such as youth tobacco usage and tobacco dependence.

Subject the tobacco industry to severe financial surcharges in the event underage tobacco use does not decline radically over the next decade.

Empower the federal government to set national standards controlling the manufacturing of tobacco products and the ingredients used in such products.

Provide new and flexible regulatory enforcement powers to ensure that the tobacco industry works to develop and introduce "less-hazardous tobacco products," including, among other things, vesting FDA with the power to regulate the levels of nicotine in tobacco products.

Require the manufacturers of tobacco products to disclose all previously non-public internal laboratory research and all new internal laboratory research generated in the future relating to the health effects or safety of their products.

Establish a minimum federal standard with tough restrictions on smoking in public places with enforcement funding from the Industry Payments, while preserving the authority of state and local governments to enact even more severe standards.

Authorize and fund from Industry Payments a $500 million annual, national education-oriented counter-advertising and tobacco control campaign seeking to discourage the initiation of tobacco use by children and adolescents and to encourage current tobacco product users to quit use of the products.

Authorize and fund from Industry Payments the annual payment to all states of significant, ongoing financial compensation to fund health benefits program expenditures and to establish and fund a tobacco products liability judgments and settlement fund.

Authorize and fund from Industry Payments a nationwide program, administered through state governments and the private sector, of smoking cessation.

The sale of tobacco products to adults would remain legal but subject to restrictive measures to ensure that they are not sold to underage purchasers. These measures respond directly to concerns voiced by federal and state public health officials, the public health community and the public at large that the tobacco industry should be subject to the strictest scrutiny and regulatory oversight. This statute imposes regulatory controls, including civil and criminal penalties, equal to, and in many respects exceeding, those imposed on other regulated industries. Further, it imposes on tobacco manufacturers the obligation to provide funding from Industry Payments for an array of public health initiatives.

The sale, distribution, marketing, advertising and use of tobacco products are activities substantially affecting interstate commerce. Such products are sold, marketed, advertised and distributed in interstate commerce on a nationwide basis, and have a substantial effect on the nation's economy. The sale, distribution, marketing, advertising and use of such products are also activities substantially affecting interstate commerce by virtue of the health care and other costs that federal and state governmental authorities have attributed to usage of tobacco products.

Various civil actions are pending in state and federal courts arising from the use, marketing or sale of tobacco products. Among these actions are cases brought by some 40 state attorneys general, cases brought by certain cities and counties, the

Commonwealth of Puerto Rico and other third-party payor cases seeking to recover monies spent treating tobacco-related diseases and for the protection of minors and consumers. Also pending in courts throughout the United States are various private putative class-action lawsuits brought on behalf of individuals claiming to be dependent upon and injured by tobacco products. Additionally, a multitude of individual suits have been filed against the tobacco products manufacturers and/or their distributors, trade associations, law firms and consultants.

All of these civil actions are complex, slow moving, expensive and burdensome, not only for the litigants but also for the nation's state and federal judiciaries. Moreover, none of those litigations has to date resulted in the collection of any monies to compensate smokers or third-party payors. Only national legislation offers the prospect of a swift, fair, equitable and consistent result that would serve the public interest by (1) ensuring that a portion of the costs of treatment for diseases and adverse health effects linked to the use of tobacco products is borne by the manufacturers of these products; and (2) restricting nationwide the sale, distribution, marketing and advertising of tobacco products to persons of legal age. The unique position occupied by tobacco in the nation's history and economy; the magnitude of actual and potential tobacco-related litigation; the need to avoid the cost, expense, uncertainty and inconsistency associated with such protracted litigation; the need to limit the sale, distribution, marketing and advertising of tobacco products to persons of legal age; and the need to educate the public, especially young people, of the health effects of using tobacco products all dictate that it would be in the public interest to enact this legislation to facilitate a resolution of the matters described.

Public health authorities believe that the societal benefits of this legislation, in human and economic terms, would be vast. In particular, FDA has found that reducing underage tobacco use by 50% "would prevent well over 60,000 early deaths." FDA has estimated that the monetary value of its present regulations will be worth up to $43 billion per year in reduced medical costs, improved productivity and the benefit of avoiding the premature death of loved ones. This statute, which extends far beyond anything FDA has previously proposed or attempted, can be expected to produce human and economic benefits many times greater than such existing regulations.

As part of this settlement, the tobacco companies recognize the historic changes that will be occurring to their business. They will fully comply with increased federal regulation, focus intense efforts on dramatic reductions in youth access and youth tobacco usage, recognize that the regulatory scheme encourages the development of products with reduced risk and acknowledge the predominant public health positions associated with the use of tobacco products.

[Source/precedent: FDA Rule]

TITLE I:
Reformation of the Tobacco Industry

Title I of the legislation would incorporate and expand upon FDA's recent regulation of nicotine-containing tobacco products.

The following rules would apply to all tobacco products sold in the United States (including all its territories and possessions, as well as duty-free shops within U.S. borders). The new regime would be allowed to operate as described below for five years. FDA would have authority to make revisions even within this period under extraordinary circumstances. Thereafter, the FDA would be authorized to review and revise the rules under applicable Agency procedures.

A. *Restrictions on Marketing and Advertising*

The advertising and marketing of tobacco products would be drastically curtailed, including in ways that exceed the FDA Rule as originally promulgated and in ways that have previously been challenged on First Amendment grounds. As in the FDA Rule the new regime would:

Prohibit the use of non-tobacco brand names as brand names of tobacco products except for tobacco products in existence as of January 1, 1995 (897.16(a)) (The citations in this and in the next section are to Part 897 of the FDA's tobacco regulations, 61 Fed. Reg. 44396 [August 28, 1996].

Restrict tobacco product advertising to FDA-specified media (897.30(a)(1)–(2)).

Restrict permissible tobacco product advertising to black text on a white background except for advertising in adult-only facilities and in adult publications (897.32(a)–(b)).

Require cigarette and smokeless tobacco product advertisements to carry the FDA-mandated statement of intended use ("Nicotine Delivery Device") (897.32(c)).

Ban all non-tobacco merchandise, including caps, jackets or bags bearing the name, logo or selling message of a tobacco brand (897.34(a)).

Ban offers of non-tobacco items or gifts based on proof of purchase of tobacco products (897.34(b)).

Ban sponsorships, including concerts and sporting events, in the name, logo or selling message of a tobacco brand (897.34(c)).

Further, building on and going beyond the FDA Rule, the new regime would:

Ban the use of human images and cartoon characters—thereby eliminating Joe Camel and the Marlboro Man—in all tobacco advertising and on tobacco product packages.

Ban all outdoor tobacco product advertising, including in enclosed stadia as well as brand advertising directed outside from a retail establishment (modifies 897.30(a)(1) and extends 897.30(b)).

Prohibit tobacco product advertising on the Internet unless designed to be inaccessible in or from the United States.

Establish nationwide restrictions in non-adult-only facilities on point of sale advertising with a view toward minimizing the impact of such advertising on minors. These provisions, which are detailed in Appendix VII, restrict point of sale advertising that was otherwise permitted in retail establishments by the FDA Rule.

Ban direct and indirect payments for tobacco product placement in movies, television programs and video games.

Prohibit direct and indirect payments to "glamorize" tobacco use in media appealing to minors, including recorded and live performances of music.

Without limiting the FDA's normal rule-making authority in this area, require that the use, in both existing and future brand styles, of words currently employed as product descriptors (e.g., "light" or "low 'tar'") be accompanied by a mandatory disclaimer in advertisements (e.g., "Brand X not shown to be less hazardous than other cigarettes"); exemplars of all new advertising and tobacco products labeling shall be submitted to FDA concurrently with their introduction into the marketplace for FDA's ongoing review.

[Source/precedent: FDA Rule; 21 C.F.R. 101.70]

B. Warnings, Labeling and Packaging

The federally mandated warning labels on cigarettes were last changed in 1984. Since then a number of countries, including Canada and members of the European Union, have imposed new warning labels. Further, the Federal Trade Commission's methodology to measure the "tar" and nicotine yields of cigarettes has been criticized as producing misleading information.

1. The legislation, through amendments to the Federal Cigarette Labeling and Advertising Act and the Comprehensive Smokeless Tobacco Health Education Act, would mandate new rotating warnings, to be introduced concurrently into

the distribution chain on all tobacco product packages and cartons, and to be rotated quarterly in all advertisements. For cigarettes, the warnings would be:

"WARNING: Cigarettes are addictive"
"WARNING: Tobacco smoke can harm your children"
"WARNING: Cigarettes cause fatal lung disease"
"WARNING: Cigarettes cause cancer"
"WARNING: Cigarettes cause strokes and heart disease"
"WARNING: Smoking during pregnancy can harm your baby"
"WARNING: Smoking can kill you"
"WARNING: Tobacco smoke causes fatal lung disease in non-smokers"
"WARNING: Quitting smoking now greatly reduces serious risks to your health"

For smokeless tobacco products, the warnings would be:

"WARNING: This product can cause mouth cancer"
"WARNING: This product can cause gum disease and tooth loss"
"WARNING: This product is not a safe alternative to cigarettes"
"WARNING: Smokeless tobacco is addictive"

For cigarettes, the warnings would occupy 25% of the front panel of the package (including packs and cartons) and would appear on the upper portion thereof. The legislation would contain a grandfather provision for existing brands with flip-top boxes comprising less than 25% of the front panel. For smokeless tobacco products, the warnings would appear on the principal display panel (e.g., a band around the can for moist smokeless tobacco products) and would occupy 25% of the display panel. The warnings would be printed in line with current Canadian standards (e.g., 17-point type with appropriate adjustments depending on length of required text) and in an alternating black-on-white and white-on-black format. The size and placement of warnings in advertisements would follow the requirements set forth in the existing U.K. standards. As described in Appendix I, the warning text and, where relevant, "tar" and nicotine (or other constituent) yield information would occupy 20% of press advertisements.

Cigarette and smokeless tobacco product packages would also carry the FDA-mandated statement of intended use ("Nicotine Delivery Device") on the side of the pack.

2. The FDA would be required to promulgate a rule governing the testing, reporting and disclosure of tobacco smoke constituents that the Agency determines the public should be informed of to protect public health, including, but not limited to "tar," nicotine and carbon monoxide. This authority would be transferred from the FTC and would include the authority to require label and advertising disclosures relating to "tar" and nicotine, as well as disclosures by other means relating to other constituents.

[Source/precedent: Canadian warning regulations; FDA Rule; FDCA, 21 U.S.C. Section 360h, with conforming amendment in light of FCLAA]

C. Restrictions on Access to Tobacco Products

Preventing youth access to tobacco products is a major objective of this legislation and the FDA Rule. Without preventing state and local governments from imposing stricter measures, the legislation would incorporate every access restriction of the FDA Rule, and more. As in the FDA Rule, the legislation would:

Set a minimum age of 18 to purchase tobacco products (897.14(a)).

Require retailers to check photo identification of anyone under 27 (897.14 (b)(1)–(2)).

Establish the basic requirement of face-to-face transactions for all sales of tobacco products (897.14(c)).

Ban the sale of tobacco products from opened packages (897.14(d)).

Establish a minimum package size of 20 cigarettes (897.16(b)).

Impose retailer compliance obligations to ensure that all self-service displays, advertising, labeling and other items conform with all applicable requirements (897.14(e)).

Ban the sampling of tobacco products (897.16(d)).

Ban the distribution of tobacco products through the mail, including redemption of coupons, except for sales subject to proof of age, with a review after two years by FDA to determine if minors are obtaining tobacco products through the mail (goes beyond 897.16(c)(2)(i)).

Building on and going beyond the FDA Rule, the legislation would:

Ban all sales of tobacco products through vending machines (goes beyond 897.16(c)(2)(ii)).

Ban self-service displays of tobacco products except in adult-only facilities. In all other retail outlets, tobacco products must be placed out of reach of consumers (i.e., behind the counter or under lock and key) or, if on the counter, not visible or accessible to consumers (goes beyond (897.16(c)(2)(ii)).

[Source/precedent: FDA Rule]

D. Licensing of Retail Tobacco Product Sellers

The legislation would mandate minimum federal standards for a retail licensing program that the federal government and state and local authorities would enforce through funding provided by the Industry Payments. Any entity that sells directly to consumers—whether a manufacturer, wholesaler, importer, distributor or retailer—would require a license.

Elements of the licensing program would include:

Mandating compliance with the Act as a condition to obtain and hold a license.

Penalties for violations (See Appendix II).

Suspension or revocation of licenses (on a site-by-site basis) for certain violations (see Appendix II).

A requirement that distribution of tobacco products for resale to consumers be made only to licensed entities.

Licensing fees to cover the administrative costs of issuing state licenses (all other costs covered as noted above).

Comparable federal licensing programs (with federal enforcement) for military facilities, U.S. government installations abroad, and other U.S. territories and possessions not otherwise under the jurisdiction of the states (including duty-free shops within U.S. borders).

Comparable licensing programs to govern tobacco product sales on Indian lands (see Appendix III).

[Source/precedent: Various state laws governing sales of tobacco products and alcoholic beverages]

E. Regulation of Tobacco Product Development and Manufacturing

This legislation, for the first time, would impose a regulatory regime to govern the development and manufacturing of cigarettes and smokeless tobacco products, including FDA approval of the ingredients used in such products and imposition of standards for reducing the level of certain constituents, including nicotine.

Elements of the regulatory regime would include:

1. Tobacco products shall have the same definition as contained in the FDA

Rule. Jurisdiction shall also cover Roll Your Own, Little Cigars, Fine Cut, etc.

2. Tobacco will continue to be categorized as a "drug" and a "device" under the Food, Drug and Cosmetic Act ("FDCA"). The Agency's authority to regulate the products as restricted medical devices will be explicitly recognized and tobacco products will be classified as a new subcategory of a Class II device pursuant to 21 U.S.C. Section 360c. FDCA shall apply to these products as provided by the Act and the amendments to FDCA contained herein.

3. The Class II classification shall permit FDA to require product modification of tobacco products, including the regulation of nicotine content, and shall provide that the sale of tobacco products to adults in the form that conforms to Performance Standards established for tobacco products pursuant to Section 514 ("Section 514") of the FDCA (21 U.S.C. Section 360d) shall be permitted notwithstanding 21 U.S.C. Sections 360f, 352(j) and 360h(e).

4. Reduced Risks Products

Products sold that an objective, reasonable consumer would believe pose less of a health risk:

> Tobacco product manufacturers will be barred from making claims that could reasonably be interpreted to state or imply a reduced health risk unless the manufacturer demonstrates to FDA that the product scientifically does in fact "significantly reduce the risk to health" from ordinary tobacco products. Currently employed product descriptors such as "light" and "low 'tar'" will be regulated as described in 1(A) above.

> FDA would have to approve all health claims (direct or implied), as well as the content and placement of any such claims in advertisements, to prevent the public from being misled and to prevent the advertisement from being used to expand, or prevent the contraction of, the marketplace.

> For "less-hazardous tobacco products," FDA will be authorized to permit scientifically based specific health claims and to permit exceptions to the advertising restrictions that apply to other products if FDA determines that such advertising would reduce harm and promote the public health. The FDA will promulgate a rule to govern how these determinations will be made.

> The manufacturers will be required to notify FDA of any technology that they develop or acquire and that reduces the risk from tobacco products and, for a commercially reasonable fee, to cross-license all such technology, but only to those companies also covered by the same obligations. Procedural protections will be built in to resolve license-fee disputes, if the private parties cannot agree among themselves first. If the technology reported to the FDA is in

the early development stages, the manufacturer will be provided confidentiality protection during the development process.

The Agency shall also have the authority to mandate the introduction of "less-hazardous tobacco products" that are technologically feasible, after a formal rule making subject to the Administrative Procedures Act ("APA"), with the right of judicial review. In doing so, the Agency shall have the authority to mandate that a manufacturer subject to this Act who owns such technology (at such manufacturer's election) either introduce such products, or, at a commercially reasonable market rate, license such technology to a manufacturer who agrees to bring the technology to market in a reasonable time frame. In the event that no manufacturer or licensee introduces such "less-hazardous tobacco products," within a reasonable time frame set by FDA, then the U.S. Public Health Service may produce either itself, or through a licensing arrangement, any such product.

The goal of any rule mandating the introduction into the marketplace of "less-hazardous tobacco products" for which the technology exists is to guarantee that a mechanism exists to ensure that products which appear to hold out the hope of reducing risk are actually tested and made available in the marketplace and not held back.

5. Performance Standards

To further the public health, to promote the production of "reduced risk" tobacco products and to minimize the harm to consumers of tobacco products by insuring that the best available, feasible safety technology becomes the industry standard, FDA will have the authority to promulgate Performance Standards pursuant to Section 514 that require the modification of tobacco products to reduce the harm caused by those products (including the components that produce drug dependence), provided that the standard shall not require the prohibition on the sale to adults of traditional tobacco products in the basic form as described in the August 28, 1996 FDA Rule at 61 Fed. Reg. at 44616 (to be codified at 21 C.F.R. Section 897.3).

Specifically:

A. For a period of no fewer than 12 years following the effective date of the Act, the product Performance Standards will be governed by the following: The Agency shall be permitted to adopt Performance Standards that require the modification of existing tobacco products, including the gradual reduction, but not the elimination, of nicotine yields, and the possible elimination of other constituents or other harmful components of the tobacco product, based upon a finding that the modification: (a) will result in a significant reduction of the health risks associated with such products to consumers thereof; (b) is technologically feasible; and (c) will not result in the creation of a significant demand for contraband or other tobacco products that do not meet the product safety standard. In determining the risk of the demand for a market in contraband products, the FDA shall take into account the number of dependent tobacco product users and the availability, or lack thereof, of alternative products then on the market and such other factors as the Agency may deem relevant.

The authority to require such product modification can be exercised upon a showing of "substantial evidence," based upon an administrative record developed through a formal rule making subject to the Administrative Procedures Act, with the right of judicial review, and any such modification shall be subject to the current procedures of the Regulatory Reform Act of 1996 to provide time and a process for Congress to intervene should it so choose. In the event a party subsequently files a petition seeking an administrative review of whether a modification has, in fact, resulted in the creation of a significant demand for contraband or other tobacco products that do not meet the safety standard and FDA denies the petition, the petitioner shall have the right to seek judicial review of the denial of the petition.

Additionally:

Within one year of the effective date of this Act, the FDA shall establish a Scientific Advisory Committee to examine and determine the effects of the alteration of nicotine yield levels and to examine and determine whether there is a threshold level below which nicotine yields do not produce drug dependence and, if so, to determine that level, and also review any other safety, dependence or health issue so designated by FDA.

Separate from and without detracting from the Agency's authority under the requirements of the Section 514 Performance Standards noted above, effective three years from the date of enactment of this Act, no cigarette shall be sold in the United States which exceeds a 12 mg "tar" yield, using the testing methodology now being used by the Federal Trade Commission.

B. After the initial twelve-year period, the Agency will be permitted to set product safety standards that go beyond the standards it is authorized to set pursuant to the above noted provisions and, if it does so, any such product Performance Standards shall be governed by the following: The Agency will be permitted to require the alteration of tobacco products then being marketed, including the elimination of nicotine and the elimination of other constituents or other demonstrated harmful components of the tobacco product, (the elimination of nicotine or other harmful constituent shall not be deemed to violate the prohibition on the sale of traditional tobacco products to adults, even if it results in a reduction of the number of the consumers who use the tobacco products then remaining on the market), based upon a finding that: (a) the safety standard will result in a significant overall reduction of the health risks to tobacco consumers as a group (this includes the reduction in harm which will result from decreased drug dependence from the reduction and/or elimination of nicotine from [i] those who continue to use tobacco products, but less often and [ii] those who stop using tobacco products); (b) the modification is technologically feasible; and (c) the modification will not result in the creation of a significant demand for contraband or other tobacco products that do not meet the safety standard. In determining the overall health benefit of a change, the Agency shall consider the number of dependent tobacco users then in existence, the availability and demonstrated market acceptance of alternate products then on the market, and the effectiveness of smoking-cessation techniques and devices then on the market and such other factors as the Agency may deem relevant.

Given the significance of such an action, the Agency will be permitted to require the elimination of nicotine or take such other action that would have an effect comparable to the elimination of nicotine based upon a "preponderance of the evidence" pursuant to, at a manufacturer's election, a Part 12 hearing, or notice and comment rule making, with a right of judicial review. Any such action shall be phased in, and no such phase-in shall begin in less than two years, to permit time for a meaningful congressional review pursuant to the current procedures of the Regulatory Reform Act of 1996. In the event a party subsequently files a petition seeking an administrative review of whether a modification has, in fact, resulted in the creation of a significant demand for contraband or other tobacco products that do not meet the safety standard and the FDA denies the petition, the petitioner shall have the right to seek judicial review of the denial of the petition. In any judicial review, the deference accorded to the Agency's findings shall depend upon the extent to which the matter at issue is then within the Agency's field of expertise.

6. Manufacturing Oversight

The legislation would subject tobacco product manufacturers to good manufacturing practice standards ("GMPs") comparable to those applicable to medical device manufacturers, food companies and other FDA regulated industries, but tailored specifically to tobacco products. In this regard there would be:

Implementation of a quality control system (e.g., to prevent contamination).

Inspection of tobacco product materials (e.g., to ensure compliance with quality standards).

Requirements for proper handling of finished product.

Tolerances for pesticide chemical residues in or on commodities in the possession of the manufacturer; existing EPA authority and oversight is retained.

Inspection authority comparable to FDA's authority over other FDA-regulated products, including the ability to enter manufacturing plants and demand certain records.

Record-keeping and reporting requirements.

Tobacco farmers will face no greater regulatory burden than the producers of other raw products regulated by the federal government.

[Source/precedent: FDA Rule; FDCA, 21 U.S.C. Sections 346a, 360]

7. Access to Company Information

The Act would ensure that previously non-public or confidential files of the tobacco industry—including internal documents—are disclosed to FDA and private litigants. The details of the arrangement are set forth in documents from health research and the public as given in Appendix VI II.

Any subpoena authority FDA has with respect to manufacturers of medical devices generally would also apply to tobacco product manufacturers.

F. Non-Tobacco Ingredients

Currently, at the federal level, tobacco manufacturers are required only to submit aggregated ingredient information (not by brand or company) to HHS for monitoring and review. Nor do tobacco products manufacturers currently disclose to consumers ingredients information for each of the tobacco products they sell.

The legislation would supersede the current often-criticized federal ingredient law and confirm FDA's authority to evaluate all additives in tobacco products. No non-tobacco ingredient could be used in manufacturing tobacco products unless the manufacturer can demonstrate that such ingredient is not harmful under the intended conditions of use. Further, the legislation would require the manufacturers to disclose to FDA the ingredients and the amounts thereof in each brand. In addition, it would require manufacturers to disclose ingredient information to the public under regulations comparable to what current federal law requires for food products, reflecting the intended conditions of use.

Under this proposed legislation:

Manufacturers would be required to provide FDA on a confidential basis a list of all ingredients, substances and compounds (other than tobacco, water or reconstituted tobacco sheet made wholly from tobacco) which are added by the manufacturer to the tobacco, paper or filter of the tobacco product by brand and by quantity in each brand. For each such item, the manufacturer would identify whether or not it believes that the item would be exempt from public disclosure under the legislation.

Manufacturers would be required to submit, within five years of the enactment of the Act, for each ingredient currently added to the tobacco product, a safety assessment, based on the best available evidence, that there is a reasonable certainty in the minds of competent scientists that the ingredient (up to a specified amount) is not harmful under the intended conditions of use. FDA shall promulgate applicable regulations within 12 months.

Within a statutory time period, FDA must review assessment(s) in accordance with the applicable standard; within 90 days, FDA shall approve or disapprove an ingredient's safety, and if FDA takes no action, the ingredient is deemed approved. FDA may also challenge any manufacturer's assertion that an ingredient would be exempt from disclosure to consumers under applicable regulations comparable to what current federal law requires for food products.

New ingredients or use of current ingredients beyond the specified maximum amount are subject to a comparable process prior to use.

FDA would be required to protect as strictly confidential ingredient information not otherwise subject to public disclosure. If not subject to such disclosure, this information will be treated as trade secrets under federal law, exempt from FOIA requests and protected by procedures which shall include the designation of an agent who will store it in a locked cabinet, maintain a record of any person who has access to the information and require a written confidentiality commitment from any such person.

Manufacturers would be required to disclose to the public ingredients information pursuant to regulations comparable to what current federal law requires for food products. During an initial five-year period, each ingredient that would be exempt from disclosure under the food regime would be presumed not to be subject to disclosure unless FDA disproves its safety. However, manufacturers would be required to disclose all ingredients which they have been compelled to publicly disclose with respect to a particular brand in order to comply with a statute or regulation (e.g., MA Chapter 94 Section 307B).

Manufacturers would be required to have procedures for the selection, testing, purchase, storage and use of ingredients.

The Act would:

Provide for record keeping regarding ingredients.

Allow FDA access to such records, with protection of proprietary information.

[Source/precedent: MA Chapter 94, Section 307B; 21 C.F.R. Sections 101.4, 101.105 and 101.170; 18 U.S.C. Section 1905; 5 U.S.C. Section 552(b)(4); MA proposed reg. 105 C.M.R. Section 660.200(G)]

G. Compliance and Corporate Culture

A key element in achieving the Act's goals will be forcing a fundamental change in the way the tobacco industry does business. Accordingly, the Act will provide for means to ensure that the industry will not only comply with the letter of the law but will also have powerful incentives to prevent underage usage of tobacco products and to strive to develop and market less-hazardous tobacco products.

First, manufacturers would be required to create plans, with an annual review and update, to:

Ensure compliance with all applicable laws and regulations.

Identify ways to achieve the goals of reduced youth access to and incidence of underage consumption of tobacco products and provide internal incentives for doing so.

Provide internal incentives to develop products with reduced risk.

Second, with a special emphasis on laws and regulations that make it unlawful to sell tobacco products to underage persons and other laws directed at the issue of underage tobacco use, the manufacturers must implement compliance programs that include, at a minimum, the following elements:

Compliance standards and procedures to be followed by employees and agents that are reasonably capable of reducing the prospect of violations.

Assignment to specific individual(s) within high-level personnel of the organization of overall responsibility to oversee compliance with the relevant standards and procedures, especially in regard to preventing underage tobacco use.

Use of due care not to delegate substantial discretionary authority to individuals who the organization knows, or should have known through the exercise of due diligence, have a propensity to disregard corporate policy.

Steps to communicate relevant standards and procedures to all employees and other agents (including lobbyists), e.g., by requiring participation in training programs or by disseminating publications that explain in a practical manner what is required.

Internal audits, hotlines and other measures to promote compliance.

Appropriate disciplinary mechanisms and measures (e.g., discipline of employees who violate marketing restrictions).

Reasonable steps to respond appropriately to a violation and to prevent further similar violations.

Furthermore, the Act would provide "whistle-blowers" in the tobacco industry with the maximum protection available under current federal statutes.

Beyond compliance with the letter of the law, manufacturers would be required to take affirmative steps in furtherance of the spirit of the new regime, including:

Promulgating corporate principles that express and explain the company's commitment to compliance, reductions of underage tobacco use, and development of reduced risk tobacco products.

Designating a specific individual within high-level personnel of the organization with appropriate responsibility and authority to promote efforts to attain these new standards.

Providing reports to shareholders on compliance as well as progress toward meeting these new standards.

Manufacturers would also be required to work with retail organizations on compliance, including retailer compliance checks and financial incentives for compliance.

Third, each tobacco manufacturer would require all contract lobbyists (and any other third parties who may engage in lobbying activities on behalf of a manufacturer) to agree that they will not support or oppose any state or federal legislation, or seek or oppose any governmental action on any matter, without the manufacturer's express authorization. Manufacturers would also require anyone lobbying on their behalf to agree in writing that: (a) they are aware of and will fully comply with all applicable laws and regulations; (b) they have reviewed and will fully comply with the Act as it applies to them; (c) they have reviewed and will fully comply with the consent decree as it applies to them; and (d) they have reviewed and will fully abide by the manufacturer's business conduct policies and any other policies and commitments as they apply, especially those related to prevention of youth tobacco usage.

Fourth, within 90 days after the Act's effective date, the Tobacco Institute and the Council for Tobacco Research, U.S.A. would be dissolved and disbanded. Tobacco product manufacturers would be permitted to form new trade associations only in accordance with strict procedures and federal oversight designed to ensure compliance with antitrust and other applicable laws. (See Appendix IV.)

Finally, companies would be subject to fines and penalties (including "Scarlet Letter" advertising) for breaching their obligations vis-à-vis the development, implementation and enforcement of compliance plans and corporate principles. These penalties shall follow the scheme set forth in the Clean Air Act, up to $25,000 per day per violation with a total not to exceed $200,000. In addition, each manufacturer's employees shall be directed to report to that manufacturer's compliance officer any known or alleged violations of this Act by retailers or distributors. In accordance with procedures established by FDA, the compliance officer shall be required to furnish all such reports to FDA for reference to appropriate federal or state enforcement authorities. The manufacturer shall be subject to fines or penalties in the event its compliance officer fails to furnish any such reports to FDA.

[Source/precedent: Federal organizational sentencing guidelines; various federal consent decrees; various corporate environmental programs]

H. Effective Dates

Many of the foregoing requirements relating to the reformation of the tobacco industry will become effective shortly after the Act is signed by the president; including the following categories of new rules, which will be implemented on the dates indicated:

Category / Effective dates on final passage
Retail product displays / 9 months
Retail signage / 5 months
Advertising / 9 months
Package labeling / 1/3 in 90 days
    1/3 in 120 days
    1/3 in 180 days
Sponsorships / 12/31/98
Vending machines / 12 months
Sampling / 3 months
GMPs / 24 months in accordance with rule making, whichever is later
Corporate compliance / 12 months
Face-to-face transactions / 3 months
Ban on sales of open packs / 3 months
20-cigarettes-per-pack minimum / 3 months
Puerto Rico pack size / 12 months

TITLE II:
"Look-Back" Provisions/State Enforcement Incentives

A central aim of this legislation is to achieve dramatic and immediate reductions in the number of underage consumers of tobacco products. The legislation accordingly contains a "look-back" provision giving tobacco product manufacturers significant economic incentives to take every possible step to ensure that the advertising, marketing and distribution requirements of this Act are met, and imposing substantial surcharges on the manufacturers in the event that underage tobacco-use reduction targets are not achieved.

The "look-back" provision sets targets for the dramatic reduction of current levels of underage tobacco use (as measured by the University of Michigan's National High School Drug Use Survey, "Monitoring the Future"). Underage use of cigarette products must decline by at least 30% from estimated levels over the last decade by the fifth year after the legislation takes effect, by at least 50% from estimated levels over the last decade by the seventh year after the legislation takes effect by at least 60% from estimated levels over the last decade by the tenth year after the legislation takes effect and remain at such reduced levels or below thereafter. (These required reductions amount to even steeper declines from current levels of underage smoking.) Underage use of smokeless tobacco products must decline by at least 25% from current levels by the fifth year after the legislation takes effect, by at least 35% from current levels by the seventh year after the legislation takes effect by at least 45% from current levels by the tenth year after the legislation takes effect and remain at such reduced levels or below thereafter. FDA will annually assess the prevalence of underage tobacco use (based on the methodology employed by the University of Michigan survey) to determine whether these targets have been met.

If a target has not been met, FDA will impose a mandatory surcharge on the relevant industry (cigarette or smokeless tobacco) based upon an approximation of the present value of the profit the industry would earn over the lives of all underage users in excess of the target (subject to an annual cap of $2 billion for the cigarette industry [adjusted each year for inflation] and a comparably derived cap for the smokeless tobacco industry). Tobacco product manufacturers could receive a partial abatement of this surcharge (up to 75%) only if they could thereafter prove to FDA that they had fully complied with the Act, had taken all reasonably available measures to reduce youth tobacco use and had not taken any action to undermine the achievement of the required reductions.

A fuller description is provided in Appendix V.

In addition, the proposed Act goes well beyond the provisions of the Synar Amendment's "no tobacco sales to minors" law and related regulations, 42 U.S.C. Section 300x-26, and the Final Rule promulgated thereunder, which became effec-

tive February 20, 1996 (61 Fed. Reg., June 19, 1996). The proposed Act requires
the several states to undertake significant enforcement steps designed to dramati-
cally reduce the incidence of youth smoking and youth access to tobacco products.
These enforcement obligations are funded by Industry Payments. Each state must
maintain specific levels of enforcement effort, or the state risks the loss of a significant portion of the health care program funds otherwise payable to the state under
the Act. Amounts withheld from states not doing an adequate enforcement job will
be reallocated to states with a superior "no sales to minors" enforcement record. No
state will be held responsible for sales to underage consumers outside that state's
jurisdiction.

The details of these state enforcement incentives are set forth in Appendix VI.

TITLE III:
Penalties and Enforcement/Consent Decrees/
Non-Participating Companies

A. Penalties and Enforcement

This legislation will be enforceable both by the federal government, including
FDA and civil and criminal divisions of the Department of Justice, and by the
several states. FDA will also have the authority to contract directly with state
agencies to assist with enforcement. If conduct is subject to a particular state's
consumer protection law or similar statute, such state may proceed under that
law.

State enforcement actions—whether brought under the Act or a state's consumer protection law—could not impose obligations or requirements beyond
those imposed by the legislation (except where the legislation does not specifically preempt additional state-law obligations), and would be limited to the civil
and criminal penalties established by the legislation and by the prohibition on
duplicative penalties. State enforcement proceedings under the Act (or predi-
cated on conduct violating the Act), except those exclusively local in nature,
would be removable to federal court. Nothing in the Act precludes a state from
enforcing its laws in the ordinary fashion as to matters not covered by the Act or
Protocol.

Civil and criminal penalties for violations of the legislation based on those governing other drugs or devices regulated under the Food, Drug and Cosmetic Act
and, where applicable, under Title 18 of the *United States Code*.

In addition, the industry faces civil penalties of up to $10 million per violation for
any violations of the obligations to disclose to the FDA research about tobacco product health effects and information regarding the toxicity of non-tobacco ingredients
and constituents used in their products. This penalty is 10 times the largest penalty

faced by other drug or device manufacturers for similar violations.

To reflect the fact that not all states have filed lawsuits against the tobacco industry, but that the intent of the negotiators is to provide the benefits of the settlement to all states, the industry also will enter into a binding and enforceable national tobacco control Protocol embodying certain terms of the proposed resolution. As an enforceable contract, which would not be subject to facial constitutional challenge, this Protocol will provide benefits and enforcement rights to the federal government and all states.

B. Consent Decrees

Certain terms of the agreement will also be reiterated in consent decrees between the tobacco industry and the states that will not take effect until after enactment of the Act. These consent decrees will be identical to, and will reiterate, the terms of the agreement with respect to: (1) restrictions on advertising, marketing and youth access to tobacco products; (2) trade associations; (3) restrictions on lobbying; (4) disclosure of tobacco smoke constituents; (5) disclosure of non-tobacco ingredients; (6) disclosure of existing and future industry documents relating to health, toxicity and addiction; (7) compliance and corporate culture; (8) obligations to make monetary payments to the states reflecting their reasonable share of the total provided by the Act; (9) obligations of the industry to deal only with distributors and retailers that operate in compliance with applicable provisions of law respecting the distribution, sale and marketing of tobacco products; (10) warnings, labeling and packaging (to the extent noted below); and (11) dismissal of other pending litigation specified by the parties.

The consent decrees will not contain provisions as to: (1) product design, performance or modification; (2) manufacturing standards and good manufacturing practices; (3) testing and regulation with respect to toxicity and ingredients approval; and (4) the national FDA "look-back" provisions.

The consent decrees will provide that their terms are to be construed in conformity with the Act and the Protocol and with each other. State proceedings to enforce the provisions of the consent decrees may be brought in state court, subject to an acceptable procedure to ensure consistent rulings with respect to conduct that is not exclusively local in character. State proceedings to enforce the consent decrees may seek injunctive relief only, and may not seek criminal or monetary sanctions. A state shall not be limited from seeking criminal or other sanctions for a company's subsequent violation of an injunction entered by the court in an action brought to enforce the consent decree.

The provisions of the consent decrees will remain enforceable regardless of whether subsequent changes in the Act or in any other provision of law diminish the obligations of the companies in the areas covered by the consent decrees,

except: (1) where such changes create federal requirements that produce obligations in conflict with those contained in the consent decrees; (2) with respect to
the allocation of funds; and (3) with respect to warnings, labeling and packaging.
With respect to warnings, labeling and packaging, if the requirements of the Act
are later modified, or if Congress subsequently prohibits warnings on tobacco
products, the consent decrees will be modified to conform to such requirements.
However, if Congress later eliminates altogether the warning requirement in the
Act, the warnings originally set forth in the Act (the so-called Canadian warnings)
shall be mandated and enforceable under the consent decrees.

In addition, the parties recognize that certain provisions of the consent decrees
and the agreement may require them to act (or refrain from acting) in a manner
that they might otherwise claim would violate the federal or state constitutions.
They will therefore in the consent decrees expressly waive any claim that the provisions of the consent decrees or the agreement violate the federal or state constitutions. The consent decrees will also state that if a provision of the Act covered by the decrees is subsequently declared unconstitutional, the provision
remains an enforceable term of the consent decrees.

C. Non-Participating Companies

The regime envisioned by the resolution would be substantially undercut if certain companies were free to ignore the limitations it imposes, and were instead
able to sell tobacco products at lower prices (because they were not making the
payments described above) and through less-restricted advertising and marketing activities. The resolution accordingly anticipates the possibility that some
manufacturers of tobacco products may not consent to the institution of this
regime. Rather than seeking to impose on such manufacturers the advertising
restrictions, full required payments and corporate culture changes set forth
above, the resolution avoids constitutional questions that might otherwise be
raised by establishing a separate regime for non-participating manufacturers.

Non-participating manufacturers would be subject to the access restrictions and
regulatory oversight set forth above. They would receive none of the civil liability protections described in Title VIII. Their product would be subject to a user
fee equal to the portion of the payments by participating manufacturers allocated to fund public health programs and federal and state enforcement of the
access restrictions.

The resolution further recognizes that—unlike the participating manufacturers
—non-participating manufacturers will not have made consensual payments to
settle governmental actions for health care costs, to settle class actions and to
provide consideration for the partial settlement of individual tort actions (including punitive damages claims). Because such actions would remain wholly unsat-
isfied, it is vital that the claimants be ensured that funds will be available to sat-

isfy any judgments that may be obtained. Accordingly, the resolution requires that each non-participating manufacturer place into an escrowed reserve fund each year an amount equal to 150% of its share of the annual payment required of participating manufacturers (other than the portion allocated to public health programs and federal and state enforcement). These escrowed funds would be earmarked for potential liability payments, and the manufacturer would reclaim them with interest 35 years later to the extent they had not been paid out in liability.

Moreover, the resolution also recognizes that—because non-participating manufacturers are not subject to the corporate culture commitments requiring manufacturers to monitor distributor and retailer compliance with the underage access restrictions—distribution and retail sales of those manufacturers' products present a particularly great obstacle to the achievement and enforcement of the access restrictions. Accordingly, the resolution provides that the exemption from civil liability applicable to distributors and retailers of the products of participating manufacturers will not apply to distributors and retailers who handle tobacco products of non-participating manufacturers.

Title IV:
Nationwide Standards to Minimize Involuntary Exposure to Environmental Tobacco Smoke

Until now, there has been no minimum or other federal standard governing smoking in public places or at work. The legislation would:

Restrict indoor smoking in "public facilities" (i.e., any building regularly entered by 10 or more individuals at least one day per week) to ventilated areas with systems that:

Exhaust the air directly to the outside;
Maintain the smoking area at "negative pressure" compared with adjoining areas; and
Do not recirculate the air inside the public facility.

Ensure that no employee shall be required to enter a designated smoking area while smoking is occurring. Cleaning and maintenance work in a designated smoking area shall be conducted while no smoking is occurring.

Exempt restaurants (but not "fast-food" restaurants; "fast-food" restaurant means any restaurant or chain of restaurants which primarily distributes food via customer pickup [either at a counter or drive-through window]. In addition, OSHA would be authorized to issue regulations clarifying this definition to the extent necessary to ensure that the intended inclusion of establishments catering largely to minors is achieved. Any such regulation may consider such factors as whether a restaurant either has attached playgrounds or play areas for children, uses ad campaigns that feature or prominently include cartoon characters and/or toy giveaways or advertises "happy meal" or other comparable kids' combination platters, and other factors OSHA deems relevant) and bars (including those in hotels), private clubs, hotel guest rooms, casinos, bingo parlors, tobacco merchants and prisons.

Direct OSHA to issue, not later than one year after the effective date of the legislation, regulations implementing and enforcing the preceding standards, with enforcement costs paid out of the Industry Payments. The smoking restrictions outlined in this Title would take effect on the first anniversary of the enactment of the legislation irrespective of whether the implementing regulations have been promulgated.

The legislation would not preempt or otherwise affect any other state or local law or regulation that restricts smoking in public facilities in an equal or stricter manner. Nor would the legislation preempt or otherwise affect any federal rules that restrict smoking in federal facilities.

[Source/precedent: H.R. 3434, as reported out of committee; WISHA workplace smoking rule; state law exemptions for the "hospitality sector"]

TITLE V:
Scope and Effect

A. Scope of FDA Authority

All product sold in U.S. commerce.

Covers new entrants; imports; U.S. duty-free, etc.

BATF to retain fiscal authority over tobacco products.

FTC to retain existing authority, except for "tar," nicotine and carbon monoxide testing.

Grower limitation: FDA jurisdiction does not extend to the growing, cultivation or curing of raw tobacco (USDA has exclusive authority).

B. State Authority

1. Preservation of state and local government laws and legal authority

   While setting a federal "floor" for tobacco control measures in many substantive areas, this legislation preserves, to the maximum extent, state and local government authority to take additional tobacco control measures that further restrict or eliminate the product's use by and accessibility to minors.

This legislation also permits state and local governments to enact measures that further restrict or eliminate employee and general public exposure to smoking in workplaces and in other public and private places and facilities.

The legal authority of a state or local government to further regulate, restrict or eliminate the sale or distribution of tobacco products, and to impose state or local taxes on such products, also remains unchanged.

The legislation retains similar flexibility for Indian tribes, military facilities and other federal agencies.

2. Uniformity of warning labels, packaging, labeling and other advertising requirements; manufacturing requirements

Current federal law providing for national uniformity of warning labels, packaging and labeling requirements and advertising and promotion requirements related to tobacco and health, is preserved, except that this legislation gives FDA express authority to require changes in the language of the warnings, subject to the standard requirement that it provide public notice and a hearing opportunity prior to making such changes.

Similarly, the provisions of FDCA designed to provide uniformity in product manufacturing and design requirements relating to medical devices will apply to tobacco products, except that any application by a state or locality for an exemption permitting it to adopt additional or different requirements relating to performance standards or good manufacturing practices may only be granted if the requirement would not unduly burden interstate commerce. Further, to ensure that FDA has an adequate opportunity to evaluate non-tobacco ingredients as described in Title 1(F), no exemption relating to ingredients may be applied for until the fifth anniversary of the effective date of the Act.

TITLE VI:
Programs/Funding

Total 25-Year-Package Face Value—$368.5 Billion

A. Up-Front Commitment—Lump Sum Cash Payment—$10 Billion

1. Payable on statute signing date.

B. Base Annual Payments—25-Year-Total Face Value—$358.5 Billion

(Figures are subject to inflation protection and volume adjustments)

1. Duration—annual payments in perpetuity.

2. Commencement—12/31 of first full year after statute signing.

3. Face amounts (include payments from all industry sources):

Payment year:	1	2	3	4	5	6–8	9	after
Total Payments:	$8.5B	$9.5B	$11.5B	$14.0B	$15.0B	$15.0B	$15.0B	$15.0B
Base Amount:	$6.0B	$7.0B	$8.0B	$10.0B	$10.0B	$12.5B	$15.0B	$15.0B
Public Health Trust:	$2.5B	$2.5B	$3.5B	$4.0B	$5.0B	$2.5B		

4. Inflation protection for annual payments

   Greater of 3% or CPI applied each year on previous year, beginning with first annual payment.

5. Adjustment for volume decrease (adult volume only) or total volume increase

   Beginning in year 1; payment is made equal to the scheduled annual payment times the ratio of actual relevant domestic tobacco product unit-sales volume to relevant base volume. In the event of a decline in volume, relevant actual volume and relevant base volume are adult-volume figures; in the event of an increase in volume, relevant actual volume and relevant base volume are total-volume figures. Base volume is 1996 volume.

   Any reduction in an annual payment will be reduced by 25% of any increase above the industry's base-year net operating profits (after application of inflator discussed above) from domestic sales of tobacco products.

6. Payment protection

   Provide for payment priority/continuation during bankruptcy/reorganization proceedings. Protocol cannot be rejected in bankruptcy. Obligation for annual payments responsibility only of entities selling into domestic market.

7. Passthrough

   In order to promote maximum reduction in youth smoking, the statute would provide for the annual payments to be reflected in the prices manufacturers charge for tobacco products.

C. *Applicability*

1. Applicable to all Sellers of tobacco products

Through protocol and statute to protocol signatories.

Through alternative statutory provisions to non-signatories.

D. *Tax Treatment*

All payments pursuant to this agreement (including those pursuant to Title II) shall be deemed ordinary and necessary business expenses for the year of payment, and no part thereof is either in settlement of an actual or potential liability for a fine or penalty (civil or criminal) or the cost of a tangible or intangible asset.

TITLE VII:
Public Health Funds from Tobacco Settlement As Recommended by the Attorneys General for Consideration by the President and the Congress

BASED ON THE PREMISE OF $1 BILLION FOR THE FIRST YEAR AND GRADUALLY INCREASING TO $1.5 BILLION THEREAFTER, ADJUSTED FOR INFLATION AFTER THE FIRST YEAR.

BASED ON THE PREMISE OF $1 BILLION FOR SMOKING CESSATION FOR THE FIRST FOUR YEARS AND $1.5 BILLION THEREAFTER, ADJUSTED FOR INFLATION.

A. *Allocation of Grant Monies Among Programs*
The use of moneys under this Section shall be limited to programs established under this Section, shall be adjusted for inflation annually from the effective date, and shall be allocated among such programs as follows:

1. $125,000,000 for the first three years and $225,000,000 annually thereafter to the Secretary of HHS to accomplish the purposes described in Paragraph (B) of this Section (Reduction in Tobacco Usage)

2. $300,000,000 annually for the FDA to carry out its obligations under and to enforce the terms of this Act, including for grants to the states to assist in the enforcement of the provisions of the Act

3. $75,000,000 for the first two years; $100,000,000 in the third year; and

$125,000,000 annually thereafter to fund state and local tobacco control community-based efforts modeled on the ASSIST program, designed to encourage community involvement in reducing tobacco use and the enactment and implementation of policies designed to reduce the use of tobacco products

4. $100,000,000 annually to fund research and the development of methods for how to discourage individuals from starting to use tobacco and how to help individuals to quit using tobacco

5. Beginning in the second year, $75,000,000 annually for a period of 10 years to compensate events, teams or entries in such events who lose sponsorship by the tobacco industry as a result of this Act, or who currently receive tobacco industry funding to sponsor events and elect to replace that funding, provided that the event, team or entry is otherwise unable to replace its tobacco industry sponsorship during those given years. Funds used for this purpose shall promote a Quit Tobacco Use theme. After a 10-year period, no additional funds shall be used for this purpose and the funds previously allocated to this purpose shall be used as follows: 50% to supplement funding of the multimedia campaigns in Paragraph (1) of this subsection; 25% to supplement the funding of the enforcement provisions of Paragraph (2) of this subsection; and 25% to supplement the funding of community action programs in Paragraph (3) of this subsection.

B. Establishment of Programs by the Secretary

The secretary shall establish programs to accomplish the following purposes:

1. The reduction of tobacco product usage, both by seeking to discourage the initiation of tobacco use by persons under the age of 18 and by encouraging current tobacco users to quit through media-based and non-media-based education, prevention and cessation campaigns. The secretary may make grants to state health departments to assist in carrying out the purposes of this provision.

2. The research into and development and public dissemination of technologies and methods to reduce the risk of dependence and injury from tobacco product usage and exposure

3. The identification, testing and evaluation of the health effects of both tobacco and non-tobacco constituents of tobacco products

4. The promulgation of such other rules and regulations as are necessary and proper to carry out the provisions of this Act, as well as the development of such other programs as the secretary determines are consistent with the goals of the Act.

C. Public Education Campaign

$500,000,000 shall be spent annually in such multimedia campaigns designed to discourage and deglamorize the use to tobacco products. To carry out such efforts, an independent non-profit organization with a board made up of prestigious individuals and the leaders of the major public health organizations shall be created which shall contract or make grants to non-profit private entities who are unaffiliated with tobacco manufacturers or tobacco importers, who have a demonstrated record of working effectively to reduce tobacco product use and expertise in multi-media communications campaigns. The independent body shall be authorized to contract with state health departments, where appropriate, to run campaigns for their states and communities. In creating the program the secretary or independent body shall also take into account the needs of particular populations. The goal shall be the reduction of tobacco product usage, both by seeking to discourage the initiation of tobacco use by persons under the age of 18 and by encouraging current tobacco users to quit.

D. Tobacco Use Cessation

For the first four years, $1 billion, and thereafter, $1.5 billion of the total amount paid by the tobacco industry shall be paid into a Trust Fund to be used to assist individuals who want to quit using tobacco to do so.

Within 12 months the secretary shall promulgate regulations to govern: (1) the establishment of criteria and a procedure for the approval of cessation programs and devices for which payment may be made under the program; (2) the eligibility requirements for individuals seeking to use moneys from the trust to fund the tobaccocessation efforts; and (3) the procedures to govern the tobacco-cessation program.

The goal of the tobacco-cessation program shall to enable the most tobacco users possible to receive assistance in their effort to quit using tobacco by providing financial assistance, and identifying the programs, techniques and devices that have been shown to be safe and effective. Benefits to individuals should not be limited to a single effort, but should be tailored to the needs of individual smokers according to standards established by the secretary using the best available scientific guidelines.

E. Public Health Trust Fund Presidential Commission

A presidential commission will be appointed to include representatives of the public health community, attorneys general, Castano attorneys and others to determine the specific tobacco-related medical research for which the $25 billion Public Health Trust Fund will be used.

TITLE VIII:
Civil Liability

The following provisions would govern actions for civil liability related to tobacco and health.

A. *General*

1. Present attorney general actions (or similar actions brought by or on behalf of any governmental entity), *parens patriae* and class actions are legislatively settled. No future prosecution of such actions. All "addiction"/dependence claims are settled and all other personal injury claims are reserved. As to signatory states, pending congressional enactment, no stay applications will be made in pending actions, based upon the fact of this resolution, without mutual consent of the parties.

2. Third-party payor (and similar) actions pending as of 6/9/97 are not settled, but governed by provisions regarding past conduct set forth in Section B below.

B. *Provisions as to Civil Liability for Past Conduct*

The following provisions apply to suits for relief arising from past conduct—i.e., suits by persons claiming injury or damage caused by conduct taking place prior to the effective date of the Act.

1. All punitive damages claims resolved as part of overall settlement. No punitive damages in individual tort actions.

2. Individual trials only: i.e., no class actions, joinder, aggregations, consolidations, extrapolations or other devices to resolve cases other than on the basis of individual trials, without defendant's consent. Action removable by defendant to federal court upon receipt of application to, or order of, state court providing for trial or other procedure in violation of this provision.

3. Except as expressly provided in the Act, FCLAA and applicable case law unchanged by the Act.

4. Provided that the five negotiating companies enter into the Protocol. Protocol manufacturers to enter into joint sharing agreement for civil liability. Protocol manufacturers not jointly and severally liable for liability of non-Protocol manufacturers. Trials involving both protocol and non-Protocol manufacturers to be severed.

5. Permissible parties:

Plaintiffs

a. Claims of individuals, or claims derivative of such claims, must be brought either by person claiming injury or heirs.

b. Third-party payor (and similar) claims not based on subrogation that were pending as of 6/9/97.

c. Third-party payor (and similar) claims based on subrogation of individual claims; no extrapolations, etc.

Defendants

a. Maintained only against companies, their assigns, any future fraudulent transferee and/or entity for suit designated to survive defunct manufacturer. Actions may be manufacturing successors and

b. Manufacturers of agents' agencies and liable vicariously for acts (including advertising attorneys).

6. No removal except under Paragraph 2 above.

7. The development of "reduced risk" tobacco products after the effective date of the Act is neither admissible nor discoverable.

8. Statute of limitations: for all actions, individual state laws governing time periods from injury, discovery, notice or contamination/violation.

9. Annual aggregate cap for judgments/settlements: 33% of annual industry base payment (including any reductions for volume decline). If aggregate judgments/settlements for a year exceed annual aggregate cap, excess does not have to be paid that year and rolls over.

Any judgments/settlements run against defendant but give rise to 80-cent-on-the-dollar credit against annual payment in year paid. Suitable provision for settlement consultation and permission. Manufacturers control insurance claims, and any insurance recovery obtained by manufacturers (net of cost) on account of judgment and/or settlement covered by above sharing arrangement allocated 80% to annual payments. Manufacturers retain any insurance proceeds on account of defense costs.

Provision with respect to individual judgments above $1 million: amount in excess of $1 million not paid that year unless every other judgment/settlement can be satisfied within the annual aggregate cap. Excess rodlls forward without interest and is paid at the rate of $1 million per year, until the first year that the annual aggregate cap is not exceeded (at which time the remainder is paid in full). For purposes of this provision, a third-party payor (or similar) action not based on subrogation is treated as having been brought by a single plaintiff and is subject to the $1 million rollover on that basis.

10. In the event that the annual aggregate cap is not reached in any year, a commission appointed by the president will determine the appropriate allocation of the amount representing the unused amount of the credit. The commission will be entitled to consider, among public health, governmental entities and other uses of the funds, applications for compensation from persons, including non-subrogation claims of third-party payors, not otherwise entitled to compensation under the Act.

11. Defense costs paid by manufacturers.

C. Provisions as to Civil Liability for Future Conduct

The following provisions apply to suits for relief arising from future conduct—i.e., suits claiming injury or damage caused by conduct taking place after the effective date of the Act.

1. Paragraphs 2, 3, 5, 6, 7, 8, 9, 10 and 11 in Section B apply.

2. No third-party payor (or similar) claims not based on subrogation.

TITLE IX: Board Approval

The terms of this resolution are subject to approval by the boards of directors of the participating tobacco companies.

APPENDICES

Appendix I—Warnings in Advertisements

The space in press and poster advertisements for tobacco products that is to be devoted to the warning and, where relevant, the "tar," nicotine and any other constituent yield statements will be 20% of the area of the advertisement. The size of the printing of the warning and the yield statements shall be pro rata to the following examples:

a) Whole-page broadsheet newspaper—45-point type

b) Half-page broadsheet newspaper—39-point type

c) Whole-page tabloid newspaper—39-point type

d) Half-page tabloid newspaper—27-point type

e) DPS magazine—31.5-point type

f) Whole-page magazine—31.5-point type

g) 28 cm times 3 columns—22.5-point type

h) 20 cm times 2 columns—15-point type

FDA may revise the required type sizes within the 20% requirement.

Appendix II—Retail Tobacco Product Seller Penalties

1. The sale of tobacco products to consumers by an unlicensed seller shall be a criminal violation, and be subject to a minimum penalty of $1,000, or imprisonment for six months, or both, if an individual; or in the case of a corporation, a maximum penalty of $50,000. Any state or local jurisdiction may provide by statute or code more severe penalties.

2. In addition to any criminal penalties which may be imposed under any applicable state or local law, a tobacco product licensee may be subjected to civil sanctions, including penalties, or license suspension or revocation (on a site-by-site basis), or a combination thereof, for any violation of the provisions of the state licensing laws regarding sales to minors. Such sanction shall not exceed the following:

(a) For the first offense within any two-year period: $500 or a three-day license suspension, or both.

(b) For the second offense within any two-year period: $1,000 or a seven-day license suspension, or both.

(c) For the third offense within any two-year period: $2,000 or a 30-day license suspension, or both.

(d) For the fourth offense within any two year period: $5,000 or a six-month license suspension or both.

(e) For the fifth offense within any two year period: $10,000 or one-year license suspension, or both.

(f) For the sixth and any subsequent offenses within any two-year period: $25,000 or a revocation of license with no possibility of reinstatement for a period of three years.

(g) Permanent license revocation is mandatory for the tenth offense within any two-year period.

Each state must enact a statutory or regulatory enforcement scheme that provides substantially similar penalties to the minimum federal standards for a retail licensing program.

[Source/precedent: Washington state Alcohol Licensing Act]

Appendix III—Application to Indian Tribes

A. *Application of Act*

1. The provisions of the FDCA, the regulations of the FDA and the Act relating to the manufacture, distribution and sale of tobacco products shall apply on Indian lands as defined in 18 U.S.C Section 1151 and on any other trust lands subject to the jurisdiction of an Indian tribe. To the extent that an Indian tribe engages in the manufacture, distribution or sale of tobacco products, the provisions of this Act shall apply to such tribe.

2. Any federal tax or fee imposed on the manufacture, distribution or sale of tobacco products shall be paid by any Indian tribe engaged in such activities, or by persons engaged in such activities on such Indian lands, to the same extent such tax or fee applies to other persons under the law.

B. *Tribal Programs and Authority*

1. For the purposes of the provisions of this Act, FDA is authorized to treat any federally recognized Indian tribe as a state, and is authorized to provide any such tribe grant and contract assistance to carry out the licensing and enforcement functions provided by this section.

2. Such treatment shall be authorized only if:

(a) the Indian tribe has a governing body carrying out substantial governmental powers and duties;
(b) the functions to be exercised by the Indian tribe under this section pertain to activities on trust lands within the jurisdiction of the tribe; and
(c) the Indian tribe is reasonably expected to be capable of carrying out the functions required under this Act.

[Source/precedent: Clean Air Act, 42 U.S.C. Section 7601(d)]

3. FDA regulations which establish a retail licensing program shall apply on Indian trust lands, and each tribe's program shall be no less strict than the program of the state in which the tribe is located.

4. If FDA determines that an Indian tribe does not qualify for treatment as a state, FDA will directly administer the retailer licensing program, or may delegate such authority to the state.

C. *Tobacco Compensation and Public Health Grants*

1. A portion of the settlement funds to which a state is otherwise entitled shall be paid to HHS for distribution to the Indian tribes which have been certified by FDA for treatment as states. The funds to be paid for such purposes on behalf of Indian tribes shall be determined by the proportion of registered tribal members resident on the reservation to the total population of the state in which the tribe is located. The funds to be distributed to Indian tribes shall be used for the same purposes as those funds are to be used by the states and be subject to the same compliance requirements for retail sales to minors as are the states under the Act.

2. The Department of Health and Human Services will annually pay to the governing body of each Indian tribe its share of the funds for use under an FDA-approved plan after annual certification by FDA, under the same standards that apply to the states, that the Indian tribe is in compliance with the requirements of the Act and any applicable regulations.

3. If HHS does not distribute all, or a portion, of an Indian tribe's share of the

funds in any given year because the tribe has not qualified under the terms of this section or has not met the compliance requirements for retail sales to minors, those funds will be distributed to other qualified tribes in the same state for the same purposes and on the same proportional basis, less the non-qualified tribe's population, as other settlement funds are to be distributed to the tribes.

D. Obligations of Tobacco Manufacturers

1. Tobacco manufacturers shall not engage in any activity on Indian lands subject to this Act which activity the manufacturers may not otherwise do within a state.

2. Tobacco manufacturers also agree not to sell tobacco products for manufacture, distribution or sale to an Indian tribe, or to a manufacturer, distributor or retail seller subject to the jurisdiction of an Indian tribe, except under the same terms and conditions as the tobacco manufacturers impose under other manufacturers, distributors and retail sellers under the Act, or any applicable regulations.

Appendix IV—Industry Associations

Within 90 days of the effective date of the Act, the tobacco product manufacturers shall disband and dissolve the Council for Tobacco Research, U.S.A. and the Tobacco Institute. In addition, with respect to any new trade associations:

A. Tobacco product manufacturers may form or participate in any new tobacco industry trade association. Any such new trade association shall have an independent board of directors, in accordance with the following requirements. For at least 10 years after the formation of the new association, a minimum of 20% of the directors, but at least one director, shall be other than a current or former director, officer or employee of any association member or affiliated company. No other director of a new trade association may be, at the same time, a director of any association member or affiliated company. The officers shall be appointed by the board and shall be employees of the association and during their term shall not be employed by any association member or affiliated company. Legal counsel for any such association shall be independent and not serve as legal counsel to any association member or affiliated company while counsel to the association.

B. Any new tobacco product manufacturers trade association shall adopt by-laws governing the association's procedures and the activities of its members, board, employees, agents and other representatives. The bylaws shall include, among other things, provisions that:

(1) members who are competitors in the tobacco industry shall not meet on

the association's business except under sponsorship of the association;

(2) every board of directors meeting, board subcommittee meeting, general association or committee meeting, and any other association-sponsored meeting, shall proceed under and strictly adhere to an agenda, approved by legal counsel and circulated in advance; and

(3) minutes describing the substance of the meetings shall be prepared for all such meetings, and shall be maintained by the association for a period of five years.

C. Moreover, under the new regime:

1. The structure, bylaws and activities of tobacco industry trade associations shall be subject to continuing oversight by the U.S. Department of Justice and by state antitrust authorities. For a period of 10 years from the creation of a new trade association, such authorities may, without limitation on whatever other rights to access they may be permitted, upon reasonable prior notice:

(a) have access during regular office hours to inspect and copy all books, records, meeting agenda and minutes, and other association documents; and

(b) interview the association's directors, officers and employees, who may have counsel present.

The inspection and discovery rights provided in (a) and (b) above shall be exercised through a multistate states attorneys general oversight committee. Any documents and information provided to any state pursuant to (a) and (b) above shall be kept confidential by and among the states and shall be utilized only for governmental purposes of enforcing the Act and ancillary documents.

2. In order to achieve the goals of this agreement and the Act relating to tobacco use by children and adolescents, the tobacco product manufacturers may, notwithstanding the provisions of the Sherman Act, the Clayton Act, or any other federal or state antitrust law, act unilaterally, or may jointly confer, coordinate or act in concert, for this limited purpose. Manufacturers must obtain prior approval from the Department of Justice of any plan or process for taking action pursuant to this section; however, no approval shall be required of specific actions taken in accordance with an approved plan. Approval or non-approval of a plan shall not be grounds for abatement of any surcharge to a manufacturer for failure to meet the reductions in underage tobacco use contemplated in this resolution and the Act.

Appendix V—"Look Back"

A summary of the "look-back" provision is as follows:

A. *The Reduction Requirements*

1. The required reductions in underage tobacco use are measured against a base percentage. For underage use of cigarettes, the base percentage is the average weighted by relative population of such age groups in 1995 as determined by the U.S. Census Bureau, of: (a) the average of the percentages of 12th-graders (ages 16 and 17) from 1986 to 1996 who used cigarette products on a daily basis; (b) the average of the percentages of 10th-graders (ages 14 and 15) from 1991 to 1996 who used cigarette products on a daily basis; and (c) the average of the percentages of 8th-graders (age 13) from 1991 to 1996 who used cigarette products on a daily basis. The percentages are those measured by the University of Michigan's National High School Drug Use Survey, "Monitoring the Future," or by such comparable index using identical methodology as is chosen by FDA after notice and hearing. For underage use of smokeless tobacco products, the base percentage is the average, weighted by relative population of such age groups in 1995 as determined by the U.S. Census Bureau, of: (a) the percentage of 12th-graders (ages 16 and 17) in 1996 who used smokeless tobacco products on a daily basis; (b) the percentage of 10th-graders (ages 14 and 15) in 1996 who used smokeless products on a daily basis; and (c) the percentage of 8th-graders (age 13) in 1996 who used smokeless tobacco products on a daily basis. These percentages are to be derived from the same source as are the percentages with respect to use of cigarette products.

2. After the fifth year after enactment of the Act and annually thereafter, the FDA will calculate the incidence of daily use of tobacco products by those under 18 years of age as follows:

For cigarette product use, the FDA will calculate the average, weighted by relative population of such age groups in 1995 as determined by the U.S. Census Bureau of the percentages of 12th-graders (ages 16 and 17), 10th-graders (ages 14 and 15) and 8th-graders (age 13) who used cigarette products on a daily basis during the preceding year. The percentages used in this calculation are to be those measured: (a) by the University of Michigan survey; or (b) by such comparable index using identical methodology as is chosen by the FDA after notice and hearing. If the methodology of the University of Michigan survey is hereafter changed in a material manner from that employed in 1986–96 (including by changing the states or regions on which that survey is based), the FDA shall use the percentages measured by an index chosen by it after notice and hearing having a methodology identical to that employed by the University of Michigan survey in 1986–96.

For smokeless tobacco product use, the FDA will calculate the average, weighted by relative population of such age groups in 1995 as determined by the U.S. Census Bureau of of the percentages of 8th- (age 13), 10th- (ages 14 and 15) and 12th- graders (ages 16 and 17) who used smokeless tobacco products on a daily basis during the preceding year. This calculation is to be made using the same methodology as with respect to cigarette product use.

Any data underlying the University of Michigan survey shall be available by request from FDA.

3. The reduction requirements (expressed as reduction from the base percentage) for cigarette products are as follows:

Year after Enactment Reduction Requirement
Years 5–6:   30% reduction
Years 7–9:   50% reduction
Year 10 and after: 60% reduction

The reduction requirements (expressed as reduction from the base percentage) for smokeless tobacco products are as follows:

Year after Enactment Reduction Requirement
Years 5–6:   25% reduction
Years 7–9:   35% reduction
Years 10 and after: 45% reduction

B. The Surcharge

Where the FDA's calculation (per the procedure set forth above) shows that the reduction requirements with respect to underage use of cigarette products were not met in the preceding year, the FDA will impose a surcharge on the manufacturers of cigarette products. Where the FDA's assessment shows that the reduction requirements with respect to underage use of smokeless tobacco products were not met in the preceding year, the FDA will impose a surcharge on the manufacturers of smokeless tobacco products.

1. The surcharge with respect to the cigarette industry will be calculated as follows:

(a) The FDA will the determine the percentage point difference between:

(1) the required percentage reduction applicable to a given year, and
(2) the percentage by which the percent incidence of underage use of cigarette products for that year is less than the base incidence percentage. (In the event that the FDA's calculation of the percent incidence of underage

use of cigarette products for that year is greater than the base incidence percentage, the number of percentage points used will be: (i) the required percentage reduction for that year; plus (ii) the percentage by which the actual percent incidence for that year is greater than the base incidence percentage.)

(b) The surcharge will be $80 million for each percentage point derived per the above procedure. This amount reflects an approximation of the present value of the profit the cigarette industry would earn over the life of underage smokers in excess of the required reduction (at current levels of population and profit). This calculation will be subject to the following:

(1) The $80 million will be adjusted proportionately for percentage increases or decreases compared with 1995 in the population of persons resident in the United States aged 13–17, inclusive.

(2) The $60 million will be adjusted proportionately for percentage increases or decreases compared with 1996 in the average profit per unit (measured in cents and weighted by annual sales) earned by the cigarette industry. (The average profit per unit in 1996 will be derived from the industry's operating profit as reported to the SEC and the average profit per unit for the year in which the surcharge is being determined will be calculated and certified to the FDA by a major, nationally recognized accounting firm having no existing connection to the tobacco industry using the same methodology as employed in deriving the average profit per unit for 1996.)

(3) The surcharge will be reduced to prevent double counting of persons whose smoking had already resulted in the imposition of a surcharge in previous years (to the extent that there were not underage smokers of comparable age in those previous years on whom a surcharge was not paid because of the cap set forth in Paragraph [4] below).

(4) The surcharge may not exceed $2 billion in any year (as adjusted for inflation).

2. The surcharge with respect to the smokeless tobacco industry will be derived through a comparable procedure based upon a base per-percentage point amount and a cap specific to that industry.

3. The surcharge payable by cigarette manufacturers will be the joint and several obligation of those manufacturers, allocated by actual market share. The surcharge payable by smokeless tobacco product manufacturers will be the joint and several obligation of those manufacturers, as allocated in the same manner. Within each such respective product market, the FDA will make such allocations

according to each manufacturer's relative market volume in the U.S. domestic cigarette or smokeless tobacco markets in the year for which the surcharge is being assessed, based on actual federal excise tax payments.

4. The surcharge for a given year, if any, will be assessed by the FDA by May 1 of the subsequent calendar year. Surcharge payments will be paid on or before July 1 of the year in which they are assessed by the FDA. The FDA may establish, by regulation, interest at a rate up [sentence incomplete in original].

5. After payment of its share of the surcharge, a tobacco product manufacturer may seek return of up to 75% of that payment through the abatement procedures described below.

C. Use of the Surcharge

The surcharge funds would be used in a manner designed to speed the reduction of the levels of underage tobacco use. Upon final completion and review of any abatement petition, the FDA would transfer as grants to state and local government public health agencies, without further appropriation, 90% of all monies paid as surcharge amounts. As a condition of such transfers, the recipients of the transferred funds would be required to spend them on additional efforts by state and local government agencies, or by contract between such agencies and private entities, to further reduce the use of tobacco products by children and adolescents. The FDA may retain up to 10% of such surcharge amounts for administrative costs—the administration of the Surcharge provisions of the Act and related proceedings, and for other administrative requirements imposed on the FDA by the Act. If 10% of the surcharge amounts exceed the administrative costs, the FDA may: (1) transfer any portion of the excess to other federal agencies, or to state and local government agencies, to meet the objective of reduction of youth tobacco usage; or (2) may expend such amounts directly to speed the reduction of underage tobacco use.

D. Abatement Procedures

Upon payment of its allocable share of any surcharge, a tobacco product manufacturer may petition the FDA for an abatement of the surcharge, and shall give timely written notice of such petition to the attorneys general of the several states.

1. The FDA shall conduct a hearing on an abatement petition pursuant to the procedures set forth in Sections 554, 556 and 557 of Title 5 of the *U.S. Code*.

2. The attorneys general of the several states shall be entitled to be heard and to participate in such a hearing.

3. The burden shall be on the manufacturer to prove, by a preponderance of the evidence, that the manufacturer should be granted an abatement.

4. The FDA's decision on whether to grant an abatement, and the amount thereof if any, shall be based on whether:

(a) the manufacturer has acted in good faith and in full compliance with the Act; any FDA rules or regulations promulgated thereunder; and all applicable federal, state or local laws, rules or regulations;

(b) in addition to full compliance as set forth in (a) above, the manufacturer has pursued all reasonably available measures to attain the required reductions;

(c) there is evidence of any action, direct or indirect, taken by the manufacturer to undermine the achievement of the required reductions or other terms and objectives of the Act; and

(d) any other relevant evidence.

5. Upon a finding by the FDA that the manufacturer meets the grounds for an abatement under the standards set forth above, it shall order an abatement of up to 75% of the surcharge with interest at the average U.S. 52-week Treasury-Bill rate for the period between payment and abatement of the surcharge. The FDA may consider all relevant evidence in determining what percentage to order abated.

6. Any manufacturer or state attorney general aggrieved by an abatement petition decision of the FDA may seek judicial review thereof within 30 days in the United States Court of Appeals for the District of Columbia Circuit. Unless otherwise specified in this Act, judicial review under this section shall be governed by Sections 701–706 of Title 5 of the *U.S. Code.*

7. Notwithstanding the foregoing, a tobacco product manufacturer may neither file an abatement petition or seek judicial review of a decision denying an abatement if it has failed to pay the surcharge in a timely fashion.

8. No stay or other injunctive relief enjoining imposition and collection of the surcharge amounts pending appeal or otherwise may be granted by the FDA or any court.

[Source/precedent: 5 U.S.C. Sections 554, 556–57, 701–06]

Appendix VI—State Enforcement Incentives

The details of the state enforcement incentives are as follows:

In addition to FDA and other federal agency, state attorney general and other existing state and local law enforcement authority under current law, the proposed Act requires the following:

A. States must have in effect a "no sales to minors" law providing that it is unlawful for any manufacturer, retailer or distributor of tobacco products to sell or distribute any such products to any persons under the age of 18 (42 U.S.C. Section 300-26(a)(1); 45 C.F.R. Section 96.130(b)). This state statutory requirement remains in addition to the federal regulatory prohibitions on retail sales of tobacco products to children and adolescents (also defined as persons under the age of 18) adopted by the FDA in its August 28, 1996 Final Rule (to be codified at 21 C.F.R. Section 897.14 et seq.).

B. States must conduct random, unannounced inspections at least monthly, and in communities geographically and statistically representative of the entire state and its youth population to ensure compliance with the "no sales to minors" law, and implement "any other actions which the state believes are necessary to enforce the law" (goes further than 45 C.F.R. Sections 96.130(c), 96.130(d)(1)—(2)).

C. States must conduct at least 250 random, unannounced inspections of retailer compliance with the "no sales to minors" law per year for each one million of resident population, as determined by the most recent decennial census. In the case of tribes, tribes must conduct no fewer than 25 such inspections per location of point of sale to consumers per year, conducted throughout the year.

A. *Annual State Reporting Requirements*

As a condition to receiving any moneys due and payable pursuant to the Act, states must annually submit a report to the FDA and the states must make their reports public (except as provided in 3 below) within the state. Such state reports must include at least the following:

1. A detailed description of enforcement activities undertaken by the state and its political subdivisions during the preceding federal fiscal year.

2. A detailed description of the state's progress in reducing the availability of tobacco products to individuals under the age of 18, including the detailed statistical results of the mandated compliance checks.

3. A detailed description of the methods used in the compliance checks, and in identifying outlets which were tested, with the FDA providing the state appropriate confidentiality safeguards for information provided to the agency regarding the timing and investigative techniques of state compliance checks that depend for their continued efficacy upon such confidentiality.

4. A detailed description of strategies the state intends to utilize in the current and succeeding years to make further progress on reducing the availability of

tobacco products to children and adolescents

5. The identity of the "single state agency" responsible for fulfilling the Synar amendment and the Act's requirements, including the coordination and report of state efforts to reduce youth access to tobacco products sold or offered for sale in the state (strengthens and extends beyond 45 C.F.R. Section 96.130(e) by adding greater detail to the requirements and transferring reporting obligation of states to FDA from HHS).

B. Required Attainment Goals for State Enforcement

The FDA is required to make an annual determination, prior to allocating any moneys allocated to the states under the proposed Act for the purposes of defraying public health care program expenditures (but not including or conditioning moneys made available under the Act for the payment of private claims), as to whether each state has "pursued all reasonably available measures to enforce" the prohibition on sales of tobacco products to children and adolescents.

In addition to the criteria set forth in 45 C.F.R. Section 96.130, the proposed Act will require the FDA to find presumptively that the state has not "pursued all reasonably available measures to enforce" the "no sales to minors law" unless the state has achieved, in the following years, the following compliance rate results for the retail compliance checks required by the Act:

Federal Fiscal Year under Review	Retail Compliance Check Performance Target
5th year after year of enactment of Act	75%
7th year after year of enactment of Act	85%
10th year after year of enactment of Act and annually thereafter	90%

These compliance percentages are expressed as the percentage of the random, unannounced compliance checks conducted pursuant to the Act for which the retailer refused sale of tobacco products to the potential underage purchaser. (Note: these performance targets are far more stringent on the states than those in the Synar amendment, which sets as a "final goal" a target of no less than 80% [i.e., an inspection failure rate of no more than 20%] within "several years. See 45 C.F.R. Section 96.130. In addition, the proposed Act's targets are mandatory, uniform national minimum performance requirements, while the Synar amendment calls for HHS simply to "negotiate" an "interim performance target" beginning in 1998.)

C. Reduction of Money Allocated to State Not Meeting Performance Targets

If a state does not meet the Act's "no sales to minors" performance targets for retail compliance checks, then the FDA may refuse to pay to that non-complying state certain moneys otherwise payable to that state under the proposed Act. No state shall be held responsible for sales to underage consumers outside that state's jurisdiction. Specifically, the FDA may withhold from such state an amount equal to 1% of moneys otherwise payable to that state under the Act to defray health care expenditures of public programs of medical assistance for each percentage point by which the state's performance on its mandatory compliance checks fails to meet the required performance targets for that year. In no event may the FDA withhold more than 20% of the money otherwise allocable to such state under the Act for such purposes.

The FDA shall reallot any Withhold Amounts, once final, to states that exceed the Act's performance targets, in amounts and by an allocation formula determined by the Agency to reward those states with the best record of reducing youth access to tobacco products.

D. Appeal Following Withhold

Upon notice from the FDA of a withhold of moneys (the "Withhold Amount") allocable to the state under the Act, a state subject to such notice of withhold may petition the Agency for a release and disbursement of the Withhold Amount, and shall give timely written notice of such petition to the attorney general for that state and to all tobacco product manufacturers. The Agency shall hold, and invest in interest-bearing securities of the U.S. government or its agencies, any Withhold Amounts subject to a pending petition for release and disbursement or related appeal until final disposition of such petition and appeal.

In the case of petition by a state for a release and disbursement of a Withhold Amount, the Agency's decision on whether to grant such a petition, and the amount thereby released and disbursed if any, shall be based on whether:

(1) the state has acted in good faith and in full compliance with the Act, and any Agency rules or regulations promulgated thereunder;
(2) the state has pursued all reasonably available measures to attain the retail compliance check performance targets and youth smoking reduction goals of the Act;
(3) there is evidence of any action, direct or indirect, taken by the state to undermine the achievement of the retail compliance check performance targets and youth smoking reduction goals or other terms and objectives of the Act; and
(4) any other relevant evidence.

The burden shall be on the state to prove, by a preponderance of the evidence, that the state should be granted a release and disbursement of the Withhold Amount or any portion thereof. Prior to decision, the Agency shall hold a hearing on the petition, with notice and opportunity to be heard given to the attorney general of that state and to all domestic tobacco product manufacturers.

Upon a finding by the Agency that the state meets the grounds, as set forth above, and the burden of proof for a release and disbursement of a Withhold Amount, then it shall order a release and disbursement of up to 75% of the Withhold Amount appealed, and it shall so release and disburse to the state that amount, with interest at the average U.S. 52-week Treasury-Bill rate for the period between notice and release of such Withhold Amount. The Agency may consider all relevant evidence in determining that percentage of the Withhold Amount to order released and disbursed.

Any manufacturer or state attorney general aggrieved by a Withhold Amount decision of the Agency may seek judicial review thereof within 30 days in the United States Court of Appeals for the District of Columbia Circuit. Unless otherwise specified in this Act, judicial review under this Section shall be governed by Sections 701–706 of Title 5 of the *U.S. Code*.

No stay or other injunctive relief enjoining imposition of the Withhold Amount Pending appeal or otherwise may be granted by the FDA or any court.

No appeal may be taken from an Agency decision denying a petition to release and disburse a Withhold Amount unless filed within 30 days following notice of such decision. No stay or other injunctive relief, enjoining imposition of the Withhold Amount pending appeal or otherwise, may be granted, by any court or administrative agency. Appeals filed hereunder shall be made to the United States Court of Appeals for the District of Columbia Circuit and, on appeal, shall be governed by the procedural and evidentiary provisions of the Administrative Procedures Act, unless otherwise specified in this Act. The judgment of the United States Court of Appeals for the District of Columbia on appeal shall be final.

Appendix VII—Restrictions on Point of Sale Advertising

The details with respect to point of sale advertising restrictions are as follows:

1. There shall be no point of sale advertising of tobacco products, excluding adults-only stores and tobacco outlets, except as provided herein:

A. Each manufacturer of tobacco products may have not more than two separate point of sale advertisements in or at each location at which tobacco products are offered for sale, except any manufacturer with 25% of market share may have one additional point of sale advertisement. A retailer may have one sign for its own or its wholesaler's contracted-house retailer or private-label brand. No supplier of tobacco products may enter into any arrangement with a retailer that limits the retailer's ability to display any form of advertising or promotional material originating with another supplier and permitted by law to be displayed at retail.

B. Point of sale advertisements permitted herein each shall be of a display area not larger than 576 square inches (either individually or in the aggregate) and shall consist of black letters on white background or recognized typographical marks.

Point of sale advertisements shall not be attached to nor located within two feet of any fixture on which candy is displayed for sale. Display fixtures are permitted signs consisting of brand name and price, not larger than two inches in height.

2. Except as provided herein, point of sale advertising shall mean all printed or graphical materials bearing the brand name (alone or in conjunction with any other word), logo, symbol, motto, selling message or any other indicia of product identification identical or similar to, or identifiable with, those used for any brand of cigarettes or smokeless tobacco, which, when used for its intended purpose, can reasonably be anticipated to be seen by customers at a location at which tobacco products are offered for sale.

3. Audio and video formats otherwise permitted under the FDA Rule may be distributed to adult consumers at point of sale but may not be played or shown at point of sale (i.e., no "static video displays").

Appendix VIII—Public Disclosure of Past and Future Tobacco Industry Documents and Health Research

The legislation would ensure that previously non-public or confidential documents from the files of the tobacco industry—including the results of internal health research—are disclosed to the federal government, the states, public and private litigants, health officials and the public. The legislation also would provide for binding, streamlined and accelerated judicial determinations with nationwide effect in the event that disputes remain over the legitimacy of claims of privileges or protections, including attorney-client privilege, and work-product and trade-secret protections.

1. Under the Act, the manufacturers, CTR and TI would establish a national tobacco document depository that is open to the public and located in the Washington, D.C., area. This depository would serve as a resource for litigants,

public health groups and anyone else with an interest in the tobacco industry's corporate records on the subjects of smoking and health, addiction or nicotine dependency, safer or less-hazardous cigarettes and underage tobacco use and marketing. Specifically:

The depository would include all of the documents produced to the other side by the manufacturers, CTR and TI in the attorneys general actions (including all documents selected by plaintiffs from the Guilford, U.K., repository), Philip Morris Companies, Inc.'s defamation action against Capital Cities/ABC News, the FTC's investigation concerning Joe Camel and underage marketing, the *Haines* and *Cipollone* actions and the *Butler* action in Mississippi.

In the event there are additional existing documents discussing or referring to health research, addiction or dependency, safer/less hazardous cigarettes, studies of the smoking habits of minors and the relationship between advertising or promotion and youth smoking that the manufacturers or trade associations have not yet completed, producing as agreed or required in the above actions, such additional documents shall be placed in the depository commencing within 90 days of the effective date of the Act, and concluding as soon as practicable thereafter.

Except for privileged and trade-secret materials (which shall be exempt from disclosure into the depository), all documents placed in the depository shall be produced without any confidentiality designations of any kind.

Along with these document collections, the manufacturers and trade associations shall place into the depository all indices (as defined by the court's order in the Minnesota attorney general action) of documents relating to smoking and health, including all indices identified by the manufacturers in the Washington, Texas and Minnesota attorney general actions. Any computerized indices shall be produced in both a computerized and hard-copy form. (If reductions of any such indices are required in order to protect any privileged or trade-secret information, such reductions shall be subject to the procedures set forth below for adjudicating any disputes over claims of privilege and trade secrecy.)

All documents placed into the depository shall be deemed produced for purposes of any litigation in the United States. The court in each underlying action shall retain the discretion to determine the admissibility on a case-by-case basis of any such produced document.

The tobacco industry shall bear the expense of maintaining the depository.

2. Immediately upon finalizing a resolution of these litigations with the attorney general, without waiting for Congress to embody these requirement in the proposed legislation, the manufacturers, CTR and TI shall:

> Commence to conduct a good-faith, de novo, document-by-document review of all documents previously withheld from production in tobacco litigation on grounds of privilege. The purpose of this review shall be to identify documents which the reviewer concludes are not privileged. All documents so identified shall be placed in the depository as soon as practicable.

> Prepare and place in the national depository as soon as practicable a comprehensive new privilege log of all documents that the manufacturers, CTR and TI, based on their de novo review, continue to deem to be legitimately privileged against disclosure.

> Itemize on this new privilege log all of the descriptive detail that the court has required defendants to furnish document by document on their privilege logs in the Minnesota attorney general action, thereby ensuring that there will be sufficient detail on the privilege logs to enable any interested person to determine whether he or she wishes to challenge claims of privilege or trade secrecy on any particular documents.

3. The Act also would establish a panel of three federal Article III judges, appointed by the judicial conference, to hear and decide all disputes over claims of privilege or trade secrets, except for those disputes that already have been determined by other federal or state courts at the time the Act is enacted, or are pending in cases prior to the time the court has had an opportunity to begin to review privilege claims.

> The three-judge panel shall decide all privilege or trade-secrecy challenges asserted by the federal government, the states, public and private litigants, health officials and the public with respect to tobacco industry documents.

> The Act would vest exclusive federal jurisdiction for the three-judge panel to decide any such disputes in accordance with the ABA/ALI Model Rules and/or principles of federal law with respect to privilege and the Uniform Trade Secrets Act with respect to trade secrecy. Any such adjudication shall be reviewable only in the manner prescribed by 28 U.S.C. [Sec. 1 25-certiorari].

> The panel's adjudications shall be binding upon all federal and state courts in all litigation in the United States.

> The panel shall be authorized to appoint special masters pursuant to Fed. Reg. Civ. P.53, with the cost to be borne by the tobacco industry.

Once the Act becomes effective and the three-judge panel is appointed, all disputes that may arise concerning privilege claims by the manufacturers or trade associations relating to smoking and health subjects must be resolved through this process, except for disputes in pending cases that can be resolved prior to the time the court has had an opportunity to begin to renew privilege claims.

If a claim of privilege is not upheld, the three-judge panel shall consider whether the claimant had a good faith factual and legal basis for an assertion of privilege and, if the claimant did not, shall assess against the claimant costs and attorneys' fees and may assess such additional costs or sanctions as the panel may deem appropriate.

4. In order to expedite the process of judicial review and to ensure that the federal government, the states, public and private litigants, health officials and the public no longer need to be concerned that claims of privilege and trade secrecy are being asserted improperly or without legal basis, the legislation would create an accelerated process by which any public or private person or entity, subject to a right of intervention by any other interested person or entity, may challenge any claims of privilege or trade secrecy before the three-judge panel. Under the Act, a person or entity filing such an action to challenge to privilege or trade secrecy will not need to make any prima facie showing of any kind as a prerequisite to in-camera review of the document or documents at issue.

5. The manufacturers would also be subject to certain continuing disclosure obligations over and above the aforementioned provisions and whatever further judicial discovery may be required in pending or future civil actions. Specifically, for the first time ever, the manufacturers would be required to disclose all original laboratory research relating to the health or safety of tobacco products, including, without limitation, all laboratory research relating to ways to make tobacco products less hazardous to consumers.

Whenever such research is performed in the future, the manufacturers shall disclose its results to the FDA.

In addition, all such research (except for legitimate trade secrets) shall be produced to the national document depository described above. In addition, the manufacturers and trade associations shall produce into the depository on an ongoing basis any future studies of the smoking habits of minors or documents discussing or referring to the relationship, if any, between advertising and promotion and underage smoking.

No original laboratory research relating to the health or safety of tobacco products shall be withheld from either the FDA or the depository on grounds of attorney/client privilege or work-product protection.

6. The tobacco manufacturers' and CTR's and TI's compliance with any of the provisions of this Act shall not be deemed a waiver of any applicable privilege or protection.

7. The Act will also incorporate reasonable and appropriate provisions to protect against the destruction of documents bearing on matters of public health or safety.

Selected Bibliography

THESE BOOKS AND articles were useful in the preparation of the book. They include some of the most authoritative histories and analyses of the tobacco industry and its long struggle with health advocates, federal and state authorities, and sick smokers.

Books

Burrough, Bryan and John Helyar. *Barbarians at the Gate: The Fall of RJR Nabisco*. New York: Harper & Row, 1990.

Glantz, Stanton. *The Cigarette Papers*. Berkeley, California: University of California Press, 1996.

Hilts, Philip. *Smokescreen: The Truth Behind the Tobacco Industry Cover-Up*. Reading, Massachusetts: Addison-Wesley Press, 1996.

Kluger, Richard. *Ashes to Ashes: America's Hundred-Year Cigarette War, the Public Health, and the Unabashed Triumph of Philip Morris*. New York: Alfred A. Knopf, 1996.

Articles

Barstow, David. "The Thief and the Third Wave," *St. Petersburg (Florida) Times*, April 6 and 7, 1997.

Brenner, Marie. "The Man Who Knew Too Much," *Vanity Fair*, May 1996.

Freedman, Alix and Suein Hwang. "Peace Pipe: Philip Morris, RJR, and Tobacco Plaintiffs Discuss a Settlement," *Wall Street Journal*, April 16, 1997.

——. "How Seven Individuals with Diverse Motives Halted Tobacco's Wars," *Wall Street Journal*, July 11, 1997.

——. "Burning Questions: Tobacco Pact's Limits—And Its Loopholes—Presage Fierce Debate," *Wall Street Journal*, June 23, 1997.

Greising, David. "The Big Four Who Battle Big Tobacco," *Business Week*, April 16, 1997.

Orey, Michael. "Fanning the Flames," *American Lawyer*, April 1996.

Sellers, Patricia. "Geoff Bible Won't Quit," *Fortune*, July 21, 1997.

Schwartz, John. "A Maverick's Complaint," *Washington Post,* July 24, 1997.
Weiser, Benjamin. "Tobacco's Trials," *Washington Post Magazine,* December 8, 1996.

Web Sites

Tobacco Bulletin Board System. Gene Borio (http:/www.tobacco.org).
State Tobacco Information Center. Northeastern University (http://stic.neu.edu).
Galen II Tobacco Control Archives: Brown & Williamson Collection. University of California at San Francisco (http://www.library.ucsf.edu/tobacco/bwsearch.html). (9/10/97).

Index

ABOUT BLOOMBERG

Bloomberg Financial Markets is a global, multimedia-based distributor of information services, combining news, data, and analysis for financial markets and businesses. Bloomberg carries real-time pricing, data, history, analytics, and electronic communications that are available 24 hours a day and currently accessed by 250,000 financial professionals in 94 countries.

Bloomberg covers all key global securities markets, including equities, money markets, currencies, municipals, corporate/Euro/sovereign bonds, commodities, mortgage-backed securities, derivative products, and governments. The company also delivers access to Bloomberg News, whose more than 540 reporters and editors in 80 bureaus worldwide provide around-the-clock coverage of economic, financial, and political events.

To learn more about Bloomberg—one of the world's fastest-growing, real-time financial information networks—call a sales representative at:

Frankfurt:	49-69-920-410
Hong Kong:	852-2521-3000
London:	44-171-330-7500
New York:	1-212-318-2000
Princeton:	1-609-279-3000
San Franciso:	1-415-912-2960
São Paulo:	5511-3048-4500
Singapore:	65-226-3000
Sydney:	61-29-777-8686
Tokyo:	81-3-3201-8900

ABOUT THE AUTHORS

CARRICK MOLLENKAMP has covered tobacco for Bloomberg News in Atlanta for the past two years. Prior to joining Bloomberg, Mollenkamp worked at the *Raleigh (North Carolina) News & Observer.*

ADAM LEVY has been Bloomberg News's Atlanta Bureau chief for the past two years and before that was a reporter in Bloomberg's Atlanta Bureau for three years. Prior to joining Bloomberg, Levy was a securities analyst on Wall Street and travelled around the world. Levy and his wife, Julia, have two sons, Michael and Sam, and live in Decatur, Georgia.

JOSEPH MENN, legal reporter for Bloomberg News, has covered tobacco for Bloomberg since 1994. Previously, Menn was an award-winning investigative business reporter at the *Charlotte (North Carolina) Observer* and principal editor of *The Chronology: The Documented Day-by-Day Account of the Secret Military Assistance to Iran and the Contras.*

JEFFREY ROTHFEDER, Bloomberg News's national news editor, was formerly an editor at *Business Week* and a reporter at the *Washington Post.* Rothfeder is the author of three previous books: *Privacy for Sale* (1992), *Heart Rhythms* (1985), and *Minds Over Matter* (1982). He has two children, Alexis and Benjamin.